A Proactive Practitioner's Guide to Section 11(b) of the *Charter*

Second Edition

A Proactive Practitioner's Guide to Section 11(b) of the *Charter*, Second Edition
© Tracy Kozlowski & Joanne Stuart, 2025

Irwin Law
An imprint of University of Toronto Press
Toronto Buffalo London
utppublishing.com
Printed in Canada

ISBN 978-1-4875-6892-4 (paper) | ISBN 978-1-4875-6894-8 (UPDF)
ISBN 978-1-4875-6895-5 (EPUB)

Library and Archives Canada Cataloguing in Publication

Title: A proactive practitioner's guide to section 11(b) of the Charter /
    Tracy Kozlowski & Joanne Stuart.
Names: Kozlowski, Tracy, author. | Stuart, Joanne (Crown Counsel), author.
Description: Second edition. | Includes bibliographical references and index.
Identifiers: Canadiana (print) 20250143453 | Canadiana (ebook) 20250143461 |
    ISBN 9781487568924 (paper) | ISBN 9781487568948 (PDF) |
    ISBN 9781487568955 (EPUB)
Subjects: LCSH: Canada. Canadian Charter of Rights and Freedoms. | LCSH: Speedy
    trial—Canada. | LCSH: Court congestion and delay—Canada. | LCSH: Criminal
    justice, Administration of—Canada.
Classification: LCC KE8815 .K69 2025 | DDC 345.71/056—dc23

We wish to acknowledge the land on which the University of Toronto Press operates. This land is the traditional territory of the Wendat, the Anishnaabeg, the Haudenosaunee, the Métis, and the Mississaugas of the Credit First Nation.

University of Toronto Press acknowledges the financial support of the Government of Canada, the Canada Council for the Arts, and the Ontario Arts Council, an agency of the Government of Ontario, for its publishing activities.

Cover designer: John Beadle

I would like to dedicate this book to my husband and daughter, Mike and Yvonne "The Vonz" Kozlowski, for their constant love and support. I would also thank my parents, Edward and Marie Stapleton, for showing me by example that the harder you work, the luckier you get. I must also acknowledge my dedicated assistant and friend, Alla "The Great" Fabbroni, who never fails.

—TK

My work in this book is dedicated to my father, Professor Don Stuart, who has generously shared his passion for criminal law with me for my whole life, to my mother Pam, sisters Lisa and Chloë, steadfast friends and co-workers (past and present) for their encouragement, to the memory of my grandmother (and hero) Joy, to my daughters Evangeline and Beatrice who are the two reasons behind everything that I do, and, above all, to my husband and champion, Alexis, for his unwavering love, belief, and support, and without whom this would not have been possible.

—JKS

Summary Table of Contents

Detailed Table of Contents

CHAPTER 4

APPEALS AND EXTRAORDINARY REMEDIES 69

CHAPTER 5

POST-TRIAL DELAY 74

Foreword

The authors of this book are, among their other qualities, both brilliant and generous. It has been my privilege to get to know them as co-workers within the Crown Law Office—Criminal at the Ministry of the Attorney General. I have worked with them as students, as newly minted lawyers, and as superb senior counsel. As it pertains to the subject-matter of this book, I have also had the unique pleasure of serving with them as co-counsel in the Supreme Court of Canada dealing with the topic of section 11(b) of the *Charter*.

In this book, the authors continue a strong tradition within the criminal bar of passing on to others what they have learned through their research, their courtroom experience, and the wisdom and expertise of those who, by their own example, have led and equipped their colleagues. They have prepared and argued many cases that concern the right to be tried within a reasonable time. Whether because of innate fascination with the subject-matter or from pure necessity driven by their case assignments (I suspect the latter, which sometimes feeds the former), they have accumulated a vast knowledge and a thorough conceptual understanding which they have now shared with the profession at large.

Students of the Canadian Constitution, and in particular the *Charter of Rights and Freedoms*, will know that the right to be tried within a reasonable time, encompassed within section 11(b), stands somewhat apart from many of the other entrenched rights and freedoms. While many individual rights and freedoms are intended to constrain government activity, section 11(b) is cast in positive terms to impose upon government the obligation to act in a particular way. Therefore, if the government, acting through its prosecution services, determines to invoke the jurisdiction of the courts to try a person for a criminal offence, the government has an affirmative obligation to do so "within a reasonable time." What does that mean? How do we know whether, as a society, we are delivering on this guarantee? Likewise, how do we know when we have failed, or are at risk of failing, to do so?

These are important questions. Our courts, including the Supreme Court of Canada, have wrestled with them over the years. The Supreme Court in *Jordan v The Queen*, 2016 SCC 27, saw both a need and an opportunity to provide greater clarity. The Court decided that it is not always helpful to merely develop jurisprudence based upon litigation that looks retrospectively at whether a particular right has been infringed; rather, it concluded that guidance is needed to help courts, prosecutors, and defence counsel work proactively to achieve the *Charter's* promise.

In the pages that follow, the authors have written, in the spirit of the *Jordan* decision, to help us all with the questions listed above.

Chapters 1–3 of the book give the reader a learned and well-researched, yet practical, analysis of the *Jordan* framework from the starting of the "clock" to the stopping of the time calculation insofar as it pertains to the now well-known presumptive "ceilings." This section includes helpful discussions of the special considerations applicable to prosecutions under the *Youth Criminal Justice Act* and to the situation of retrials ordered following successful appeals.

Chapters 4 and 5 address particular features of the criminal process that were not expressly the subject of comment in relation to the operation of the presumptive ceilings in *Jordan*: specifically post-verdict proceedings such as sentencing and applications such as stays for entrapment, as well as appeals and extraordinary remedies.

Chapter 6 is very important, as it contains a thorough discussion of the doctrine of waiver as it pertains to section 11(b), and its distinction from various kinds of delays that are attributed specifically to the defence in the *Jordan* calculus.

Chapters 7 and 8 deserve special mention in the context of a book that seeks to assist the "proactive practitioner," whether the lawyer acts for the prosecution or for the defence. They serve a two-fold function. On one hand, they provide well-researched jurisprudential guidance on the "exceptional circumstances" that can justify trial delay that exceeds the presumptive ceilings and on how a delay that falls below these ceilings may nevertheless be unreasonable. On the other hand, these chapters work from the same body of jurisprudence to give the practitioner, in the spirit of *Jordan's* focus on delivering on the promise of trials within a reasonable time, practical suggestions for bringing trials to a conclusion in a timely fashion.

The book concludes with three chapters dealing with miscellaneous issues: the transitional cases "in the system" when *Jordan* was released; appellate issues concerning review of section 11(b) determinations; and the question of whether, in the post-*Jordan* world, a stay of proceedings continues to be the minimum remedy for a section 11(b) infringement.

I could say more but would rather that you move on to read the book. It is an important one. It is well-researched. It will enhance your understanding of what section 11(b) is all about.

Finally, whether you are prosecuting or defending criminal cases, it will help you be creative in making our justice processes work more effectively and efficiently to serve those for whom they were created.

Eric Siebenmorgen
March 2023

Preface

The Supreme Court of Canada's decision in *R v Jordan*, 2016 SCC 27, was intended to simplify section 11(b) *Charter* litigation. While it will likely achieve this in the long-term, in the short-term, *Jordan* threw into question much of what was previously understood about how to litigate and assess unreasonable delay. Over the past seven years, we have had the privilege of participating in significant litigation and providing guidance that has contributed to the clarification and development of the *Jordan* framework and assessments pursuant to section 11(b) of the *Charter*: *R v Williamson*, 2016 SCC 28 (the companion case to *Jordan*); *R v Cody*, 2017 SCC 31; *R v KJM*, 2019 SCC 55; *R v KGK*, 2020 SCC 7; *R v JF*, 2022 SCC 17; *R v Safdar*, 2022 SCC 21; and *R v Hanan*, 2023 SCC 12. Several crucial aspects of the *Jordan* framework remain unsettled and will feature in upcoming litigation and jurisprudence. This book, now in its second edition, is intended to provide readers with guidance on the recently developed jurisprudence and on the issues that remain unresolved. We hope our work will help Crown counsel, defence counsel, and judges to easily and proactively navigate what lies ahead for section 11(b) of the *Charter*.

Tracy Kozlowski and Joanne Stuart
November 28, 2024

Acknowledgements

The authors would like to thank the following people for their encouragement and guidance: Professor Don Stuart, Professor Stephen Coughlan, Leslie Paine, Jeffrey Miller and Lesley Steeve from Irwin Law (who gave us our start), and to the wonderful team at University of Toronto Press, particularly Antonia Pop, Josephine Mo, Kai Toh, Tina Eng and her team, Vesna Micic, and Lily Bergh. We are especially grateful to our former colleague and mentor, Eric Siebenmorgen, for kindly taking the time to write the Foreword for this book. Eric's contributions to the development of the law on section 11(b) of the *Charter* cannot be overstated. Most importantly we thank our families and friends for their unfailing support.

CHAPTER 1

Introduction

Section 11(b) of the *Canadian Charter of Rights and Freedoms*[1] states that "any person charged with an offence has the right to be tried within a reasonable time," but what does this mean? Who is a person for the purposes of this section? What does it mean to be charged with an offence? When can an accused be said to have been tried, and, most complicated, what *is* a reasonable period of time for someone to be tried for an offence? If the Crown prosecutor fails to bring someone to trial within a reasonable time, how can that be remedied, if at all? The purpose of this book is to offer answers to these questions to the extent that they have been definitively answered in the jurisprudence, to provide a guide to applying the framework for assessing whether the time required to try an accused is reasonable, and to consider some of the emerging issues in the law related to section 11(b) of the *Charter*. Each chapter tracks each step in the analysis of the reasonableness of time to trial, followed by considerations of the remedy for a breach of section 11(b) of the *Charter* and issues that arise in the appellate context. To place the discussion in context, it is important to understand what the right pursuant to section 11(b) is intended to protect, the history of the jurisprudence before *R v Jordan*,[2] and the Supreme Court of Canada's intentions in implementing the new *Jordan* framework.

---

1   *Canadian Charter of Rights and Freedoms*, Part I of the *Constitution Act, 1982*, being Schedule B to the *Canada Act 1982* (UK), 1982, c 11, s 11(b) [*Charter*].

2   *R v Jordan*, 2016 SCC 27 [*Jordan*].

A. THE INTERESTS THAT SECTION 11(B) OF THE *CHARTER* SEEKS TO PROTECT

First, section 11(b) of the *Charter* is intended to protect the liberty interests of an accused person. That is to say, someone who has been charged with an offence should not be subject to restrictions on their liberty, whether subject of bail conditions while awaiting trial or in custody, for any longer than is reasonable. As Moldaver J wrote in *Jordan*,[3] "Security of the person is impacted because a long-delayed trial means prolonging the stress, anxiety, and stigma an accused may suffer."[4] Second, the right to a fair trial can be prejudiced by unreasonable delay in getting to trial. Where it takes too long to try an accused person for an offence, the risk that evidence will be lost or denuded in some way, or the memories of witnesses diminished as a result of the passage of time, is heightened. An accused may be prejudiced in their ability to defend themself in such circumstances.

In addition to the harm caused to personal security and fair trial interests for individuals charged with criminal offences when trials are delayed, are more general concerns related to the public's confidence in the administration of justice. Society has an interest in seeing trials conducted swiftly, such that those who are found to be guilty of an offence are punished, and those who are not are left alone by the state. Victims of crime and their families, who are also subject to strain and anxiety awaiting the adjudication of a criminal complaint, are likewise entitled to see the matter reach its end within a reasonable period of time. Collective faith in our system of criminal justice is dependent upon the efficient prosecution of criminal charges.[5]

B. A BRIEF HISTORY OF THIRTY YEARS OF SECTION 11(B) *CHARTER* JURISPRUDENCE

The Supreme Court's first opportunity for consideration of section 11(b) of the *Canadian Charter of Rights and Freedom* arose in *R v Mills*.[6] At issue as it related to section 11(b) was whether a provincial court

---

3   *Ibid.*

4   *Ibid* at para 20.

5   *Ibid* at paras 22–23.

6   1986 CanLII 17 (SCC) [*Mills*].

judge at the preliminary hearing stage of proceedings possesses jurisdiction to grant a remedy for a *Charter* breach pursuant to section 24(1). The Court held that a judge at the preliminary hearing stage was not a "court of competent jurisdiction" within the meaning of section 24 having regard to the limited jurisdiction conferred to the preliminary hearing judge pursuant to Part XV of the *Criminal Code.*[7] Accordingly, an application for relief must be brought as a pre-trial motion in advance of the trial and before the trial judge.[8] The majority would have allowed for whatever remedy was appropriate in the circumstances, with a stay of proceedings saved for only the most serious or compelling cases.[9] Chief Justice Dickson and Lamer J, dissenting, held that jurisdiction is lost upon a breach of section 11(b) of the *Charter* such that a stay was the minimum remedy in the event of a breach.[10]

The next year, in *R v Rahey*,[11] the Court affirmed that an application pursuant to section 11(b) was properly heard in nearly all instances by the trial court, but with the superior court holding parallel jurisdiction to hear the application where it is inappropriate for the trial judge to hear it, as in instances where the trial judge is alleged to be responsible for the unreasonable delay.[12] The remedy for a breach of section 11(b) of the *Charter* was also revisited by the Court.[13] The majority now established that the minimum remedy for a breach is a stay of proceedings.[14]

In *Mills* and *Rahey* can also be seen the development of the test and legal framework for assessing the reasonableness of trial delay. In *Mills*, Lamer J, writing for the minority, proffered an analysis that required a balancing between impairment of the accused's liberty and fair trial interests over time against waiver of delay, the time requirements inherent to the needs of the case, and the limits of institutional resources.[15] The test was reiterated by Lamer J in *Rahey*, whereas Beetz

---

7   RSC 1985, c C-46.

8   *Mills*, above note 6 at paras 37–76, 99, 264–68, and 288–91; *R v Carter*, 1986 CanLII 18 (SCC).

9   *Mills*, above note 6 at paras 276–77 and 297–303.

10   *Ibid* at paras 78, 99, and 229–41.

11   *R v Rahey*, 1987 CanLII 52 (SCC) [*Rahey*].

12   *Ibid* at paras 16–18; *R v Smith*, 1989 CanLII 12 (SCC) [*Smith*].

13   *Rahey*, above note 11 at paras 48–52 and 58.

14   A fulsome discussion as to the remedy for a breach of s 11(b) of the *Charter* is found in Chapter 10.

15   *Mills*, above note 6 at paras 160–218; *Rahey*, above note 11.

and Le Dain JJ held that the test for assessing reasonableness should be a weighing as between:

> (a) whether the delay complained of is *prima facie* unreasonable, having regard to the inherent time requirements of the particular case; (b) the reasons or responsibility for the delay, having regard to the conduct of the prosecution and the accused, including the question of failure to object or waiver, as well as the conduct of the court and any responsibility which may be reasonably assigned to the unacceptable inadequacy of institutional resources; and (c) the prejudice caused to the accused by a particular delay.[16]

Also at issue in the developing law was the extent to which prejudice to the accused's rights could be presumed to be present as a function of the passage of time or whether prejudice had to be established as "actual prejudice" arising from the delay and particular to the accused, and not arising from the fact of having been charged alone. In *Mills*, La Forest J was of the view that "actual, proven prejudice, need not, indeed is not, relevant to establishing a violation of s. 11(b)."[17] This was so as from the time of the charge there immediately exists prejudice that section 11(b) of the *Charter* seeks to limit. Actual prejudice would, however, be relevant to a determination as to the appropriate relief.[18] Justice Wilson, dissenting, disagreed that prejudice ought to be presumed, instead holding that what an accused applicant had to prove was "that he has suffered an impairment of his liberty and security interests as a result of the Crown's failure to bring him to trial within a reasonable time, not as a result of the Crown's having charged him."[19] In *Rahey*, Beetz and Le Dain JJ held that prejudice to the right to a fair trial, and in particular the ability to raise a defence, was of particular importance, and could be inferred from a lengthy delay, but that prejudice related to the accused's personal circumstances arising from the delay was less salient. Instead, a "general weight" ought to apply as to prejudice to an accused's security interests.[20] In *R v Conway*,[21] Lamer J disagreed,

---

16   *Rahey*, above note 11 at para 55.

17   *Mills*, above note 6 at para 165.

18   *Ibid* at paras 161–68.

19   *Ibid* at paras 280–82.

20   *Rahey*, above note 11 at paras 56–57.

21   1989 CanLII 66 (SCC) [*Conway*].

holding that the accused's ability to raise a defence was not a relevant consideration pursuant to section 11(b), but to section 11(d) of the *Charter*.[22] As well, the majority in *Conway* held that the assessment did not require a shift in the onus to the Crown to demonstrate that the delay was reasonable once a certain point was reached.[23]

The Court came to some unanimity as to the basic elements of the applicable test for assessing the reasonableness of trial delay pursuant to section 11(b) of the *Charter* in its decision in *R v Smith*,[24] the factors to consider being (1) the length of the delay; (2) the reason for the delay, including limits on institutional resources and the inherent time requirements of the case; (3) waiver of time periods; and (4) prejudice to the accused.[25] The Court also agreed on a functional approach to the assessment and found that while the onus fell to the applicant to prove a breach, that the evidentiary burden *would* shift to the Crown depending on the circumstances, as for example, where the Crown requested an unusually long adjournment.[26] The Court did not settle upon the import of prejudice to the analysis as the length of the delay in *Smith* made the existence of prejudice to the accused a foregone conclusion in that case.

R v Askov[27] was decided by the Supreme Court soon thereafter. Following a detailed review of the above-noted cases, Cory J, writing for the Court, determined that section 11(b) of the *Charter* primarily seeks to protect individual rights, namely fair trial and security of the person, with a related societal interest in ensuring those who break the law are dealt with and that people who have been charged with offences are treated fairly. Justice Cory also noted that, in some instances, accused persons have an interest in avoiding a trial, such that the courts must guard against the use of section 11(b) as a sword rather than as a shield.

The Court then outlined the framework for the assessment of the reasonableness of trial delay pursuant to section 11(b) of the *Charter*, the analysis (soon thereafter modified in *R v Morin*[28]) that would apply

---

22   *Ibid.*

23   *Ibid.*

24   Above note 12.

25   *Ibid.*

26   *Ibid.*

27   [1990] 2 SCR 1199 [*Askov*].

28   1992 CanLII 89 (SCC) [*Morin*].

for the next twenty-five years in Canada. Justice Cory summarized the framework as follows:

(i) The Length of the Delay.

The longer the delay, the more difficult it should be for a court to excuse it. Very lengthy delays may be such that they cannot be justified for any reason.

(ii) Explanation for the Delay.

(a) Delays Attributable to the Crown.
Delays attributable to the action of the Crown or officers of the Crown will weigh in favour of the accused. The cases of *Rahey* and *Smith* provide examples of such delays.

Complex cases which require longer time for preparation, a greater expenditure of resources by Crown officers, and the longer use of institutional facilities will justify delays longer than those acceptable in simple cases.

(b) Systemic or Institutional Delays.
Delays occasioned by inadequate resources must weigh against the Crown. Institutional delays should be considered in light of the comparative test referred to earlier. The burden of justifying inadequate resources resulting in systemic delays will always fall upon the Crown. There may be a transitional period to allow for a temporary period of lenient treatment of systemic delay.

(c) Delays Attributable to the Accused.
Certain actions of the accused will justify delays. For example, a request for adjournment or delays to retain different counsel.

There may as well be instances where it can be demonstrated by the Crown that the actions of the accused were undertaken for the purposes of delaying the trial.

(iii) Waiver.

If the accused waives his rights by consenting to or concurring in a delay, this must be taken into account. However, for a waiver to be valid it must be informed, unequivocal and freely given. The burden of showing that a waiver should be inferred falls upon the Crown. An example of a waiver or concurrence that could be inferred is the consent by counsel for the accused to a fixed date for trial.

(iv) Prejudice to the Accused.
There is a general, and in the case of very long delays an often virtu-
ally irrebuttable presumption of prejudice to the accused resulting from
the passage of time. Where the Crown can demonstrate that there was
no prejudice to the accused flowing from a delay, then such proof may
serve to excuse the delay. It is also open to the accused to call evidence to
demonstrate actual prejudice to strengthen his position that he has been
prejudiced as a result of the delay.[29]

In the year that followed the release of the Supreme Court's decision
in *R v Askov*, in Ontario alone approximately 47,000 cases were stayed
arising from breaches of section 11(b) of the *Charter*. Consequently, the
Court in *R v Morin*[30] determined to give greater weight to what the
Court termed the "secondary societal interest" requiring that those who
are charged with serious offences are not permitted to avoid responsibility on a strict application of the *Askov* framework. Justice Sopinka,
writing for the majority, held that "[a]s the seriousness of the offence
increases so does the societal demand that the accused be brought to
trial."[31] Accordingly, the *Askov* framework was revisited.

The overall analytical factors as outlined in *Smith* and *Askov* remained
the same, as did the onus of proof, with the ultimate legal burden on
the applicant, and the potential for the evidentiary burden to shift to
the Crown where circumstances warranted it. However, the Court
now instituted guidelines for reasonable institutional delay—between
eight and ten months in the provincial courts and between six to eight
months in the Superior Court.[32] The guidelines were only intended
as suggested time periods, however, both flexible and modifiable, and
could give way to other considerations, including the complexity of the
matter, the seriousness of the offence charged, and the extent to which
the accused could demonstrate having suffered some prejudice to their
security or fair trial interests as a result of the delay.[33] Over the nearly
twenty-five years that followed, largely due to the flexible nature of the
analysis, the adjudication of section 11(b) *Charter* applications became

---

29   *Askov*, above note 27 at 1231–32.
30   Above note 28.
31   *Ibid.*
32   *Ibid.*
33   *Ibid.*

increasingly complex and time-consuming, while lengthier periods of delay were adjudged to be reasonable.

C. NEW FRAMEWORK — *R V JORDAN*

On 8 July 2016, the Supreme Court released its decision in *R v Jordan*.[34] The analytical approach to the assessment of the reasonableness of delay pursuant to section 11(b) of the *Charter* was entirely overhauled. The decision allowed for an adjustment period in acknowledgement that the parties could not have acted in accordance with the new framework prior to the release of the decision and to allow the system to get in step with the new *Jordan* principles, now that the *Morin* framework was abandoned.

The rationale for the new framework was made clear by Moldaver J, writing for the majority, and, it is suggested, can be distilled into three main principles. First, the complexity and uncertainty of the *Morin* framework as it had developed over time (its doctrinal problems, as the court termed it) had itself contributed to the burden on a criminal justice system already overburdened with litigation. Second, the backward-looking nature of the analysis was such that it did nothing to incentivize front-end cooperation between the parties or encourage efficient use of the system. Instead, a "culture of complacency"[35] had taken hold. Third, the acceptance of more and more delay in bringing accused Canadians to trial had the effect of denuding both fair trial and security rights of the accused and public confidence in the administration of justice.[36]

In reading this book and moving through the development of the law since the Supreme Court's decision in *R v Jordan*, it will be readily apparent that every revisitation of the framework by the Court has been guided by these fundamental rationales. The analysis must be clear, straightforward and strictly applied such that the parties know the perimeters in advance of trial and are therefore encouraged to move a matter forward with them in mind right at the outset when a charge is laid.

Stated succinctly, *R v Jordan* imposes strict caps for delay to the end of trial. Delay beyond that applicable cap is presumptively unreasonable

---

34   *Jordan*, above note 2.

35   *Ibid* at para 4.

36   *Ibid* at paras 19–45.

and it falls to the Crown to show why it should be determined to be otherwise. Failing that, a breach of section 11(b) of the *Charter* is established and the prosecution must come to a permanent end. The presumptive time periods within which an accused must be brought to trial—eighteen months for cases in provincial court, and thirty months for cases tried in superior court or in provincial court following a preliminary inquiry.[37] In cases where the total delay, less delays either waived or exclusively caused by the defence, exceeds the presumptive ceiling, the onus shifts to the Crown to demonstrate that the delay was nevertheless reasonable.[38] Where the delay falls below the ceiling, the defence must demonstrate that the period of time to the end of trial was nevertheless unreasonable.[39] Stays of proceedings for delays that fall below the ceilings will be rare and limited to clear cases.[40]

The *Jordan* framework applies to *any* case "in the system" on the day the decision was released (8 July 2016). However, its application is subject to a built-in "transitional exception" which acknowledges that, for matters already in the system, the parties would have placed reasonable reliance on the legal framework provided in *Morin*[41] and its progeny and could not have been aware of the *Jordan* framework prior to the release of the decision.[42] Application of the transitional exception was intended to prevent a recurrence of the type of situation that led to the stay or withdrawal of tens of thousands of criminal charges in Ontario alone that resulted in the wake of the Supreme Court's decision in *Askov*.[43] The cases remaining in the system that fall into that exception are likely few to none at present. Nevertheless, it will be important to be aware of it given that it was applied to many precedential decisions since *Jordan*. Further, the transitional exception can still arise in other contexts aside from trial delay, for example, in Ontario, in delay before sentencing.

The steps in the analysis are outlined in more detail in the chapters that follow.

---

37   *Ibid* at paras 5 and 46.
38   *Ibid* at para 47.
39   *Ibid* at para 48.
40   *Ibid*.
41   *Morin*, above note 28.
42   *Jordan*, above note 2 at paras 5, 21, and 92–104.
43   *Askov*, above note 27.

CHAPTER 2

Application of the *Jordan* Framework

A. STEPS IN THE ANALYSIS

The general analytical steps to be taken in applying the *Jordan*[1] framework are outlined below. This analysis is applicable to trial delay only. As will be seen, a separate analysis is applicable to each of the following: judicial deliberation time to arrive at a verdict (Chapter 3); post-verdict applications (Chapter 5); and the period required for sentencing (Chapter 5). For trial delay, each of the highlighted terms in the outline below will be considered in detail in the chapters that follow.

The steps in the analysis to assess the reasonableness of delay to the end of trial are as follows:

1) Calculate the **total delay**, which is the period from the laying of the charge to the actual or anticipated end of trial—that is, the end of evidence and argument (Chapter 3);
2) Subtract **defence delay**, including delay that is waived, from the total delay, which results in the **net delay** (Chapter 6);
3) Compare the **net delay** to the presumptive ceiling;
4) If the net delay exceeds the presumptive ceiling, the Crown must establish the presence of **exceptional circumstances,** otherwise a stay will follow. Exceptional circumstances fall under two categories: **discrete events** and **particularly complex cases** (Chapter 7);
5) Subtract delay caused by discrete events from the **net delay** (leaving the **remaining delay**);

---

1   *R v Jordan*, 2016 SCC 27 [*Jordan*].

6) If the **remaining delay** exceeds the presumptive ceiling, the court must consider whether the case was particularly complex such that the time the case has taken is justified and the delay is reasonable (Chapter 7);

7) If the **remaining delay falls below the presumptive ceiling**, the onus is on the defence to show that the delay is nevertheless unreasonable (Chapter 8);

8) The new framework, including the presumptive ceiling, applies to cases already in the system when *Jordan* was released. For cases in the system at the time *Jordan* was released, if the remaining delay exceeds the presumptive ceiling and is not determined to be justified on the basis of the complexity of the case, then it is necessary to also consider whether the delay is reasonable under the **transitional exceptional circumstance**.[2] If the parties can be said to have reasonably relied on the *Morin*[3] framework because some portion of the prosecution was conducted prior to the *Jordan* decision, the delay, though it exceeds the ceiling, may still be found to be reasonable.[4] If not, then the proceedings will be stayed (Chapter 9).

B. TIMING OF THE APPLICATION

The Supreme Court and provincial appellate courts have made clear that an application for a remedy pursuant to section 11(b) of the *Charter* must be brought in a timely fashion.[5] In most cases, this means prior to the start of trial as it is a given that the anticipated end of trial will be known

---

2   As the Supreme Court released the *Jordan* decision on 8 July 2016, such cases remaining in the system are now rare. The transitional exception does not apply to cases not in the system on that date.

3   *R v Morin*, 1992 CanLII 89 (SCC) [*Morin*].

4   *R v Coulter*, 2016 ONCA 704 at paras 34–41; *R v KN*, 2018 BCCA 246 at para 5; *R v Rai*, 2019 BCCA 377 at paras 94–95; *R v Shlyk*, 2021 BCCA 472 at paras 32–42; *R v Mamouni*, 2017 ABCA 347 at paras 57–58, leave to appeal refused (without reasons) 2018 CanLII 89741 (SCC); *R v Boehmer*, 2019 SKCA 74 at para 29; *R v Lemioer*, 2019 SKCA 95 at para 17; *R v Schenkels*, 2017 MBCA 62 at para 16, leave to appeal refused (without reasons) 2017 CanLII 78703 (SCC); *R v Bulhosen*, 2019 ONCA 600 at paras 41–54, leave to appeal refused (without reasons), 2020 CanLII 17613 (SCC); *R v Daponte*, 2021 ONCA 14 at para 14; *R v Shaikh*, 2019 ONCA 895 at paras 5–10; *R v JCP*, 2018 ONCA 986 at para 8; *R v Mallozzi*, 2017 ONCA 644 at paras 27–30, leave to appeal refused, 2018 CanLII 30058 (SCC); *Pelletier v R*, 2019 NBCA 9 at paras 8–9.

5   *R v Allison*, 2022 ONCA 329 at paras 57–70 [*Allison*].

to all parties on the date the trial dates are set. Where a section 11(b) application is brought against the applicable rules of court requiring that such motion be brought prior to the start of trial,[6] to hear the application will be exceptional and requires the applicant to demonstrate cogent reasons why it would be in the interests of justice to grant an order permitting the application to be brought.[7] In the absence of some material change in the legal or factual landscape, leave to bring the motion will not be granted. This is not a new approach arising from *Jordan*. In *R v Rabba*,[8] for example, Arbour JA (as she then was) held that to fail to bring an application before or during trial would in most instances be "fatal" to the claim.[9]

The Supreme Court of Canada's most recent consideration of the obligation to raise a *Charter*[10] claim for delay pursuant to section 11(b) was in *R v JF*.[11] The Court held that as the anticipated end of trial will be known when the trial dates are set, the accused has a duty to raise the issue and bring an application before the start of the trial. Even in instances where the delay issue has crystallized mid-trial (such as when continuation dates have been added), the accused is required to act diligently and bring the application before the end of the trial. Applying the Supreme Court's decision in *JF*, where an accused failed to bring an application before the end of the trial (defined as the conclusion of evidence and argument on the trial proper pursuant to the Court's decision in *R v KGK*,[12] discussed in Chapter 3), the accused will arguably be

---

6   See, for example, in Ontario, Rule 34.03 re Dismissal for Non-Compliance with Rules, *Criminal Proceedings Rules for the Superior Court of Justice (Ontario)* (SI/2012-7) and Rule 2 re Effect of Non-Compliance, *Rules of the Ontario Court of Justice in Criminal Proceedings* (SI/97-133). The timing for when a s 11(b) application must be heard depends on the Rules and Practice Directions of a jurisdiction. For example, in Ontario, a s 11(b) motion must be heard sixty days before the start of trial: see *R v Hobeika*, 2018 ONSC 85 at para 12 [*Hobeika*], referring to *Part VI, (B) Timing for service e-filing of s. 11(b) application* of the Ontario Superior Court of Justice *Consolidated Provincial Practice Direction for Criminal Proceedings*; *R v Ibrahim*, 2022 ONCJ 450 [*Ibrahim*], referring to Rule 2.4(1) of the *Criminal Rules of the Ontario Court of Justice*; see also *R v Callahan-Tucker*, 2022 NSPC 58 at para 15, referring to the *Nova Scotia Provincial Court Rules*.

7   *Allison*, above note 5 at paras 57–70; *Hobeika*, above note 6 at paras 2–3 and 12–56; *R v Warring*, 2017 ABCA 128 at paras 9–12.

8   1991 CanLII 7073 (Ont CA).

9   *Ibid* at paras 4 and 5.

10   *Canadian Charter of Rights and Freedoms*, Part I of the *Constitution Act, 1982*, being Schedule B to the *Canada Act 1982* (UK), 1982, c 11 [*Charter*].

11   2022 SCC 17 [*JF*].

12   2020 SCC 7.

barred from bringing the application, unless there are exceptional circumstances that account for the lateness of it. Though in *JF* the Court was tasked to consider whether an accused could raise the issue for the first time on appeal, the Court also held that:

> As a general rule, in the context of a single trial, an accused who believes that their right to be tried within a reasonable time has been infringed must act diligently and apply for a remedy before their trial is held. However, an accused may in some circumstances be justified in bringing such an application later, as is the case exceptionally on appeal.[13]

It can be taken from this passage that unless there are exceptional circumstances justifying it, the application *must* be brought prior to the start of trial or prior to trial's end where the delay issue crystallized mid-trial, with failure to do so being potentially fatal to the claim.

Trial judges also have the authority to summarily dismiss a motion, including section 11(b) *Charter* applications.[14] Though the motion is pursued prior to the end of trial, where there has not been compliance with applicable rules as to the timing of the application, the record is deficient, and the Crown has raised a claim that the motion is without merit, the judge can refuse to hear it. The determination to summarily dismiss the motion should be informed, not only by the interests of the accused, but by broader administration of justice concerns, "including the need to conduct all litigation in a fair, orderly and efficient manner."[15] Whether to allow the motion to proceed will cause prejudice to the Crown's ability to respond, the state of completeness of the motion record, or whether the application itself has the potential to cause further delay in the proceedings should also be considered. However, the power to dismiss motions involving constitutional claims must still be exercised cautiously, and procedural fairness respected.[16] Indeed, the Supreme Court recently held that that the correct threshold for the

---

13   *JF*, above note 11 at para 3; see also: *R v Yizhak*, 2022 ONCJ 476 (s 11(b) Application) at paras 25–35; *R v Fraser*, 2022 ONCJ 580 at paras 19–21; *contra*: *Ibrahim*, above note 6.

14   *R v Cody*, 2017 SCC 31 at paras 36–42 [*Cody*]; *R v Kutynec*, 1992 CanLII 7751 (Ont CA); *R v Vukelich*, 1996 CanLII 1005 (BCCA).

15   *R v Kazman*, 2020 ONCA 22 at para 15, leave to appeal refused 2020 CanLII 48927 (SCC) [*Kazman*].

16   *R v Greer*, 2020 ONCA 795 at paras 107–15; *R v D'Allesandro*, 2018 BCCA 118 at paras 17–20; *R v Felderhof*, 2003 CanLII 37346 (Ont CA) at para 40; *R v Blom*, 2002 CanLII 45026 (Ont CA) at para 22.

summary dismissal of applications made in the criminal law context is whether the underlying application is manifestly frivolous.[17] That the accused had delayed the case previously, then, is not good enough reason on its own to prevent the accused from bringing a potentially meritorious application. This is particularly so where the accused is unrepresented, as was the case in *R v Imola*,[18] for example. Nor can the standard that there is "no reasonable prospect of success" be sufficient for summary dismissal of an application. That said, even unrepresented accused, "can[not] be allowed to ignore court orders and deadlines while the constitutional clock runs down and valuable court resources are consumed."[19] Where the application is manifestly frivolous, the court should summarily dismiss it.[20]

Even in instances where the accused has failed to act diligently in advancing a claim for delay prior to the end of trial, but has nevertheless been permitted to proceed, inaction in this regard that has caused delay of the proceedings cannot be attributed to the state. Inaction that winds up causing delay does not necessarily amount to waiver of the period of delay, though it is a relevant factor as to whether the delay was waived. That said, delay caused as a result of a late application need not be classified as having been waived since in such circumstances the delay is likely to be attributable to defence-caused delay and to be deducted at any rate (see discussion in Chapter 6).[21]

C. APPLICATION RECORD

A complete application record is essential to advancing a claim under section 11(b) of the *Charter*.[22] Given the obligation to raise the claim when the delay issue crystallizes, the applicant must order all of the transcripts for every court appearance and for both levels of court, where applicable, as quickly as possible. Delay in this regard has the potential to cause further delay in the proceedings.

---

17   *R v Haevischer*, 2023 SCC 11.

18   2019 ONCA 556 at paras 14–22.

19   *Kazman*, above note 15 at paras 14–99.

20   *Cody*, above note 14 at para 38.

21   *JF*, above note 11 at paras 51–52; *Cody*, above note 14 at para 33; *Jordan*, above note 1 at paras 63, 113, and 121; *contra*: *R v Spencer*, 2022 SKCA 135 at para 52.

22   *R v Allen*, 1996 CanLII 4011 (Ont CA) [*Allen*].

Alternatively, and in some instances preferably, an Agreed Statement of Fact can be placed before the court where the parties agree on what occurred, and on how most of each portion of delay ought to be classified within the *Jordan* framework. The Supreme Court has made clear that the obligation to cooperate for the purpose of ensuring efficient use of the criminal justice system applies as it relates to motions, including motions for a stay for delay pursuant to section 11(b).[23] Accordingly, where possible, the parties should endeavour to restrict the issues to a consideration of the areas where there is actual disagreement. This can be achieved in the context of a pre-motion discussion. Where consensus in this regard cannot be reached, a complete record, including every appearance, as well as all relevant correspondence between the parties, must be filed. While in some instances a trial judge might be amenable to deciding the application on only a partial record, it is not recommended. Even a short appearance may include reference to something on record that is of importance to the characterization of some segment of delay. As well, on appeal, the full record will be required, whether or not it was before the trial court, in the absence of an Agreed Statement of Fact.[24]

The record must also include a factum outlining the applicant's position and legal argument and referring to the filed transcripts. A chart summarizing each appearance, the delay between each appearance and the next, and the proposed characterization of that delay period pursuant to *Jordan* will be essential. Indicate plainly, both in the introductory portion of the factum and at the bottom of the chart, the applicant's calculation of the total delay and net delay figures. The respondent should do the same. In this way, the points of contention as to the facts and legal characterizations of delay will be brought into focus for the application judge. Sidebar those portions of the record that support your position and cite them in the legal argument portion of your factum. Where the record is large, filing a compendium in advance of oral argument can only assist in focusing the judge on contentious issues and portions of the record that support your argument, as well as the relevant jurisprudence in that regard. In addition, include the cases that support your position, side-barring relevant passages. A separate Book of Authorities might also be included.

---

23   *Jordan*, above note 1 at paras 5 and 138; *Cody*, above note 14 at paras 32–33.
24   *Allen*, above note 22.

An application for a stay for delay applying the pre-2016 *Morin*[25] framework nearly always required an affidavit from the applicant outlining the prejudice suffered by the accused as a result of the delay in getting the matter to trial. The result was often protracted litigation, with the Crown cross-examining the applicant for the purpose of establishing that they were not prejudiced by the delay. It very often also included argument as to whether the prejudice the accused has suffered was more properly attributable to the delay to trial or the fact of simply having been charged, as though this distinction could be readily made. This is no longer needed under *Jordan.* Prejudice is presumed to be present where the ceiling has been breached. Indeed, the Supreme Court has recently made plain that prejudice is not a consideration on application of the *Jordan* framework at all.[26] Unless the applicant is advancing a section 11(b) delay application in a case that was commenced prior to the release of the *Jordan* decision, whether the applicant was or was not prejudiced by the delay is irrelevant to the analysis. Only in a transitional case (discussed in detail in Chapter 9) will there be some consideration of the *Morin*[27] framework, including prejudice to the accused, as that framework applied before *Jordan* and the parties would have reasonably relied on it through that period. Otherwise, an affidavit from the applicant as to the effect of the delay is no longer needed.

---

25   *Morin,* above note 3.

26   *JF,* above note 11 at para 17.

27   *Morin,* above note 3.

CHAPTER 3

Calculating the Total Delay Period

A. APPLICABLE CEILINGS

1) Presumptive Ceilings

The *Jordan* framework was created to focus the section 11(b) analysis and to encourage all participants in the criminal justice system to be proactive and cooperate in achieving reasonably prompt justice, with a view to fulfilling section 11(b)'s important objectives. The "heart" of the *Jordan* framework are the presumptive ceilings, beyond which delay, from the charge to the actual or anticipated end of trial, is presumed to be unreasonable unless exceptional circumstances justify it.[1] The presumptive ceilings mark the point at which the burden shifts from the defence to prove that the delay was unreasonable, to the Crown to justify the length of time the case has taken.[2] By creating the presumptive ceilings that mark where the burden of proof shifts to the Crown, the Court developed a prospective approach that allows the various participants to know, from the outset of the proceedings, the temporal limits within which the trial must take place.[3]

The Court prescribed that delay is presumptively unreasonable for a case tried in a single-stage proceeding in the provincial or territorial court if the trial exceeds eighteen months. This ceiling also applies

---

1   *R v Jordan*, 2016 SCC 27 at para 47 [*Jordan*].
2   *Ibid* at para 58.
3   *R v JF*, 2022 SCC 17 at para 1 [*JF (SCC)*].

to provincial offences prosecutions[4] and has been adopted for use in court martials.[5] The Court further prescribed that delay is presumptively unreasonable for a case tried in provincial court following a preliminary hearing or in superior court if the trial exceeds thirty months.[6] The Court declined to apply the framework to sentencing although they acknowledged that section 11(b) protection applies to sentencing proceedings.[7]

Delay attributable to or waived by the defence does not count toward the presumptive ceiling. If the total delay from the charge to the actual or anticipated end of trial (minus defence delay or a period of delay attributable to exceptional circumstances) falls *below* the presumptive ceiling, then the onus is on the defence to show that the delay is unreasonable.[8] To do so, the defence must establish that (1) it took meaningful steps that demonstrate a sustained effort to expedite the proceedings, *and* (2) the case took markedly longer than it reasonably should have.[9] The Court noted the expectation that stays beneath the ceiling will be rare and limited to clear cases. If the total delay from the charge to the actual or anticipated end of trial (minus defence delay) *exceeds* the ceiling, then the delay is presumptively unreasonable and the burden shifts to the Crown. To rebut this presumption, the Crown must establish the presence of exceptional circumstances. If the Crown cannot do so, the delay is unreasonable, and a stay will follow. Exceptional circumstances lie outside the Crown's control in that (1) they are reasonably unforeseen or reasonably unavoidable, and (2) they cannot reasonably be remedied.

2)   Purpose of the Presumptive Ceilings

In creating the ceilings beyond which trial delay is presumptively unreasonable, the Court developed a prospective approach that allows the various participants to know, from the outset of the proceedings,

---

4   *Tristan Construction v Technical Standards and Safety Authority (TSSA)*, 2022 ONCJ 129 at para 31; *R v Nguyen*, 2020 ONCA 609 at paras 22–26; *R v KJM*, 2019 SCC 55 at para 65 [*KJM (SCC)*]; *R v Sangha*, 2022 BCSC 874 at para 57.

5   *R v Zapata-Valles AA (Corporal)*, 2022 CM 3011 at para 76.

6   *Jordan*, above note 1 at paras 5, 46, and 49; *KJM (SCC)*, above note 4 at para 44.

7   *Jordan*, above note 1 at fn 2; *R v MacDougall*, 1998 CanLII 763 (SCC) [*MacDougall*].

8   *Jordan*, above note 1 at para 48.

9   *Ibid.*

the temporal limits within which the trial must take place.[10] In *Jordan*, the Court explained that the presumptive ceilings were imposed in order to:

1) give meaningful direction to the state on its constitutional obligations and to those who play an important role in ensuring that the trial concludes within a reasonable time: court administration, the police, Crown prosecutors, accused persons and their counsel, and judges;[11]

2) provide some assurance to accused persons, to victims and their families, to witnesses, and to the public that section 11(b) is not a hollow promise;[12]

3) enhance analytical simplicity and foster constructive incentives;[13] and

4) consider compelling case-specific factors that remain relevant to assessing the reasonableness of a period of delay both above and below the ceiling.[14]

The rationale for the ceilings and the framework are a touchstone for any unresolved questions. Subsequent interpretive jurisprudence consistently underscores how predictability, simplicity, and proactivity of the bright-line approach created by the presumptive ceilings and how that is supplemented with a flexible, case-specific approach to delay below the ceiling, informs every answer about how the framework is to be applied. As the Court held in *R v KJM*, "*Jordan* marries uniformity with flexibility."[15]

The Court made plain that the applicable presumptive ceiling is not an "aspirational target."[16] Rather, it is the point at which delay becomes presumptively unreasonable. The Court explained that the public should expect that most cases can and should be resolved before reaching the ceiling. For this reason, the Crown bears the onus of justifying delays that exceed the ceiling. It is also for this reason that an

---

10   *JF (SCC)*, above note 3 at para 1.

11   *Jordan*, above note 1 at para 50.

12   *Ibid.*

13   *Ibid* at para 51.

14   *Ibid.*

15   *KJM (SCC)*, above note 4 at para 69.

16   *Jordan*, above note 1 at para 56.

accused may, in clear cases, still demonstrate that their right to be tried within a reasonable time has been infringed, even before the ceiling has been breached.[17] The Court further acknowledged that eighteen months and thirty months reflect our current realities and that these numbers might need to be revisited in future.[18]

Responding, in part, to the dissent of Cromwell J, the majority acknowledged reasonableness cannot be captured by a number alone, and that the framework did not depart from the concept of reasonableness but simply represented a different view of how reasonableness should be assessed.[19] The numbers do not mark when delay is unreasonable but rather when delay is presumptively unreasonable such that the burden shifts to the Crown.[20]

3)   What Contributed to the Presumptive Ceilings

In creating the presumptive ceilings, the Court was guided by a number of considerations. First, the Court took as a starting point the *Morin*[21] guidelines that set eight to ten months as a guide for institutional delay in the provincial court, and an additional six to eight months as a guide for institutional delay in the superior court following an accused's committal for trial. Thus, under *Morin*, a total of fourteen to eighteen months was the measure for proceedings involving both the provincial court and the superior court.[22] Second, the Court considered the inherent time requirements of the case, taking into account the increased complexity of criminal cases since *Morin* and the significant role that process now plays in the criminal justice system.[23] Third, prejudice as described in *Morin*, which the Court eliminated as no longer playing an explicit role in the section 11(b) analysis, also informed the setting of the presumptive ceiling. Once the ceiling is breached, according to the *Jordan* framework, it is inferred that the accused has suffered prejudice to their *Charter*-protected liberty,

---

17   *Ibid.*

18   *Ibid* at para 57.

19   *Ibid* at para 51.

20   *Ibid* at paras 58, 254, and 301.

21   *R v Morin*, 1992 CanLII 89 (SCC) *[Morin]*.

22   *Jordan*, above note 1 at para 52; *KJM (SCC)*, above note 4 at para 45.

23   *Jordan*, above note 1 at para 53; *KJM (SCC)*, above note 4 at para 45.

security of the person, and fair trial interests.[24] The Court made clear that this was not a rebuttable presumption: once the ceiling is breached, an absence of actual prejudice cannot convert an unreasonable delay into a reasonable one.[25] The Court concluded that the presumptive ceiling provides clarity and assurance that will build public confidence in the administration of justice.[26]

4) Eliminating the *Morin* Categories of Prejudice

The imposition of the ceilings immediately raised questions about whether the Court truly meant to do away with previously identified categories of prejudice under *Morin*, such as in instances where an accused is a young person as defined by the *Youth Criminal Justice Act (YCJA)*[27] or where an accused is awaiting a retrial. Accused persons who fit into one of these categories had their matters advanced more expeditiously through the criminal justice system by all participants due to the special priority ascribed to them under the *Morin* regime. A body of jurisprudence soon explored whether the ceilings in *Jordan* were firm or would be adjusted to reflect these recognized categories requiring priority. The short answer is that the presumptive ceilings do not change based on the *Morin* categories of prejudice.[28] Rather, the issues that were previously understood as categories of prejudice under *Morin* may inform the test under the presumptive ceiling on a case-by-case basis.[29]

a) Young Persons under the *Youth Criminal Justice Act*
The first test of whether the Supreme Court of Canada was committed to ending the *Morin* categories of prejudice was *KJM* (SCC),[30] which was a youth criminal justice matter. The majority of the Court in *KJM* definitively stated that the same eighteen-month presumptive ceiling

---

24   *Jordan*, above note 1 at para 54; *Morin*, above note 21 at para 61; *R v Godin*, 2009 SCC 26 at para 37; *KJM (SCC)*, above note 4 at para 45.

25   *Jordan*, above note 1 at para 54; *KJM (SCC)*, above note 4 at para 45.

26   *Jordan*, above note 1 at para 55; *KJM (SCC)*, above note 4 at para 45.

27   *Youth Criminal Justice Act*, SC 2002, c 1, as amended SC 2012, c 1, s 3(1)(b)(iv) & (v) [YCJA].

28   *JF (SCC)*, above note 3 at para 61.

29   *Ibid* at paras 62–73.

30   *KJM (SCC)*, above note 4 at paras 65, 78, and 85.

applies to youth criminal justice matters without modification.[31] Essentially, the Court confirmed that no lower, separate presumptive ceilings would apply to youth matters. As youth matters had perhaps the strongest claim to prejudice as a result of delay, given the documented evidence that informed the codification of this concern in the *YCJA*,[32] this decision signalled to the profession that no former category of prejudice under *Morin* was likely to succeed in altering the presumptive ceilings. The Court held that the concerns captured by the former *Morin* category of prejudice were best considered on the second branch of the test for delay below the presumptive ceiling, should the first branch of that test be met.

Following *Jordan* and before *KJM*, there was a split body of jurisprudence about whether young persons should have a separate, and lower, presumptive ceiling. It is well recognized in the jurisprudence,[33] which the *YCJA* has codified, that timely intervention in youth matters is needed to reinforce the link between the offending behaviour and its consequences, and that prompt and speedy enforcement is needed, given young persons' different perception of time as compared to adults.[34] Placed in context of the whole of the *YCJA*, the import of these principles is even greater. That context is best captured in section 3 of the *YCJA*, which states:

> 3(1) The following principles apply in this *Act*:
>
> (a) the youth criminal justice system is intended to protect the public by
>
> > (i) holding young persons accountable through measures that are proportionate to the seriousness of the offence and the degree of responsibility of the young person,
> >
> > (ii) promoting the rehabilitation and reintegration of young persons who have committed offences, and
> >
> > (iii) supporting the prevention of crime by referring young persons to programs or agencies in the community to address the circumstances underlying their offending behaviour;

---

31   *Ibid* at para 4.

32   *YCJA*, above note 27, s 3.

33   *KJM (SCC)*, above note 4 at para 56; *R v M (GC)*, 1991 CanLII 7057 (Ont CA) [*M (GC)*]; *R v HR*, 2004 BCPC 464; *R v RDR*, 2011 NSCA 86 at para 8; *R v M (K)*, 2017 ONCJ 8 at para 38; *R v PR*, 2018 SKCA 27 at para 85; *R v TR*, 2005 CanLII 18709 (Ont CA) at para 40; see also: *R v LB*, 2014 ONCA 748 at para 14.

34   *KJM (SCC)*, above note 4 at paras 59–60; *YCJA*, above note 27, s 3(1)(b)(iv) & (v).

   (b)   the criminal justice system for young persons must be separate from that of adults, must be based on the principle of diminished moral blameworthiness or culpability and must emphasize the following:

       (i)   rehabilitation and reintegration,

      (ii)   fair and proportionate accountability that is consistent with the greater dependency of young persons and their reduced level of maturity,

     (iii)   enhanced procedural protection to ensure that young persons are treated fairly and that their rights, including their right to privacy, are protected,

     (iv)   timely intervention that reinforces the link between the offending behaviour and its consequences, and

      (v)   the promptness and speed with which persons responsible for enforcing this Act must act, given young persons' perception of time;

   (c)   within the limits of fair and proportionate accountability, the measures taken against young persons who commit offences should

       (i)   reinforce respect for societal values,

      (ii)   encourage the repair of harm done to victims and the community,

     (iii)   be meaningful for the individual young person given his or her needs and level of development and, where appropriate, involve the parents, the extended family, the community and social or other agencies in the young person's rehabilitation and reintegration, and

     (iv)   respect gender, ethnic, cultural and linguistic differences and respond to the needs of aboriginal young persons and of young persons with special requirements; and

   (d)   special considerations apply in respect of proceedings against young persons and, in particular,

       (i)   young persons have rights and freedoms in their own right, such as a right to be heard in the course of and to participate in the processes, other than the decision to prosecute, that lead to decisions that affect them, and young persons have special guarantees of their rights and freedoms,

      (ii)   victims should be treated with courtesy, compassion and respect for their dignity and privacy and should suffer the minimum degree of inconvenience as a result of their involvement with the youth criminal justice system,

(iii) victims should be provided with information about the proceed-
       ings and given an opportunity to participate and be heard, and

(iv)   parents should be informed of measures or proceedings involv-
       ing their children and encouraged to support them in addressing
       their offending behaviour.

(2) This *Act* shall be liberally construed so as to ensure that young
persons are dealt with in accordance with the principles set out in sub-
section (1).[35]

In *R v KJM* (ABCA),[36] the Court of Appeal of Alberta split three ways
in their discussion of how the section 11(b) *Charter* assessment should
apply to young persons. Justice Wakeling held that the *Jordan* ceilings
apply equally to youth matters and that, even if *Jordan* left open the
possibility that a lower ceiling apply to youth matters, the record did
not assist in determining what that ceiling ought to be. In applying the
Jordan framework, Wakeling J held that the unavailability of a transcript
ordered by the trial judge was an exceptional circumstance as it was
outside of the Crown's control and as such the delay was under the presumptive ceiling. Applying the under the ceiling test, Wakeling J held
that there was no evidence that the accused had made a sustained effort
to expedite proceedings and that the case took markedly longer than
it should have. Accordingly, there was no breach of section 11(b) of the
Charter. In the alternative, any delay was justified under the transitional
exception.

Justice O'Ferrall, concurring with Wakeling J in the result, rejected
the view that any presumptive ceiling ought to apply to youth matters.[37]
His reasoning was, in part, due to the impact a ceiling might have on
the application of extrajudicial measures and the imposition of extrajudicial sanctions, which are crucial to fulfilling the mandate of the
youth criminal justice system to promote accountability, rehabilitation,
and reintegration.[38]

Justice Veldhuis dissented, holding that although new categories
of persons entitled to different presumptive ceilings ought not be created lightly, such a category should be established where young people

---

35   YCJA, above note 27, s 3.
36   *R v KJM*, 2018 ABCA 278 at para 45 [*KJM (ABCA)*].
37   *Ibid* at para 71.
38   *Ibid* at para 76.

were concerned.[39] She relied on the decision of Paciocco J, as he then was, in *R v JM*,[40] in which he established a fifteen-month presumptive ceiling for young persons under the *YCJA*.[41] She further concluded that the delay exceeded the fifteen-month ceiling, and that the transitional exception was not engaged.[42]

The Supreme Court determined that the presumptive ceilings in *Jordan* apply unchanged to youth criminal justice matters. Put differently, no lower presumptive ceiling applied to young persons.[43] Applying a separate ceiling for various categories of prejudice would reintroduce the unpredictability and complexity of the *Morin* framework that the *Jordan* framework intended to correct. As Moldaver J, for the majority, explained:

> By building the concept of prejudice into the presumptive ceilings, *Jordan* eliminated prejudice as "an express analytical factor" to be considered (see paras. 54 and 109-10). Thus prejudice is not irrebuttably presumed once the ceiling is breached meaning that "an absence of actual prejudice cannot convert an unreasonable delay into a reasonable one" (para. 54). Prejudice also has a strong relationship with the concept of defence initiative, as it can be expected that accused persons who experience heightened prejudice as a result of delay will be more proactive in moving the matter along (see para. 109). In sum, "the concept of prejudice underpins the entire framework" (para. 109).[44]

The Court acknowledged that the enhanced need for timeliness in youth matters is well-established in the jurisprudence and codified in section 3(1)(b)(iv) and (v) of the *YCJA*.[45] There were five reasons for this. First, the need to reinforce the connection between actions and consequences. Due to their different perception of time and less well-developed memory compared to adults, young persons are less able to appreciate the connection between their actions and the consequences.[46] Long delays

---

39   *Ibid* at paras 81 and 92–116.

40   2017 ONCJ 4 at paras 113–45 [*JM*].

41   *KJM (ABCA)*, above note 36 at paras 81 and 92–116; *YCJA*, above note 27.

42   *KJM (ABCA)*, above note 41 at paras 132–52.

43   *KJM (SCC)*, above note 4 at para 4.

44   *Ibid* at para 46.

45   *Ibid* at para 4.

46   *Ibid* at para 51, citing N. Bala & S. Anand, *Youth Criminal Justice Law*, 3d ed (Toronto: Irwin Law, 2012) at 439.

can obscure the connection between the offence and the disposition, whereas timely intervention reinforces it and enables the young person to learn from the experience and promotes rehabilitation and overall social development.[47] Accordingly, as the Court held, the effectiveness of the youth justice process depends at least in part on its timeliness.[48]

Second, section 11(b) of the *Charter* has special significance for young persons due to the heightened psychological impact of lengthy delays on young people. The Court held that delay may have a greater psychological impact on young persons because young persons perceive time differently than adults. The simple reality is that time spent awaiting trial occupies a greater proportion of a young person's life than an adult's. The Court observed, "the same period of delay may weigh more heavily on a young person than on an adult, which may in turn increase the overall feelings of stress, anxiety, and (where applicable) loss of liberty associated with the delay," which necessitates that youth matters, "as a general rule" proceed more expeditiously than adult matters.[49]

Third, the Court observed that young persons ought to be tried more quickly as memories tend to fade faster for young persons than for adults, which has an impact on the right to make full answer and defence.[50] In addition, as young persons have less ability to take long-term consequences into consideration and greater propensity for short-sighted decision-making, they may be less able to assist in their defence as delay accumulates and be motivated to get to the end of proceedings, regardless of the outcome.[51]

---

47   *KJM (SCC)*, above note 4 at para 51, citing P. Harris, et al, "Working 'In the Trenches' with the YCJA" (2004) 46 *Canadian Journal of Criminology and Criminal Justice* 367 at 369.

48   *KJM (SCC)*, above note 4 at para 51, citing J.A. Butts, G.R. Cusick & B. Adams, *Delays in Youth Justice* (2009) at 8.

49   *KJM (SCC)*, above note 4 at para 52, citing *Catholic Children's Aid Society of Metropolitan Toronto v M (C)*, [1994] 2 SCR 165.

50   *KJM (SCC)*, above note 4 at para 53; citing N. Bala, "*Youth as Victims and Offenders in the Criminal Justice System: A Charter Analysis—Recognizing Vulnerability*" (2008) 40 *Supreme Court Law Review*, 2d ed 595 at 616, in turn citing C.J. Brainerd, "Children's Forgetting with Implication for Memory Suggestibility," in N.L. Stein et al, eds, *Memory for Everyday and Emotional Events* (1997) at 213–17; see also *Dersch v Canada (Attorney General)*, [1990] 2 SCR 1505; *R v Khelawon*, 2006 SCC 57 at para 47; and *R v Bjelland*, 2009 SCC 38 at para 20.

51   *KJM (SCC)*, above note 4 at para 53; citing Butts, Cusick & Adams, above note 48 at 10.

Fourth, the Court noted that adolescence is a time of rapid brain, cognitive, and psychological development.[52] Delay between the offending conduct and the punishment should be minimized to avoid punishing a young person for "who they used to be," which would engender a sense of unfairness in a young person who has changed considerably since the offending conduct took place.[53]

Fifth, it serves society's interest to try young persons in a timely manner as prompt intervention in youth matters increases the likelihood of seeing the young person rehabilitated and reintegrated into society as swiftly as possible, which reduces the likelihood of recidivism.[54] Further, the Court explained, "as 'the most vulnerable members of our community' [...], it seems axiomatic that society has a particularly strong interest in ensuring young persons do not suffer prolonged delays."[55]

Justice Moldaver, for the majority, noted that, historically, the Court had avoided creating separate guidelines or constitutional thresholds for delay in youth matters.[56] In *R v D(S)*,[57] the Court noted youth as a factor to be taken into account but it stopped short of commenting one way or another on the administrative guidelines for unreasonable delay proposed by the Court of Appeal for Ontario in *R v M (GC)*.[58]

While Abella and Brown JJ, in dissent, would have introduced a fifteen-month ceiling for young persons,[59] it was the majority's view that lowering the ceiling would constitute a response to a problem in the youth criminal justice system that had not been shown to exist.[60]

---

52   *KJM (SCC)*, above note 4 at para 54, citing L Steinberg, *"Adolescent Development and Juvenile Justice"* (2009) 5 *Annual Review of Clinical Psychology* 459 at 465–71; T. Grisso, "Adolescents' Decision Making: A Development Perspective on Constitutional Provisions in Delinquency Cases" (2006) 32 *New England Journal on Criminal & Civil Confinement* 3 at 7–9; M. Levick et al, "The Eighth Amendment Involves: Defining Cruel and Unusual Punishment Through the Lens of Childhood and Adolescence" (2012) 15 *University of Pennsylvania Journal of Law and Social Change* 285 at 293–99.

53   *KJM (SCC)*, above note 4 at para 54.

54   *Ibid* at para 55, citing Butts, Cusick & Adams, above note 48 at 9.

55   *KJM (SCC)*, above note 4 at para 55, citing *R v Alicandro*, 2009 ONCA 133 at para 36, citing G.J. Fitch, QC, "Child Luring" in *Substantive Criminal Law, Advocacy and the Administration of Justice*, vol 1, presented to the National Criminal Law Program (2007).

56   *KJM (SCC)*, above note 4 at para 57.

57   1992 CanLII 58 (SCC).

58   *M (GC)*, above note 33; *KJM (SCC)*, above note 4 at para 57.

59   *Ibid* at para 62.

60   *Ibid* at para 64.

Further, to lower the applicable ceiling for *YCJA* matters would undermine the uniformity and simplicity of the *Jordan* framework and its streamlined approach and lead to a multiplicity of ceilings for various categories of prosecution, each with a unique level of prejudice experienced by the particular category or subcategory of persons in question:

> Young persons in custody, young persons out of custody, adults in custody, adults out of custody, persons whose custody status changes, persons with strict bail conditions, persons with minimal bail conditions, persons who experience heightened memory loss, and others could all lay claim to their own distinct ceiling.[61]

Furthermore, the separate system statutorily established by the *YCJA* did not dictate constitutional standards.[62]

The Court determined that the flexibility of the existing *Jordan* framework already accounted for the enhanced need for timeliness in youth cases.[63] In particular, the majority noted that the special status of young offenders, and the rationale for that status, "can, and should" be considered in applying the second branch of the test for a stay below the presumptive ceiling, namely as a case-specific factor in determining whether the case took markedly longer than it reasonably should have, assuming the first branch of the test—that the defence took meaningful steps that demonstrate a sustained effort to expedite the proceedings—has been met.[64] The majority concluded that "unless and until it can be shown that *Jordan* is failing to adequately serve Canada's youth and society's broader interest in seeing youth matters tried expeditiously, there is in my view no need to consider, much less implement, a lower constitutional ceiling for youth matters."[65] The majority added that while stays below the ceiling will be "rare" and "limited to clear cases" when considered against all criminal proceedings and the entire body of applications, this may be less so when considered against the smaller body of youth matters.[66] Tolerance for delay in the youth context has been—and will continue to be—lower than in the adult

---

61   *Ibid* at para 65.

62   *Ibid* at para 66.

63   *Ibid* at paras 4 and 64.

64   *Ibid* at paras 4 and 68–75; *Jordan*, above note 1 at para 48.

65   *KJM (SCC)*, above note 4 at para 4.

66   *Ibid* at para 78.

context.[67] The restriction to "clear cases" in considering whether delay below the ceiling is nevertheless unreasonable was intended to ensure that borderline cases were not stayed, given the significant public interest in seeing criminal matters resolved on their merits.[68] To maintain the ceilings for *YCJA* matters, while allowing that youth matters are more likely to result in a breach of section 11(b) of the *Charter* though the delay trial was below the ceiling, would ensure both that the Crown will remain proactive to ensure a case does not take markedly longer than it should have and that defence counsel will remain proactive given the requirement that the defence take meaningful steps to demonstrate a sustained effort to expedite the proceedings before a breach below the ceiling can be established.[69]

The majority added helpful guidance around the treatment of delay resulting from failed attempts at extrajudicial sanctions. The *YCJA* defines extrajudicial measures as "measures other than judicial proceedings under this *Act* used to deal with a young person alleged to have committed an offence and includes extrajudicial sanctions."[70] Extrajudicial measures are intended to respond to youth offending in "a less intrusive, more informal, and more expeditious fashion" than can be achieved through the Courts, such as warnings or cautions and referrals to programs or agencies in the community.[71] They are forms of diversion that attempt to address youth offending outside the formal court system. Their use helps minimize delays in the youth court system and within the court system more generally and is essential to the principles and proper functioning of the *YCJA* by reducing the over-reliance on incarceration for non-violent young persons and as an effective and timely means of intervention.[72] Such measures, however, require that the young person comply with the terms and conditions of the program, and it does not prevent judicial proceedings from recommencing if the young person fails to do so.

---

67   *Ibid* at para 81.

68   *Ibid* at para 78.

69   *Ibid* at paras 82–83.

70   *YCJA*, above note 27, s 2(1); *KJM (SCC)*, above note 4 at para 86.

71   *Ibid*, citing Bala & Anand, above note 46 at 340 and 350, and citing B. Jones, E. Rhodes & M.R. Birdsell, *Prosecuting and Defending Youth Criminal Justice Cases: A Practitioner's Handbook*, in B.H. Greenspan & V. Rondinelli, eds, Criminal Law Series (2016) at 128.

72   *KJM (SCC)*, above note 4 at para 87.

The Court held that extrajudicial sanctions should be treated on a case-by-case basis but that it can reasonably be expected that the time taken to attempt completion of diversion programming, where that has failed and judicial proceedings recommenced, will be deducted as defence-caused delay. Removing this delay from the calculation of net delay in applying the *Jordan* framework will minimize the risk that authorities will refrain from using extrajudicial sanctions in the first place for fear that they may increase the likelihood of a stay if efforts fail. Effectively, the *Jordan* clock stops while the matter is on a diversion track and only restarts if it returns to the court system track.[73]

b) Retrials

The Supreme Court definitively addressed the question of how to calculate delay in cases involving retrials in *R v JF*.[74] In that case, the accused attempted to raise delay that he experienced in his first trial for the first time at his retrial. The Court held that delay experienced in the first trial cannot be raised in the second trial.[75] In doing so, the Court reiterated that the purpose of the *Jordan* framework is to offer greater predictability and clarity and to encourage all parties to be proactive. To effect this purpose depends on the accused raising unreasonable trial delay in a timely manner.[76] The expectation is that an accused diligently apply for a remedy in advance of the trial. In some exceptional circumstances an accused may bring the application on appeal, but after the appeal court has ordered a new trial, the accused will no longer be able to raise the delay from their first trial.[77] The Court confirmed that the presumptive ceilings and *Jordan* framework apply to the retrial, but the time begins to count from zero on the day that an appellate court orders a new trial. While the Court acknowledged that retrials ought to be prioritized when scheduling hearings and be shorter than first trials, it specifically declined to adopt a different ceiling for retrials.[78]

The judge at first instance in *R v JF* took a "global and contextual approach" to the assessment of reasonableness of delay pursuant to

---

73   *Ibid* at paras 88–89.

74   JF (SCC), above note 3.

75   *Ibid* at para 3.

76   *Ibid*.

77   *Ibid*.

78   *Ibid* at para 4.

section 11(b) and determined that time to trial for both trials was cumulatively captured by the presumptive ceiling.[79] The Quebec Court of Appeal upheld the trial judge's stay of proceedings, but on the basis of a different rationale. The Court held that the calculation of delay must restart at zero in cases where a retrial is ordered, but that the accused ought not to be precluded from raising delay on the first trial given that he had never expressly waived the delay arising in the first trial.[80] The Court of Appeal proposed a two-step approach for calculating delay: to consider delay in the first trial and, if that is reasonable, then the delay at the retrial may be assessed, starting from the order of the new trial. The Quebec Court of Appeal upheld the stay on the basis of the delay in the first trial, applying the above-noted analysis.

Chief Justice Wagner, writing for the majority of the Supreme Court (Côté J dissenting), held that the lower courts had erred in considering delay as it relates to the first trial, allowed the appeal, and set aside the stay of proceedings.[81] The Court recognized that an accused reverts to the status of "a person charged with an offence," and therefore is under the protection of section 11(b) of the *Charter*, if a trial decision is set aside and a new trial is ordered (see Chapter 3 regarding the inapplicability of section 11(b) of the *Charter* pending appeal).[82] The Court acknowledged that prior to *Jordan*, appellate jurisprudence permitted an accused sent back for retrial to raise the delay in both their first trial and their retrial but pointed out that the Court had never opined on the right of an accused to bring such an application in a retrial in *Jordan*.[83] The new parameters prescribed by *Jordan*, the Court explained, made the situation "completely different."[84] The Court clarified that the *Jordan* framework was intended to provide a solution to delay in bringing an accused to trial and that the predictability imposed by the presumptive ceiling was central to its functioning.[85] In view of

---

79   *R c JF*, 2019 QCCQ 1236 at paras 71–78 [*JF (QCCQ)*]; *JF (SCC)*, above note 3 at paras 12–15.

80   *JF (QCCQ)*, above note 79 at paras 71–78; *JF (SCC)*, above note 3 at paras 16–20.

81   *Ibid* at para 79.

82   *Ibid* at para 23.

83   *Ibid* at para 54.

84   *Ibid* at para 55.

85   *Ibid* at paras 27, 31, and 56; *R v KGK*, 2020 SCC 7 at paras 31, 34, and 50 [*KGK (SCC)*]; *Jordan*, above note 1 at paras 2, 4, 13, 33, 49, 117, 121, and 129; *R c Rice*, 2018 QCCA 198 at para 41 [*Rice*].

this, the Court held, it "should now be understood that the computation of delay restarts at zero when a new trial is ordered" and that "what was said in *Potvin* cannot be interpreted in any other way today": the accused cannot bring a section 11(b) motion during a retrial based on delay at their first trial.[86]

After a new trial is ordered and the accused regains the status of a person charged with an offence, the Crown, once again, has the duty to bring the accused to trial within a reasonable time.[87] The Court made clear that, in restarting the *Jordan* clock at zero, the presumptive ceilings apply as established in *Jordan*, and that no lower presumptive ceiling was required though the matter is a retrial.[88] The Court outlined two reasons that this was so: First, as in *KJM*, absent a particular systemic failure in the criminal justice system, no new constitutional standard for retrials was required.[89] Second, as in *KJM*, setting ceilings that are specific to retrials or other former categories of prejudice would undermine the uniformity and predictability that *Jordan* sought to implement and would frustrate the framework's objective of simplifying and streamlining the section 11(b) *Charter* analysis.[90] The Court noted that the framework provided a flexible, case-specific approach to delay where the calculated net delay fell under the ceiling and left open the consideration of first trial delay in assessing the reasonableness of retrial delay in exceptional circumstances.[91]

In essence, while the former *Morin* categories of prejudice no longer exist, the concerns that informed them remain relevant in the contextual, case-specific analysis within the *Jordan* framework above and below the ceiling.[92] The Court proposed two factors to consider when analyzing the reasonableness of retrial delay under the ceiling. First, it made clear that the need to prioritize retrials when scheduling hearings remains unchanged and that all justice participants should be proactive about

---

86   *JF (SCC)*, above note 3 at para 55, referencing *R v Potvin*, 1993 CanLII 113 (SCC) [*Potvin*]; *R v MacIsaac*, 2018 ONCA 650 at para 31 [*MacIsaac*]; *R v JEV*, 2019 ABCA 359 at paras 36–37; *R v JAL*, 2019 ABCA 415 at para 6.

87   *JF (SCC)*, above note 3 at para 61.

88   *Ibid* at paras 61–73.

89   *Ibid* at paras 63–65.

90   *Ibid* at paras 66–67.

91   *Ibid* at paras 60 and 70–73.

92   *Ibid* at paras 66–68.

scheduling retrials in view of this.[93] Second, retrials, as a general rule, ought to conclude in less time than first trials since the evidence has already been presented a first time. The Court was quick to acknowledge that this is not always the case and that changes adopted from one trial to the next may result in a trial of comparable length.[94] Finally, the Court held that the history of the first trial will, in exceptional circumstances, inform the analysis, but ought not to be given too much weight given that the focus of the analysis remains delay from the date of the order for a new trial to the end of that subsequent trial.[95] The delay to the end of the first trial carries little, if any, weight to the analysis of the reasonableness of delay in a subsequent trial in most instances.[96]

In cases following the Court's decision in *JF*, focus has been on the Court and the Crown's efforts to prioritize the scheduling of retrials. In *R v Heintzelman*,[97] for example, McKimm J's analysis centred on the direction provided in *JF* that retrials should be given priority and should be capable of being conducted in an expeditious fashion.[98] First, he held that the Court ought to have given priority to the retrial in spite of the fact that the defence intended to exhaust leave to appeal to the Court of Appeal, which made things unpredictable. Justice McKimm was "sympathetic to the court's analytical processes in making that decision," that it was better to schedule other matters that were certain to proceed rather than waste court resources by giving priority to a matter that might not need them.[99] Still, he found that there was a failure to give priority to a retrial in spite of the Supreme Court's express direction.[100] He further found that, although defence counsel expressed some reservation about scheduling the retrial before the accused's rights of appeal were exhausted, defence counsel's reservation did not amount to express or implicit waiver.[101] Ultimately McKimm J held that most delay fell at the feet of the Crown because the Crown failed to give priority to the retrial. He determined that there was evidence that the Crown was

---

93   *Ibid* at paras 70 and 72.

94   *Ibid* at paras 71–72.

95   *Ibid* at para 73; see: *R v Heintzelman*, 2022 BCPC 150 [*Heintzelman*].

96   *JF (SCC)*, above note 3 at para 78.

97   *Heintzelman*, above note 95.

98   *Ibid* at para 22.

99   *Ibid* at para 24.

100   *Ibid.*

101   *Ibid.*

taking inconsistent positions (applying for a Crown witness to testify remotely while opposing the accused's application to appear remotely, and also requesting an adjournment when defence filed submissions late and then filing the Crown's submissions late), had failed to resort to case management processes when the rescheduling went well beyond local practice directions, estimated time requirements that were "wildly inaccurate," had not been responsive to defence counsel's suggestions to streamline the evidence, and there had been a last-minute reassignment of the matter.[102] Finally, McKimm J held that there was nothing arising in the retrial that meant it could not be conducted expeditiously and, if wrong about the delay calculation and this matter fell under the presumptive ceiling, as a retrial, the time to end of the evidence and submissions was unreasonable. In his view, the case should have been completed "in half the time" that it ultimately took to complete, and therefore, had taken markedly longer than it should have.[103]

5) Direct Indictments, Re-elections, Consent to Committal, and Mistrials

There are several events that can divert a trial from a standard trajectory, including direct indictments, re-election, consent to committal, and mistrials. The following provides some guidance on whether those events have an impact on how the presumptive ceiling is to be applied under the *Jordan* framework.

a) Direct Indictments

The presumptive ceiling for superior court matters remains thirty months even where the accused is the subject of a direct indictment, thus bypassing the preliminary inquiry process. In *R v Manasseri*,[104] the Court of Appeal of Ontario encouraged the Crown to prefer an indictment for the purpose of reducing the time to trial. It has since been held that, where the Crown has preferred an indictment, the applicable ceiling will remain thirty months for matters going to trial in the superior court, whether or not there has been a preliminary

---

102   *Ibid* at paras 23–35.
103   *Ibid* at para 37.
104   *R v Manasseri*, 2016 ONCA 703 at para 376 (fn 5) [*Manasseri*].

hearing.[105] Further, it is generally the case that the time required for the Crown to pursue a direct indictment will not be held against the Crown as such a step is a matter of prosecutorial discretion, reviewable only for abuse of process, and such a step inevitably saves trial time.[106]

In some instances, however, a court has held that delay in pursuing a direct indictment, where a trial was likely to have been scheduled sooner but for that delay, may result in a portion of the delay to trial being attributed to the Crown. For example, in *R v Agpoon*,[107] the Crown argued that the entirety of the delay between the adjournment of the preliminary inquiry in May 2020 (due to COVID-19 pandemic closures) and the preferring of the Indictment in May 2021 ought to be deducted from the net delay count. The applicant countered that the Crown ought to have sought the direct indictment at the judicial pre-trial or, at the least, in May 2020 when the shutdown arose. Had it been pursued then, a trial would have taken place sooner. Justice Leipert agreed with the applicant, holding that because the Crown had apparently been contemplating such a step in February 2020 and because it had managed to prefer a direct indictment in a similar matter within three months' time, some of the delay to trial must have been due to the Crown's delay in this regard, rather than to the pandemic closures. Only three months, the time it took the Crown to prefer an indictment in the other matter, was deducted from the net delay count in the circumstances.[108]

Additionally, preferring an indictment does not allow the Crown a thirty-month period during which it can sit back and allow delay to

---

105   *R v Perdomo Lopez*, 2020 ABCA 404 at paras 67–68; *Pennington v R*, 2020 SKQB 198 at paras 47–53; *R v Ochelo et al*, 2021 ABCA 380 at para 39; *R v Burg and Khan*, 2021 MBCA 77 at para 23; *R v Schenkels*, 2017 MBCA 62 at paras 43–50, leave to appeal refused (without reasons) 2017 CanLII 78703 (SCC); *R v DJH*, 2021 BCSC 1340 at para 66; *R v Walton*, 2022 ABCA 276 at para 124.

106   *R v Barra*, 2021 ONCA 568 at paras 30 and 34; *R v Bulhosen*, 2019 ONCA 600 at paras 67–72 and 85–94, leave to appeal refused (without reasons) 2020 CanLII 17613 (SCC) [*Bulhosen*]; *Manasseri*, above note 104 at para 376 (fn 5); *R v Nyznik*, 2017 ONSC 69 at paras 33–35 [*Nyznik*]; *R v Jones*, 2016 ABQB 691 at para 26.

107   2022 ONSC 2762 [*Agpoon*].

108   *Ibid* at paras 53–59. Note: The Ontario Court of Appeal considered this decision in *R v Agpoon*, 2023 ONCA 449, leave to appeal refused (without reasons) 2024 CanLII 45540 (SCC). The Court held that the trial judge erred in attributing any delay to the Crown for the delayed Direct Indictment application given that it did not cause any delay. Instead, the delay through that period was properly attributable to the pandemic.

run. As Nordheimer J (as he then was) explained in the decision in *R v Nyznik*:[109]

> The preferring of an indictment does not bestow 30 months of free time on the prosecution, which they can consume at their leisure on their way to a trial. It is always open to an accused person to demonstrate that a trial, that occurs below the 30 months ceiling, is still an unreasonable time for the trial to take place.[110]

Accordingly, though the ceiling sits at thirty months in these circumstances, that a direct indictment was pursued will be a relevant factor in assessing the reasonableness of delay even where the delay to trial comes in under the presumptive ceiling.

b)   Re-elections

Where the accused is scheduled to have a preliminary hearing but *prior to* the completion of the hearing either elects (not having done so already or where the election was not formally recorded) or re-elects with the consent of the Crown to be tried before the provincial court, the applicable ceiling is eighteen months.[111] Where the re-election takes place after the completion of the preliminary inquiry, the thirty-month ceiling applies.[112] As the Court of Appeal for Ontario held in *R v Shaikh*,[113] in instances "where re-election would create the risk of s. 11(b) problems, the Crown has the authority to, and should, refuse consent, absent a s. 11(b) waiver."[114] In instances where an accused does not exercise their right to re-elect in a timely fashion, such that scheduled trial dates are proven to be lost or delay is otherwise proven to be caused, such delay is defence-caused and to be deducted from the net delay count.[115] That said, where the decision to re-elect is delayed because it is tied to another source of delay that is not solely caused by the defence and is at least, in part, attributable to the Crown, such as failure to make

---

109   *Nyznik*, above note 106.

110   *Ibid* at paras 30–32.

111   *R v Shaikh*, 2019 ONCA 895 at paras 47–58 [*Shaikh*]; *R v Charity*, 2022 ONCA 226 at para 17.

112   *R v S(DM)*, 2016 NBCA 71 at para 17.

113   *Shaikh*, above note 111.

114   *Ibid* at para 57; *R v Wookey*, 2021 ONCA 68 at paras 3, 12–14, 46, and 61–76 [*Wookey*]; *R v Long*, 2023 ONCA 679 at paras 14 and 62.

115   *R v Lai*, 2021 SCC 52 at paras 2–4; *R v Sharma*, 2022 BCSC 2080 at paras 27–36.

timely disclosure, the delay may be attributed to the Crown in those circumstances.[116]

c)   Consent to Committal

Preliminary hearings are built into the presumptive ceiling of thirty months for superior court and two-stage matters in the provincial court. If an accused consents to committal and waives the preliminary hearing before trial in superior court, as with direct indictments, the ceiling of thirty months remains unchanged.[117]

d)   Mistrials

The Supreme Court has yet to pronounce on how to factor a mistrial into the *Jordan* calculation. The developing appellate jurisprudence on this issue accepts that most mistrials come under the *Jordan* ceiling as part of a first trial, but qualify as exceptional circumstances.[118] That said, there is also a recognition that mistrials "come in many flavours."[119] Some do not fall into the category of reasonably unforeseen or reasonably unavoidable, such as an inflammatory closing address by the Crown or a prejudicial statement by a Crown witness in front of a jury.[120] A Crown's conduct of the retrial following a mistrial may also be scrutinized for evidence that it failed to take any available steps that could have led to the case being heard earlier, disregarded any opportunities to cooperate with the defence, failed to bring sufficient resources to bear to conduct the trial, or failed to fulfill its duties in a timely way.[121] Similarly, where a mistrial is caused by defence conduct, it would properly be deducted as defence-caused delay.[122]

---

116   *R v LL*, 2023 ONCA 52 at paras 15–16; *R v Lee*, 2017 ONSC 4862; *R v Aden*, 2023 ONSC 766 at paras 81–86.

117   *Bulhosen*, above note 106 at paras 69–72; *R v Maone*, 2017 ONSC 3537 at paras 11–22.

118   *R v Mallozzi*, 2017 ONCA 644 at paras 40–43; *R v Christhurajah*, 2019 BCCA 210 at paras 116–17; *R v Wu*, 2017 BCSC 2373 at para 91 [*Wu*]; *R v Beckett*, 2017 BCSC 1116 at para 163 [*Beckett*]; *R v Masilamany*, 2018 ONSC 3171 at paras 24–26; *R v Way*, 2022 ABCA 1 at para 38 [*Way*]; *R v Locknick*, 2019 ONCA 625 at paras 13–18 [*Locknick*]; *R v Kuntz-Angel*, 2020 BCSC 1777 at paras 162–63 [*Kuntz-Angel*].

119   *R v Clifford*, 2022 ABQB 509 at para 25 [*Clifford*]; *Way*, above note 118 at paras 35–41.

120   *Jordan*, above note 1 at paras 69–74; *Wu*, above note 118 at para 79; *Beckett*, above note 118 at para 163; *R v JHT*, 2016 BCSC 2382 at paras 155–74; *Clifford*, above note 119 at paras 25–33; *R v JT*, 2021 ONSC 365 at para 30 [*JT*].

121   *Kuntz-Angel*, above note 118 at paras 162–63.

122   *Clifford*, above note 119 at para 30; *JT*, above note 120 at para 30.

B.   START POINT: WHEN THE INFORMATION IS SWORN

1)   Pre- and Post-Charge Delay

The portion of the prosecution that is measured against the *Jordan* framework runs from "the charge to the actual or anticipated end of trial."[123] This period encompasses the date of the laying of the charge to the end of trial. It is the date that the Information is sworn (meaning the charge is formally laid), not the arrest date, which will mark the start of the count or the "charge" for the purposes of section 11(b) of the *Charter*. In *R v Kalanj*,[124] decided during the *Morin* era, the Supreme Court determined that the date the Information is sworn (or where a direct indictment has been preferred) marked the start of the count.[125] That this was so arose from the wording, structure, and organization of section 11(b) of the *Charter*.[126] "Pre-information delay w[ould] not be a factor"[127] in assessing the reasonableness of trial delay. The Court like-wise noted that in *R v Mills*,[128] the Supreme Court majority had rejected the notion that the date of arrest could ever have been treated as the start date for assessing delay, a view which it later confirmed in *R v Cart-er*.[129] Without any flexibility as to its definition, "charged" for the pur-poses of section 11(b) of the *Charter*, referred to the date of the initiation of a prosecution via the swearing of an Information or by preferment of an indictment.[130] Accordingly, in *R v Kalanj*, though the arrest date occurred eight months prior to the date the Information was laid, the start date for the delay count pursuant to the *Morin* framework did not include any of the pre-charge delay. That is, none of what occurred prior to the swearing of the Information was relevant time to the analysis of the reasonableness of the delay to trial.

Post-*Jordan*, some lower courts have held that where there has been either too long a period between the accused's arrest and the date the Information was laid, or no explanation for the delay in that regard, the arrest date will be the start point for measuring the total delay. In

---

123   *Jordan*, above note 1 at paras 47–49, 60, and 82.

124   1989 CanLII 63 (SCC) [*Kalanj*].

125   *Ibid* at para 1.

126   *Ibid* at paras 17–19.

127   *Ibid* at para 16.

128   1986 CanLII 17 (SCC).

129   1986 CanLII 18 (SCC); *Kalanj*, above note 124 at paras 11–17.

130   *Ibid* at para 16.

R v Luoma,[131] for example, the accused had been arrested for drinking and driving offences two months prior to the date the Information was laid. After his arrest he attended the courthouse to find that his name was not on the docket. Without explanation, police had not yet laid the Information. Justice Schreck held that *Kalanj* was never intended to apply to instances where the delay between the arrest and the swearing of the Information was unexplained. In *Kalanj*, the eight months between the arrest and commencement of a prosecution was explained in that police required that time to continue to pursue an investigation.[132] Further, unexplained delay in laying an Information could be accounted for by reducing the deduction for intake that would have otherwise been treated as neutral, and therefore not counted, pursuant to the analysis in *Morin*, but could not be accounted for under the *Jordan* framework.[133] As a matter of fairness, to account for unexplained delay in commencing a prosecution required that the start date for the section 11(b) calculus be the *arrest date* in such circumstances. This was so as it should not be left to the whim of police to refuse to lay a charge as soon as is practicable though required to do so pursuant to section 505 of the *Criminal Code*.[134] The critical point in time for the purposes of commencing the *Jordan* count should be the point at which an accused becomes subject to the processes of the court. Therefore, the start date for the *Jordan* count should be when the Information was sworn or "ought to have been sworn"[135] according to the court in *Luoma*.

Other courts have not supported this view.[136] In *R v Akumu*,[137] Fisher J would not follow *Luoma*, though the delay between arrest and the laying of the Information amounted to four months in that case. That the interpretation proffered in *Luoma* should be rejected was

---

131   2016 ONCJ 670 [*Luoma*]; see also: *R v Gleiser*, 2017 ONSC 2858 at para 18; *R v Albadry*, 2018 ONCJ 114 at para 9; *R v Bolé*, 2019 ONCJ 141 at paras 22–24; *R v Gill*, 2020 ONCJ 124 at paras 24–30; *R v Elakrat*, 2020 ONCJ 343 at para 14; *R v Creglia*, 2018 ONCJ 262, at fn 2; *R v Rosenthal*, 2023 ONCJ 149.

132   *Luoma*, above note 131 at paras 24–26.

133   *Ibid* at para 21; see also: *R v Duszak*, [2013] OJ No 5015 (CJ) at para 51; *R v Hashmi*, [2016] OJ No 1116 (CJ) at para 32; *R v Kopalasingam*, [2016] OJ No 4200 (CJ) at paras 21–26.

134   *Luoma*, above note 131 at paras 22 and 27–28; *Criminal Code*, RSC 1985, c C-46.

135   *Luoma*, above note 131 at para 29.

136   See: *R v Gandhi*, 2016 ONSC 5612 at para 4; *R v Pelletier*, 2016 BCSC 2496 at paras 24–25 [*Pelletier*]; *R v Ashraf*, 2016 ONCJ 584 at paras 51–52 [*Ashraf*]; *R v Ajgirevich*, 2022 ONCJ 237 at paras 24–27; *R v Thompson*, 2022 ONSC 2712 at paras 32–39.

137   2017 BCSC 896 [*Akumu*].

supported by the binding authority of *Kalanj*.[138] Fisher J noted that one of the reasons the Court in *Kalanj* held that pre-charge delay should not factor into the section 11(b) calculus is the difficulty in assessing what can be said to be a reasonable time for the investigatory period, which is unpredictable by its nature.[139] The rights of the accused are protected by general law and guaranteed by sections 7, 8, 9, and 10 of the *Charter* during the pre-charge phase. Further, post-*Jordan*, to extend the definition of "charged" pursuant to section 11(b) of the *Charter* would risk side-tracking the analysis into considerations of the reasonableness of police investigations and the Crown charge approval process.[140]

Justice Fisher's view is supported by the decision in *R v Hunt*,[141] a matter that was argued before the Supreme Court on the same day as *R v Cody*.[142] While *Cody* related to the application of section 11(b), the issue before the Court in *Hunt* was the application of section 7 of the *Charter* to pre-charge delay. The case arose from a lengthy investigation into the actions of the senior management of a company in concealing business losses, selling company assets that had been used to secure loans, and falsifying books. The accused were not charged until ten years after the commencement of the investigation, and five years passed between the time the investigation could reasonably be taken to have resulted in charges (it was argued) and when the accused actually were charged, with little explanation for the delay. The accused were blindsided by the charges and sought a stay pursuant to section 7 of the *Charter*, alleging an abuse of process.[143] The applicants were successful in that regard at the trial stage. At the Newfoundland Court of Appeal, the majority, Welsh JA (Rowe JA concurring) agreed that the pre-charge delay was unreasonable, prejudiced the respondent's right to a fair trial, and amounted to an abuse of process applying section 7 of the *Charter*.[144]

Justice Hoegg, in dissent, would have allowed the Crown's appeal and lifted the stay. He pointed to the Supreme Court's jurisprudence,

---

138   *Kalanj*, above note 124.

139   *Akumu*, above note 137 at paras 25–26.

140   *Ibid* at para 26.

141   2017 SCC 25 [*Hunt (SCC)*], affirming Hoegg JA (in dissent) *R v Hunt*, 2016 NLCA 61 [*Hunt (NLCA)*].

142   2017 SCC 31 [*Cody*].

143   *Hunt (NLCA)*, above note 141 at paras 2–15; *Hunt (SCC)*, above note 141.

144   *Hunt (NLCA)*, above note 141 at paras 17–44; *Hunt (SCC)*, above note 141.

including in *Kalanj*,[145] where the Court held that pre-charge delay could not be considered in the section 11(b) context at all and was to be assessed pursuant to section 7 instead.[146] Justice Hoegg further observed that "*Kalanj* does not stand for the proposition that the courts are authorized to assess the efficiency of a police investigation or determine when the Crown was in a position to lay charges" on consideration of pre-charge delay pursuant to section 7.[147] In addition, the pre-charge delay had to be egregious in terms of the Crown's conduct, *not with regard to the length of the delay*.[148] Further, though the respondents argued that an abuse of process was established on the basis of delay by the Crown that was oppressive, Hoegg JA determined that to establish oppressive conduct rested on "some positive action" on the part of the Crown and must be of such a magnitude that it would "seriously compromise or tarnish the integrity of the justice system."[149] The Supreme Court (Côté J dissenting) allowed the appeal from the bench, adopting Hoegg JA's reasons.[150] That the date the Information was sworn is the start point for the section 11(b) analysis was similarly confirmed in the Supreme Court's decision in *R v KJM*,[151] where the Court identified the date of the swearing of the Information as "the point at which the *Jordan* clock starts ticking."[152]

In Ontario, whether the start of the section 11(b) ceiling count is at the date of the laying of the Information or "when it ought to have been laid" was definitively settled by the Ontario Court of Appeal in *R v Allison*.[153] Relying on *Luoma*[154] and the series of lower court decisions that followed its rationale, the appellant argued that the trial judge had erred by not treating the arrest date, seven weeks prior to the laying of the Information, as the start point for the *Jordan* analysis. The Court rejected this argument on the basis of the binding authority in *Kalanj*[155] and noted that had the Supreme Court in *Jordan* intended that the start

---

145   *Kalanj*, above note 124.

146   *Hunt (NLCA)*, above note 141 at paras 65–66 and 72; *Hunt (SCC)*, above note 141.

147   *Hunt (NLCA)*, above note 141 at para 72; *Hunt (SCC)*, above note 141.

148   *Hunt (NLCA)*, above note 141 at para 84; *Hunt (SCC)*, above note 141.

149   *Hunt (NLCA)*, above note 141 at paras 94–95; *Hunt (SCC)*, above note 141.

150   *Hunt (NLCA)*, above note 141; *Hunt (SCC)*, above note 141.

151   *KJM (SCC)*, above note 4.

152   *Ibid* at para 88.

153   2022 ONCA 329 [*Allison*]; see also: *R v Zahor*, 2022 ONCA 449.

154   *Luoma*, above note 131.

155   *Kalanj*, above note 124.

point be anything other than when the Information was sworn, it would have indicated such.[156]

The British Columbia Court of Appeal[157] and superior courts in British Columbia,[158] Quebec,[159] and New Brunswick[160] have similarly rejected the *Luoma*[161] approach. In Saskatchewan and Manitoba, some provincial courts have held that while *Kalanj*[162] stands for the proposition that the time for assessing the *Jordan* ceiling runs from the date the Information is sworn, pre-trial delay can nevertheless be relevant context as to the overall assessment of the reasonableness of delay, relying on *Morin* in this regard.[163] In Nova Scotia and Newfoundland and Labrador, it is accepted that *R v Hunt*[164] has reaffirmed *Kalanj* in the *Jordan* era and made clear that pre-charge delay can only be assessed pursuant to section 7 of the *Charter*.[165]

The issue was most recently considered at the appellate level by the New Brunswick Court of Appeal in *R v Doak*.[166] Ms. Doak was charged with one count of fraud over $5,000 with respect to theft against her employer in the amount of $130,000. While the Information arguably could have been sworn in September 2019, that did not take place until December 2021. The investigating officer testified on the section 11(b) *Charter* application as to the complexity of the investigation and noted that it had to be halted for a time as two homicide investigations had taken priority. At trial, the trial judge adopted the reasoning in *Luoma*,[167] and treated the date when the Information ought to have been sworn as the start point for the ceiling count. The ceiling having been exceeded, the prosecution was stayed.[168]

On appeal, Quigg JA, writing for the unanimous Court, held that the trial judge had erred in this regard. The start point for the analysis on

---

156   *Allison*, above note 153 at paras 35–43.

157   *R v Boima*, 2018 BCCA 297, leave to appeal refused 2019 CanLII 7958 (SCC) [*Boima*].

158   *R v Harris*, 2017 BCSC 1091; *Akumu*, above note 137.

159   *R c Bebawi*, 2018 QCCS 1476; *Paquette c R*, 2017 QCCS 677.

160   *R v Doak*, 2022 NBCA 48 [*Doak*].

161   *Luoma*, above note 131.

162   *Kalanj*, above note 124.

163   *R v Moosomin*, 2017 SKQB 182; *R v MS*, 2017 MBQB 12; *R v TSH*, 2020 SKPC 25.

164   *Hunt (NLCA)*, above note 141 at para 72; *Hunt (SCC)*, above note 141.

165   *R v PTC*, 2018 NSPC 6.

166   *Doak*, above note 160.

167   *Luoma*, above note 131.

168   *Doak*, above note 160 at paras 2–3.

delay was the date of the swearing of the Information and had been long settled by the Supreme Court.[169] Citing the repeated pronouncements by the Supreme Court on this point[170] and the negative treatments of the decision in *Luoma*,[171] the trial judge ought not to have adopted its reasoning. The appellate court also noted that to treat the date that a charge could have been laid as the start point failed to account for the Crown pre-screening process employed in New Brunswick and in other jurisdictions. An important protective measure, such a process requires the Crown to independently review a file for the reasonable prospect of a conviction and to assess whether to pursue a charge is in the public interest prior to laying a charge.

2) Withdrawals, Stays, and Recommencement of Charges

Where the Crown has sworn an Information against an accused, withdrawn the charge, and sworn a new Information, generally speaking, the clock stops on the date of the withdrawal or discharge, and starts again anew on the date the second Information is laid. In *R v Milani*,[172] the accused was initially charged with offences arising from a series of home invasion sexual assaults in 1987 and was discharged at a preliminary hearing in 1989. Eventual advancements in forensic technology allowed for identification of the accused through DNA technology many years later. The Crown preferred an indictment against Mr. Milani for the same offences in 2010 and he was arrested and charged. The judge at trial found that the period between 1987 and 2005 was inherent time, and therefore not counted within the (then applicable) *Morin* section 11(b) framework. However, because there was unexplained investigative delay through to the 2010 charges, this period was counted and the delay was found to be unreasonable, resulting in a stay of the charges.[173] The Ontario Court of Appeal overturned the stay on the basis that the accused was not a person charged with an offence through the gap

---

169   *Ibid* at paras 15–18.

170   *Kalanj*, above note 124; *R v Rahey*, 1987 CanLII 52 (SCC) [*Rahey*]; *KJM* (SCC), above note 4; *Cody*, above note 142; *R v Coulter*, 2016 ONCA 704; *Hunt (NLCA)*, above note 141 at para 72; *Hunt (SCC)*, above note 141; *Boima*, above note 157; *R v Virk*, 2021 BCCA 58.

171   *Luoma*, above note 131.

172   2014 ONCA 536 [*Milani*], leave to appeal refused (without reasons) 2015 CanLII 1293 (SCC).

173   *Ibid* at paras 9–19.

period between the first Information and the second. The clock started in 1987 but stopped on the date of the preliminary hearing discharge. It did not restart again through the investigative period, but only upon the swearing of the new Information in 2010.[174] However, included in the decision was the caveat that where the Crown acted unilaterally to withdraw and relay charges, the clock would run from the date the first Information was sworn, as the accused "remains subject to the judicial process, and his s. 11(b) interests will continue to be affected by the knowledge or expectation that further charges are imminent."[175] In other words, section 11(b) of the *Charter* would be "engaged during any period that an accused person is in fact subject to charges, or when a person no longer charged actively remains subject to the very real prospect of new charges."[176]

Post-*Jordan*, the *Milani* approach has generally been followed, with the question at issue in such cases being whether on the facts before the court, the accused could be said to have (1) remained "subject to the judicial process"; (2) with "imminent" charges on the horizon through the gap between the first Information and the second; (3) whether the accused was aware of an ongoing investigation such that her personal and privacy interests could be said to have been affected; and (4) whether the Crown had withdrawn the first charge as a means to remedy some problem.[177] Though the gap between charges may well be counted having regard to the above-noted factors, the general rule is that the clock stops and resets through this period, only starting again when a new Information is laid, and only in narrow and exceptional circumstances will it be otherwise.

In *R v Kanda*,[178] the British Columbia Court of Appeal reviewed the decisions of several courts in order to define the scope of the *Milani* caveat. The court concluded that the exception is circumscribed to instances where the Crown had withdrawn a charge for the purpose of curing some defect in the Information or the Information was withdrawn and the swearing of a new one delayed as an "end run around

---

174   *Ibid* at paras 21–47.

175   *Ibid* at paras 48–49.

176   *Ibid* at para 49; see also: *Wookey*, above note 114 at paras 49–60.

177   *R v Kanda*, 2021 BCCA 267 [*Kanda*], leave to appeal refused (without reasons) 2022 CanLII 5848 (SCC).

178   *Ibid*.

Jordan."[179] The exception, the court concluded, does not include instances where the initial Information was withdrawn for the purposes of some further investigation and that the existence of that ongoing investigation does not amount to "the very real prospect of new charges."[180] In so concluding, the court relied on *Kalanj*,[181] *Hunt*,[182] and *R v Potvin*[183] for the proposition that section 11(b) of the *Charter* was never intended to fix time limits on police investigations and that pre-charge delay is properly assessed on an abuse of process motion pursuant to section 7 of the *Charter*.[184]

Circumstances where an Information had been sworn, withdrawn, then re-sworn at some later stage, must be contrasted to instances where the Crown has stayed a prosecution pursuant to section 579 of the *Criminal Code*.[185] Section 579(1) allows that the Attorney General or counsel instructed by the Attorney General for that purpose may at any time after proceedings have commenced, but before judgment, direct the clerk to indicate in the record that the proceedings are stayed. Any release order or undertaking will be vacated in such instances. Section 579(2) allows for recommencement of the prosecution without need to swear a new Information or to prefer a new indictment until a year has passed with no notice of any recommencement to the clerk, in which case the proceedings will be deemed never to have been commenced.

In such instances, it is more likely that recommencement of the prosecution, either by the giving of notice or by the swearing of a new Information, will fit into the *Milani* exception. This is because by staying, rather than withdrawing the charges, the Crown can be taken to intend to continue pursuit of the prosecution within the year. For example, in *R v Curry*,[186] the Crown stayed the prosecution, but re-laid charges about four months later, admittedly for the purpose of allowing it more time to consider how an Information to Obtain might be properly redacted through that period. In other words, to stop the section 11(b) *Charter* clock from running. In that instance, the gap between Informations

---

179   *Ibid* at para 106; see also: *R v Antoine*, 1983 CanLII 1743 (Ont CA).

180   *Kanda*, above note 177 at paras 107–10.

181   *Kalanj*, above note 124.

182   *Hunt (NLCA)*, above note 141 at para 72; *Hunt (SCC)*, above note 141.

183   *Potvin*, above note 86.

184   *Kanda*, above note 177 at paras 103–5.

185   RSC 1985, c C-46, s 579.

186   2016 BCSC 1435 at paras 91–93.

was included in the assessment of the reasonableness of the delay. Similarly, in *R v Lanteigne*,[187] the New Brunswick Court of Appeal would not exclude the delay between Informations from the assessment. In that case, the Crown stayed serious charges arising from a motor vehicle accident on the basis that it had received information that implicated the victim, rather than the accused, as having caused the accident. The Crown required time for further investigation, including the search of two premises, neither of which were undertaken until nine months after the stay had been entered.[188] Justice Bell, writing for the Court, concluded that the accused remained subject to the court's process and legal jeopardy through this period as the Crown could choose to recommence the prosecution at any time, which it ultimately did only weeks from the end of the one-year deadline.[189] The court was likewise concerned that to find otherwise would be to allow the Crown to circumvent its obligation to bring an accused to trial within a reasonable time.[190]

In another instance, however, it was held that where the Crown admitted to a *prima facie* case at the time of the stay, this was not sufficient basis to count the gap to recommencement of the proceedings on the assessment of the reasonableness of the trial delay. In *R v Executive Flight Centre Fuel Services Ltd*,[191] a concerned citizen laid a private Information against a corporation, charging a number of regulatory offences related to an oil spill. The federal Crown intervened and stayed the charges. There was a six-month period before another Information was sworn.[192] The British Columbia Superior Court appellate judge found that the lower court had erred in including the six months as part of the delay count in that case, finding that the admission of a *prima facie* case on the basis of an incomplete investigation, conducted by a private citizen, did not rise to the level where the accused could be said to remain subject to "the very real prospect of new charges."[193]

---

187   2010 NBCA 91.
188   *Ibid* at paras 2–5.
189   *Ibid* at paras 5–6 and 13.
190   *Ibid* at para 14.
191   2018 BCSC 2212 [*Executive Flight (BCSC)*], leave to appeal granted, 2019 BCCA 139.
192   *Executive Flight (BCSC)*, above note 191 at paras 6–19.
193   *Ibid* at paras 126–39.

C. END POINT: WHEN THE EVIDENCE AND ARGUMENT ON THE TRIAL PROPER ARE COMPLETE

1) Overview

When calculating total delay for the purposes of the presumptive ceilings of the *Jordan* framework, the Court indicated in *Jordan* that the end point is the "actual or anticipated end of trial."[194] What constitutes the "end of trial," however, was not clearly defined.[195] The issue of what constituted the end of trial, and whether deliberation time ought to be included within the presumptive ceilings, arose squarely in *R v KGK*.[196] In that case, the trial judge reserved his decision for just over nine months which, if included within the presumptive ceilings, would have brought the total delay to forty-two months rather than thirty-three months. The Supreme Court's decision in *Jordan* was released more than halfway through the trial judge's deliberation in *KGK*. Even as a transitional case, the issue of whether the deliberation time counted within the presumptive ceiling made a significant difference in the delay calculus and result.

In *R v KGK*, the Supreme Court was asked to define the "end of trial," or the end point, for the calculation of "total delay" that is subject to the presumptive ceilings. While the Court[197] reiterated that the protection of section 11(b) extends up to and including the date upon which the sentence is imposed,[198] it clarified that the *Jordan* presumptive ceilings

---

194 *Jordan*, above note 1 at paras 47–49; the Court of Appeal for Ontario, in *R v Locknick*, clarified that where the actual end of trial is known, the period of delay is counted to the actual end of the trial rather than the anticipated end; see: *Locknick*, above note 118 at para 9, citing *R v Williamson*, 2016 SCC 28 [*Williamson*]; *R v Gordon*, 2017 ONCA 436; and *R v Faulkner*, 2018 ONCA 174.

195 *Jordan*, above note 1 at para 12; *R v Jordan*, 2014 BCCA 241 at para 18; *R v Jordan*, 2012 BCSC 1735 at para 12; *Williamson*, above note 194 at para 19; *Cody*, above note 142 at para 21.

196 *KGK (SCC)*, above note 85.

197 For most of the discussion in this part, reference will be made to "the Court's" decision. Justice Moldaver wrote the majority decision. Justice Abella, who wrote a concurring decision, agreed with the majority on all points except one: the use of the presumption of judicial integrity in the test for deliberation delay, which is discussed below. For all other purposes, she expressly adopted Moldaver J's decision, hence it is the Court's decision: *KGK (SCC)*, above note 85 at para 85.

198 *Ibid* at paras 3 and 26–27; *Rahey*, above note 170 at paras 39–40; *MacDougall*, above note 7 at paras 10–13 and 17–19.

and framework apply only until the end of the evidence and argument at trial, and no further.[199] The end point is the moment when the case is turned over to the trier of fact to decide.[200] The Court was clear that it does not include the time that the trier of fact takes to deliberate. As the Court pointed out, this is consistent with the design and goals of the *Jordan* framework: to provide certainty and clarity and to encourage the parties to be proactive about preventing and mitigating delay in bringing an accused to trial.[201] The *Jordan* framework—which, the Court clarified, was never intended to exhaust the section 11(b) analysis and cover all sources of delay—was designed to address a specific problem: the culture of complacency toward excessive delay associated with bringing those charged with criminal offences to trial.[202] While there is always an expectation on all justice system participants to be proactive, the ceilings, which presume unreasonable delay and shift the onus to the Crown to justify it, can only apply as long as counsel are able to be proactive. In principle, once the process is outside of the parties' control, then the *Jordan* framework can no longer apply.

Although the verdict deliberation period is not captured by the presumptive ceilings, the Court confirmed that it nonetheless remains subject to section 11(b) protection.[203] The majority of the Court in *KGK* created a stand-alone test to assess the time period between the end of evidence and argument to the verdict as being "whether the deliberation time took markedly longer than it reasonably should have in all the circumstances."[204] The accused bears the burden of demonstrating that deliberation time was unreasonable.[205] The Court described this burden as "heavy" due to the operation of the presumption of judicial integrity, which presupposes that trial judges are actively fulfilling their duty to uphold the *Charter* and are best placed to balance the various considerations that inform verdict deliberation time and that the verdict deliberation time taken by a judge in a particular case was no longer than reasonably necessary in the circumstances.[206] It was on this last

---

199   *KGK (SCC)*, above note 85 at paras 3–4, 54–57, and 65.

200   *Ibid* at paras 3, 23, 31, 33, and 50.

201   *Ibid* at paras 31–34.

202   *Ibid* at para 34; *Jordan*, above note 1 at paras 2, 4, 13, 117, 121, and 129.

203   *Rahey*, above note 170 at paras 39–40; *MacDougall*, above note 7 at para 19.

204   *KGK (SCC)*, above note 85 at paras 4, 26–28, 54–57, and 65.

205   *Ibid* at para 4.

206   *Ibid*.

point that Abella J parted company from the majority's reasons, albeit concurring in the result.

Finally, the Court offered some insight about the expectations of the counsel during the deliberation period and how to create an evidentiary foundation for an application about deliberation delay.

2) Background

After *Jordan* and prior to *KGK*, the majority of courts across the country interpreted the "end of trial" to mean the point at which the case was left in the hands of the trier-of-fact. In judge alone trials, this was at the end of closing submissions by counsel, and in jury trials, this was after the charge to the jury.[207] Still, there was conflicting jurisprudence and continued argument suggesting that the "end of trial," for the purposes of applying the presumptive ceilings, was the imposition of the verdict.[208] Under the *Morin* regime, unless itself unreasonable, there was acceptance of the view that deliberation time was included in the neutral inherent time requirements.[209] Only in rare instances would lengthy deliberations be subject to section 11(b) scrutiny pursuant to the Supreme Court's decision in *R v Rahey*.[210] As unworkable as it seemed,

---

207 *R v Basha*, 2017 ONSC 5897 at paras 110–38, affirmed in the result, 2019 ONCA 236; *R v Brown*, 2018 NSCA 62 at paras 72–75 [*Brown*]; *R v Mamouni*, 2017 ABCA 347 at paras 84–94, Slatter JA, leave to appeal refused (without reasons) 2018 CanLII 89741 (SCC); *Rice*, above note 85 at paras 41–42 and 86; *Agostine c R*, 2018 QCCA 373 at para 11; *Demers c R*, 2018 QCCA 617 at para 41; *R v King*, 2018 NLCA 66 at paras 180–81, Hoegg JA, O'Brien JA concurring; *R v Vader*, 2019 ABCA 191 at para 27; *R v Brar*, 2019 ONCJ 71 at paras 17–48, 63–89, 100–5, and 113–31, reversed on summary conviction appeal *R v Brar*, 2020 ONSC 4740 [*Brar (SCA)*]; *R v Camargo*, 2018 ONCJ 740 at paras 22–34; *Ashraf*, above note 136 at paras 73–76; *R v Zilney*, 2017 ONCJ 610 at paras 17–20; *R v Hammer*, 2017 BCPC 377 at para 21.

208 *R v SCW*, 2018 BCCA 346; *Akumu*, above note 137 paras 16, 31, and 36–37; *Pelletier*, above note 136 at paras 32–34; *R v Millar*, 2016 BCSC 1887 at paras 197–99, appeal dismissed 2019 BCCA 298; *R v Sonnenberg*, 2018 BCPC 348 at para 14; *R v Truong*, 2020 ONCJ 613 at paras 21 and 30; *R c Gauthier*, 2022 QCCA 819 at para 2; *Bergevin c R*, 2020 QCCA 658 at para 83; *R c McBride*, 2020 QCCQ 8802 at paras 69–72; *R v Safdar*, 2022 SCC 21 at para 3 [*Safdar (SCC)*]; *R v Eid*, 2020 ONCA 649 at paras 16–19.

209 *MacIsaac*, above note 85 at para 35; *R v Schertzer*, 2009 ONCA 742 at para 114, leave to appeal refused [2010] SCCA No 3; *R v Lamacchia*, 2012 ONSC 2583 at para 7; *R v Ferguson*, 2005 CanLII 28538 (ON SC) at para 213, leave to appeal refused 2008 ONCA 764.

210 *Rahey*, above note 170; see also: *Milani*, above note 172.

this provided a basis on which some courts held that deliberation time was included within the *Jordan* framework and presumptive ceilings.[211]

While the Court in *Jordan* and *Williamson*, and later, in *Cody*, had not outright defined the "end of trial" nor had it expressly addressed the issue of whether deliberation time to verdict was included in the presumptive ceilings, it had indicated that what was previously categorized under "inherent time requirements" had been absorbed into the presumptive ceilings.[212] In *R v KJM*,[213] the Court expressly determined to leave the issue for another case.

In *KGK*, more than nine of the twelve months that exceeded the presumptive ceiling was caused by judicial deliberation.[214] This case threw into sharp relief how uncomfortably deliberation time fit within the *Jordan* framework. The *Jordan* framework and its presumptive ceilings were predicated on counsel being in a position to be proactive about preventing and mitigating delay. It was incongruent to apply this framework to a period of time over which counsel, particularly the Crown, would have no expectation of control over the process and no reasonable ability to be proactive.

At first instance in *KGK*, the motion judge (who was not the trial judge) determined that deliberation time was not included within the presumptive ceiling. In finding that a separate test ought to apply, he referred to the principle of judicial independence, citing the Supreme Court's decision in *Beauregard v Canada*:

> Historically, the generally accepted core of the principle of judicial independence (*sic*) has been the complete liberty of individual judges to hear and decide the cases that come before them: no outsider —be it government, pressure group, individual or even another judge—should interfere in fact, or attempt to interfere, with the way in which a judge conducts his or her case and makes his or her decision.[215]

---

211   See also Steve Coughlan, "Patterns in the *Jordan* Case Law One Year after *Cody*" (2018) 42 CR (7th) 342; and Oliver Fitzgerald, "*Jordan* and Classifying Decision Delay: A Need for Guidance" (2017) 40 CR (7th) 72.

212   *Jordan*, above note 1 at paras 53, 83, and 184; *Williamson*, above note 194; *Cody*, above note 142; see *KGK (SCC)*, above note 85 at para 33.

213   *KJM (SCC)*, above note 4 at para 92, fn 2.

214   *KGK (SCC)*, above note 85 at paras 6–16.

215   *Beauregard v Canada*, 1986 CanLII 24 (SCC) at para 21.

In addition to noting the difficulty that "judges do not become witnesses nor do they file affidavits,"[216] the motion judge noted that including judicial deliberation time within the *Jordan* framework "would put both the Crown and the courts in the untenable position of having to schedule all matters in a manner so as to have them completed many months below the ceiling in order to accommodate potential judicial writing time."[217] The impact, he observed, would be to undermine the certainty and predictability that *Jordan* sought to bring to the section 11(b) *Charter* analysis. In determining what the stand-alone test for deliberation delay would be, the motion judge relied on the decision in *R v KGK*[218] to hold that verdict deliberation time would only be unreasonable within the meaning of section 11(b) where, in the overall context of a case, the time taken was "shocking, inordinate and unconscionable."[219] In applying this test, he found that the deliberation delay in this case, while long, was not unreasonable, and that the transitional framework applied and the delay to the end of trial was not unreasonable.

The Manitoba Court of Appeal split three ways in its decision. Justice Cameron upheld the reasons of the motion judge to find that deliberation did not come under the *Jordan* framework and was subject to the stand-alone test he set out, and agreed that, in this case, the delay was not unreasonable.[220] She held that, pursuant to the Supreme Court's decision in *Rahey*, the words "shocking, inordinate and unconscionable" were interchangeable for what is "unreasonable" in the context of assessing deliberation delay.

In dissent, Hamilton JA held that deliberation time, whether for interlocutory matters or the final verdict, is part of the time period to be considered in assessing whether the total delay is above or below the presumptive ceiling and, in this case, the delay was unreasonable.[221] Her conclusion was based on the view that under the *Morin* regime deliberation time was treated as part of the inherent time requirements, and noted that the *Jordan* framework included inherent time requirements of a case within the presumptive ceilings. The *Jordan* framework made exceptions

---

216   *R v KGK*, 2017 MBQB 96 at para 59 [*KGK (MBQB)*].
217   *Ibid* at paras 55 and 59.
218   *R v KGK*, 2019 MBCA 9 at paras 43, 77–84, 128, and 161–69 (Hamilton JA) [*KGK (MBCA)*].
219   *KGK (MBQB)*, above note 216 at para 69; *KGK (SCC)*, above note 85 at para 17.
220   *KGK (MBCA)*, above note 218 at paras 187–250.
221   *Ibid* at paras 59–170.

for discrete events and complexity only, and provided "the clear message to all players in the justice system, including judges, to address the culture of complacency with respect to delay."[222] She found that the delay was unreasonable and would have directed a stay of proceedings.

Justice Monnin concurred with Cameron JA in the result that deliberation time ought not to be included in the presumptive ceilings and that a separate and discrete approach that recognizes the "tension" between the right to trial within a reasonable time and the ability of a judge to take the time necessary to render a reasoned and just decision was required. He did not concur with Cameron JA that the "shocking, inordinate and unconscionable" criteria set out by the motion judge should apply. Rather he concurred with Hamilton JA on the point that the "shocking, inordinate and unconscionable" criteria as found by the motion judge was not in fact a test that had been enunciated by the Supreme Court in *Rahey*, but the words used by the trial judge in that case, whose decision was ultimately upheld by the Supreme Court.[223] Noting in passing the difficulty of reading the Supreme Court's decision in *Rahey*, which was unanimous in the result but split four ways on the reasons, Monnin JA determined that there was no endorsement of a test for judicial delay in *Rahey* other than "reasonableness," that the "shocking, inordinate and unconscionable" criteria set the bar too high and was not in keeping with the more recent approach of combatting complacency in the judicial system. Justice Monnin endorsed a contextual approach that balances a number of facets of the decision-making process according to the relevant evidence of the case, including a judge's or court's particular workload (which was arguably not consistent with *Jordan* which refuted that resource issues could be a legitimate explanation for delay).[224]

3) Rationale

In response to this call for clarity, the Supreme Court in *KGK* determined that the *Jordan* framework and presumption ceilings did not apply to deliberation time. The Court explained how the *Jordan* ceilings were not designed to exhaust the section 11(b) analysis and cover

222 *Ibid* at para 116.
223 *Ibid* at para 287.
224 *Jordan*, above note 1 at paras 40–42 and 117.

all sources of delay. Rather, they represent a specific solution designed to address a specific problem, namely, a culture of complacency and excessive delay associated with bringing accused persons to trial.[225] The Court observed that judicial deliberation time had not contributed to the culture of complacency, nor had it contributed in any meaningful way to the delays in bringing accused persons to trial that *Jordan* was meant to redress.[226] Finally, the Court indicated that the practical difficulties that would arise from including verdict deliberation time in the *Jordan* ceilings lend credence to the conclusion that it was not the Court's intention for that time to be included.

The Court acknowledged that section 11(b) protection, which applies through sentencing, does apply to deliberation time.[227] Justice Moldaver, for the majority (Abella J concurring on this point), continued:

> That said, the mere fact that s. 11(b) encompasses verdict deliberation time does not lead inexorably to the conclusion that this time is included in the *Jordan* ceilings. On the contrary, as will become apparent, the presumptive ceilings established in *Jordan* were not intended to cover the entire period of time to which s. 11(b) applies.[228]

The Court held that, "Properly construed, the *Jordan* ceilings apply from the date of the charge until the actual or anticipated end of the evidence and argument," when the parties' involvement on the merits of the trial is complete and the case is turned over to the trier of fact, "and no further."[229] This end point would permit the straightforward application of the *Jordan* framework in a manner consistent with its design and goals.[230]

The Court explained that the *Jordan* ceilings were "not designed to exhaust the s. 11(b) analysis and cover all sources of delay" but represented a specific solution to address a specific problem: the culture of complacency toward excessive delay in bringing those charged with criminal offences to trial.[231] As Moldaver J pointed out, there was no

---

225   *KGK (SCC)*, above note 85 at para 34.

226   *Ibid* at para 40.

227   *Ibid* at paras 26–29; see also *JF (SCC)*, above note 3 at para 23.

228   *KGK (SCC)*, above note 85 at para 30.

229   *Ibid* at paras 31–33.

230   *Ibid* at para 31.

231   *Ibid* at paras 34–38.

evidence to suggest that judicial deliberation time was a contributing cause of the culture of complacency. The call to judges in *Jordan*, he added, was to change "courtroom culture" by implementing more efficient procedures for scheduling, case management and control, and managing the conduct of trials.[232]

In addition, the Court pointed to the "host of practical problems that would arise"[233] if the presumptive ceilings were to include deliberation to verdict in order to justify its exclusion. First, it would render the argument and adjudication of pre-trial section 11(b) applications speculative, if not impossible, as there would be no way to predict in a given case whether the judge would reserve their decision or, if they did reserve, how long they might take to render a verdict.[234] Once a matter is under reserve, it is out of the parties' hands and so counsel cannot predict and plan to avoid delay, nor do anything to mitigate delay.[235] If the delay is not predictable, it would impede counsel's ability to take proactive measures to prevent or mitigate delay.

As section 11(b) applications are typically pre-trial motions, the judge, who would not have heard the evidence or submissions, would similarly not be positioned to assist counsel with a sense of whether they would need to reserve and for how long, nor would they know what pressures might arise in their judicial schedule. Justice Moldaver contrasted this with the last date of evidence and argument, which provides a workable and predictable date to use in calculating delay. He pointed out that this was the date used as the end of trial in *Jordan* and *Cody*. He further noted that including deliberation time would be especially problematic for post-trial section 11(b) applications wherein the ceiling was breached after the evidence and argument concluded and the judge had taken the case under reserve.[236] The Court subsequently affirmed the Court of Appeal for Ontario's decision in *R v Safdar* in this regard, holding that the end of the evidence and submissions was a "hard stop" to the time period assessed under the *Jordan* framework and a lingering

---

232   *Ibid* at para 41; *Jordan*, above note 1 at paras 114 and 139; *Cody*, above note 142 at paras 37–39.
233   *KGK (SCC)*, above note 85 at para 41.
234   *Ibid* at paras 24, 34–37, and 42–45.
235   *Ibid* at paras 31 and 41–47.
236   *Ibid* at para 46.

section 11(b) motion, brought after the evidence and argument were completed and before the final verdict, did not extend the delay.[237]

On the point of judicial independence, Moldaver J confirmed that while *Jordan* encourages proactivity on the part of the Crown, it made no sense to hold the Crown accountable for the time a judge takes to deliberate on a verdict. Once the matter is in the hands of the trier-of-fact, counsel can do nothing to mitigate delay. Likewise, it would be improper for the Crown to interfere or be seen to interfere with the judicial deliberation process lest it be seen as an attempt to influence the judge's decision.[238] Similarly, he acknowledged that the Crown will not be in a position to explain why the judge took the time they did to arrive at a verdict.[239] Further, even if the reasons why the judge took a lengthy period to deliberate were known to the parties, those reasons could not be meaningfully tested, as "judges do not testify or file affidavits."[240] If a judge were to become a witness in a case under reserve, it would in all likelihood compromise their ability to adjudicate that case.[241]

Finally, the majority determined that "undesirability and absurdity" would result for matters where the evidence was voluminous or the case complex. In such instances, the trial judge would be afforded less time to deliberate.[242]

4) Expectations on Counsel with Respect to Deliberation Delay

The Court in *KGK* provided "a final practical note" on how counsel can communicate with the Court to receive an update on the status of the decision when significant time has passed since the trial judge undertook the matter under reserve. The Court acknowledged that the Crown may be reluctant to probe for information lest it risk the appearance of inappropriate interference with the judicial process. Similarly, the

---

237 *R v Safdar*, 2021 ONCA 207 at paras 20–35, affirmed *Safdar (SCC)*, above note 208; *KGK (SCC)*, above note 85 at paras 31 and 33; *JF (SCC)*, above note 3 at para 27.

238 *KGK (SCC)*, above note 85 at para 47.

239 *Ibid.*

240 *Ibid* at para 48, citing *KGK (MBQB)*, above note 216 at para 59.

241 *KGK (SCC)*, above note 85 at paras 47–48.

242 *Ibid* at para 49.

accused may not wish to be seen as applying pressure on the person in whose hands their fate lies.[243]

The Court emphasized *Jordan*'s call for participants in the criminal justice system to work together to minimize delay and safeguard an accused person's section 11(b) interests. It recommended that the parties, in appropriate cases and through appropriate channels, should communicate with the trial judge and that trial judges can and should be expected to be "sufficiently resolute" to consider a request for information without consequences to counsel, the accused, or the trial.[244] Justice Moldaver, for the majority, recommended that jurisdictions set out a standardized procedure through which counsel can inquire as to the status of a verdict.[245] In the Court's view, this would attenuate the anxiety and concern that accompanies the inherent unknowability of a verdict date and delay more generally, in addition to helping the courts track judicial workload and develop a record for section 11(b) purposes.[246]

5) Deliberation Delay

Although the Court in *KGK* declined to include deliberation time within the presumptive ceilings of the *Jordan* framework, the time after the end of closing argument, through deliberation, to the imposition of verdict and sentence, all remains subject to *Charter* scrutiny. The Court acknowledged that in the pre-*Jordan* jurisprudence there was no clear test for determining whether verdict deliberation time was reasonable within the meaning of section 11(b) of the *Charter*.[247] The Court agreed with Cameron JA, of the Manitoba Court of Appeal, that there was nothing in the jurisprudence that required trial judges to estimate their deliberation time in advance of the trial in order to include that in their calculation of inherent delay in the *Morin* analysis.[248] However, the Court rejected the proposal that the verdict deliberation time would only be unreasonable within the meaning of section 11(b) where, in the overall context of a case, the time taken was "shocking, inordinate

---

243   *Ibid* at para 74.

244   *Ibid* at para 75.

245   *Ibid* at para 76.

246   *Ibid*.

247   *Ibid* at para 51.

248   *Ibid*, citing *KGK (MBCA)*, above note 218 at para 198.

and unconscionable."[249] Instead, the Court set out a separate test for the period from the end of closing argument to the verdict, to determine whether the deliberation time taken has breached section 11(b): "whether the deliberation time took markedly longer than it reasonably should have in all the circumstances."[250]

In determining whether judicial deliberation time took markedly longer than it reasonably should have in all the circumstances, the majority provided the following non-exhaustive list of factors that should be taken into account:

1) The length of verdict deliberation time; while length of verdict deliberation time is extremely unlikely to suffice on its own, there may be instances in which the time taken is so manifestly excessive that it can constitute a breach of section 11(b) on its own;[251]

2) The proximity of the case to the *Jordan* ceiling before the trial judge reserved judgment, which informs how a judge should prioritize their workload and recognizes that the impact of delay on an accused is cumulative;[252]

3) The complexity of the case (amount and nature of the evidence; number of co-accused; legal issues raised; the parties' positions) on which the necessary verdict deliberation time will depend, and which would explain whether the verdict was markedly longer than it reasonably should have been in all of the circumstances;[253]

4) Anything on the record such as correspondence from the court to the parties or the judge to the parties that the judge should deem appropriate to communicate, including reference to other obligations or illness;[254]

5) The local conditions from which inferences can be drawn about the judge's workload and institutional constraints they may face;[255] and

6) The length of time a similar case in similar circumstances might require for deliberation.[256]

---

249 *KGK (SCC)*, above note 85 at para 52.
250 *Ibid* at paras 4, 24, 51, 54–57, and 65.
251 *Ibid* at para 68.
252 *Ibid* at para 69.
253 *Ibid* at para 70.
254 *Ibid* at para 71.
255 *Ibid*.
256 *Ibid* at paras 67–72 and per Abella J at para 87; *R v Artis*, 2021 ONCA 862 at para 17.

These objective factors were intended to mirror the reasonable observer test used in cases where the accused must directly rebut the presumption of integrity and that a subject inquiry was not required by a reviewing court.[257]

The Court noted that while timeliness is a constant concern in which all parties have an interest, once the evidence is preserved on the record and the case is left in the hands of the trier of fact, trial fairness concerns about an accused's right to make full answer and defence are attenuated.[258] Trial fairness instead depends on there being necessary deliberation time so that a case may be justly adjudicated in a particular case: assessing evidence, researching points of law, and writing reasons.[259]

Taking account of the limits of judicial and court administration resources, such as the shortage of federally appointed judges as one practical constraint and in citing *R v Allen* for the proposition that "[n]o case is an island to be treated as if it were the only case with legitimate demand on court resources,"[260] the Court acknowledged that time spent on one case cannot be time spent on another. The decision called on judges to work within these institutional restrictions and manage their workloads as efficiently as possible and reiterated that the government has a responsibility to ensure that courts are sufficiently resourced to fulfill the promise of section 11(b) of the *Charter*.[261] The Court further observed that in balancing timeliness, trial fairness, and practical considerations, decisions are very often rendered within the six-month guideline set by the Canadian Judicial Council (CJC). The "adjudicative duty" set out in the CJC's *Ethical Principles for Judges* (2004), reads as follows:

> [T]he decision and reasons should be produced by the judge as soon as reasonably possible, having regard to the urgency of the matter and other special circumstances. Special circumstances may include illness, the length or complexity of the case, an unusually heavy workload or other factors making it impossible to give judgment sooner. In 1985, the

---

257   *KGK (SCC)*, above note 85 at para 73.
258   *Ibid* at paras 58–59.
259   *Ibid* at para 60.
260   *Ibid* at para 61; citing *R v Allen*, 1996 CanLII 4011 at para 27 (Ont CA).
261   *KGK (SCC)*, above note 85 at paras 61–62.

Canadian Judicial Council resolved that, in its view, reserved judgments should be delivered within six months after hearings, except in special circumstances.[262]

The Court was quick to note that this guideline is not a determinative measure of constitutionality, observing that exceeding the CJC's guidelines—which are advisory in nature—does not establish a breach of section 11(b). The guideline itself acknowledges the inherent case-specific and judge-specific nature of the balance between the considerations of the need for timeliness, trial fairness, and practical limitations.[263]

6) Presumption of Judicial Integrity

To overcome the presumption of judicial integrity is a high hurdle to clear. The burden, which remains on the accused to show that deliberation time was unreasonable, is "a heavy one due to the operation of the presumption of judicial integrity."[264] A finding that deliberation time was unreasonable will be rare and limited to clear cases. This, it was determined, is because the presumption acknowledges that judges are bound by their judicial oaths and will carry out the duties they have sworn to uphold, including upholding *Charter* rights, to the best of their abilities.[265] Judges are under an obligation to minimize delay at all stages of the trial process, including the verdict deliberation phase.[266] Accordingly, it is presumed that the trial judge took no longer than reasonably necessary to arrive at the verdict,[267] being best placed to strike

---

262 Online: https://cjc-ccm.ca/en/what-we-do/initiatives/ethical-principles-judges-o. It should be noted that there may be specific rules that apply within a specific jurisdiction. For example, in Ontario, section 123(5) of the *Courts of Justice Act*, RSO 1990, c C43, identifies six months as the point at which delay in giving judgment may warrant the intervention of the Chief Justice of the trial court to extend the time in which the decision may be given and, if necessary, relieve the judge of their other duties until the decision is given; see *R v Ansari*, 2023 ONSC 1858 at paras 47–55 [*Ansari*]. See also *R v Taylor*, 2023 ONSC 2481.

263 *KGK (SCC)*, above note 85 at para 64.

264 *Ibid* at paras 4, 56, and 65.

265 *Ibid* at paras 55 and 66; citing *R v Teskey*, 2007 SCC 25 at paras 47 and 20 and *Cojocaru v British Columbia Women's Hospital and Health Centre*, 2013 SCC 30 at para 17.

266 *KGK (SCC)*, above note 85 at para 55.

267 *Ibid* at paras 4, 54–57, and 65.

a reasonable balance between the need for timeliness and trial fairness considerations and taking only as much time as was necessary in the circumstances to render a just verdict.[268]

On this point, Abella J parted company from Moldaver J and the majority. In separate reasons (though concurring in the result) she held that the use of the presumption of judicial integrity in the assessment of whether deliberative delay violated the accused's right be tried within a reasonable time required impugning the integrity of a trial judge to find that deliberative delay is unreasonable.[269] She reasoned that requiring the accused to displace the presumption of judicial integrity had the effect of elevating the accused's burden to an almost insurmountable one. Further, she questioned what role the presumption of judicial integrity can usefully play in assessing whether a delay is "markedly longer" than is reasonable.[270]

Justice Abella elaborated upon this objection by underscoring what the presumption of judicial integrity entails:

[88] The presumption of judicial integrity "acknowledges that judges are bound by their judicial oaths and will carry out the duties they have sworn to uphold" (*Cojocaru v. British Columbia Women's Hospital and Health Centre*, 2013 SCC 30 (CanLII), [2013] 2 S.C.R. 357, at para. 17, citing *R. v. Teskey*, 2007 SCC 25 (CanLII), [2007] 2 S.C.R. 267, at para. 29, per Abella J., dissenting). It is invoked in cases which require assessing the judge's state of mind in order to determine whether "the judge has done her job as she is sworn to do" (*Cojocaru*, at para. 15). In these cases, the presumption of judicial integrity is used "to protect the judicial role from undue perceptual assault" and to avoid the "second-guessing of a judge's thought processes" (*Teskey*, at para. 47).

[89] Under this jurisprudence, in order to rebut the presumption of judicial integrity, the party assailing the outcome must present "cogent evidence" showing that a reasonable person apprised of the relevant facts would conclude that the presumption is rebutted in all the circumstances (*Cojocaru*, at paras. 18 and 27-28; *Teskey*, at paras. 21 and 33; see also *R. v. Chan* (2019), 2019 ABCA 82 (CanLII), 82 Alta. L.R. (6th) 1 (C.A.), at para. 12; *8640025 Canada Inc. (Re)*, 2019 BCCA 473, at para. 79 (CanLII)).

---

268   *Ibid* at paras 4, 56–57, and 65.

269   *Ibid* at paras 85 and 91.

270   *Ibid* at para 86.

She noted that an accused would be practically unable to proffer "cogent evidence" in the context of deliberation delay to rebut the presumption, and could only rely on the length of the delay on its face in this regard. In her view, "Adding an additional burden on the accused of demonstrating the trial judge acted without integrity, particularly without a clear way to demonstrate this, elevates the burden to an impossible threshold" that was "both conceptually irrelevant and unreachable."[271] The concern was the risk that the presumption of judicial integrity would act as a justification for a deliberative delay that, objectively, took markedly longer than it reasonably should have.[272]

Justice Moldaver expressly disputed this in his reasons, indicating that the presumption of integrity properly limits the circumstances in which a reviewing court may second-guess the trial judge's determination of how much verdict deliberation time was reasonably necessary in light of the competing considerations in play, and provides a legitimate basis upon which to presume that the trial judge actually took only as much time as was reasonably necessary in all the circumstances.[273]

7) Applying *R v KGK*

While the Court in *KGK* observed that there is no apparent systemic issue related to delay arising from judicial deliberation time, there have been a few cases post-*KGK* that have confronted *prima facie* lengthy periods of delay in receiving a verdict. The manner in which *KGK* is applied to the issue of whether deliberation delay was reasonable, has varied in these decisions. Disparate approaches have developed in terms of how to confront the evidentiary difficulties in such cases and with respect to the bounds of what counsel can and cannot do in the context of a section 11(b) application relating to deliberation delay. In particular, there is no consistent approach to factoring the presumption of judicial integrity into the analysis.

For example, in *R v Yizhak*,[274] the trial judge rendered his verdict and counsel indicated that defence might bring a section 11(b) motion. After hearing this, the judge communicated to counsel through the trial

---

271 *Ibid* at para 94.
272 *Ibid* at para 92.
273 *Ibid* at para 66.
274 2022 ONCJ 476 [*Yizhak (s 11(b) Application)*].

coordinator what portion of time he had been on a medical leave during the period in which the case was being deliberated. This led defence counsel to bring a mistrial application for reasonable apprehension of bias, in addition to the section 11(b) *Charter* application.[275] It also sparked a series of questions from defence counsel, including:

i.   *What was the portion of the deliberative period that was attributable to the health concern? This includes not only the period of leave, but any other period during which the health concern impacted functionality.*

ii.   *Was the health issue that caused the medical leave something that could be attributable to, or be considered a function of, burnout?*

iii.   *Was there an impact on other matters or was it unique to this matter? If other matters, how many?*

iv.   *If the leave was attributable to or a function of burnout, in whole or in part, was the burnout attributable to a scarcity of judicial resources?*

v.   *Is the issue of burnout unique to this matter or is it akin to a systemic concern?*[276]

In declining to answer defence counsel's questions, the trial judge held that the accused had all of the information that he was entitled to and that answering such questions would result in the judge becoming a witness in the proceedings, contrary to *KGK*.[277] While the trial judge acknowledged that *KGK* permitted communication between the court to the parties without having to fear "consequences to counsel, the accused, or the trial," he was of the view that *KGK* did not contemplate a request such as this, much less compel a trial judge to accede to it. Further he held that questions about judicial resources and other cases to be so far-reaching as to resemble a public inquiry, which, he held, is not the function of a criminal trial or a section 11(b) application. Finally, the judge exercised his own right to privacy over his personal health information: "While I have shared with the parties the *fact* of my medical leave of absence, I believe that I am entitled to privacy concerning its *nature and etiology*."[278] The presumption of judicial integrity was

---

275   *R v Yizhak*, 2022 ONCJ 360 [*Yizhak* (Mistrial Application)]; *R v Yizhak*, 2022 ONCJ 377 [*Yizhak* (Inquiries on the s 11(b) Application)]; *Yizhak* (s 11(b) Application), above note 274.

276   *Yizhak* (Inquiries on the s 11(b) Application), above note 275 at para 8.

277   *KGK (SCC)*, above note 85 at para 48.

278   *Yizhak* (Inquiries on the s 11(b) Application), above note 275 at paras 9–15 (emphasis in original).

relied upon in this case to prevent the outcome of becoming a witness and being compelled to provide personal health information.

Given the Court's suggestion in *KGK* that "it may be helpful" to consider the length of time taken in similar circumstances, counsel in *R v Esposito*[279] surveyed cases in which similar legal issues were addressed. As counsel made no attempt to try to assess the relative legal or factual complexity of these cases compared to the case at issue, the Court held that it only served to underscore the fact that every case is different, and possibly to explain the tentative nature of the Supreme Court's suggestion that this comparative process "may be helpful." What is a reasonable (or unreasonable) time requirement is informed by a trial judge's knowledge of their own jurisdiction and its typical delay.[280] The Court attributed counsel's survey as having only limited weight in the circumstances.

Other cases, such as *Mucunguzi c R*,[281] demonstrate that the evidentiary record is cleaner when a trial judge provides clear information about any delay on the record as the delay arises. This avoids any unseemly forensic investigation after the fact when deliberation delay is later raised as a concern. In this case, there was twelve-and-a-half months of judicial deliberation time before a verdict was rendered and written reasons delivered after a trial on a charge of impaired driving. At various appearances prior to delivery of the reasons, the judge indicated that issues with caseload were preventing their delivery sooner. The appellate court held that in the circumstances the appellant had not met its burden to establish that the time amounted to a marked departure such that a breach of section 11(b) was established.[282]

As Abella J predicted, including the presumption of judicial integrity into the analysis has set the stage for potential attacks against trial judge's integrity. It has also arguably set a bar to establishing a breach that is impossibly high to clear. In *R v Ansari*,[283] after a tortured history that involved a delay in reasons for judgment, the intervening plea of a co-accused, and a subsequent re-opening of the case, the trial judge set a date to render judgment. On that date, the accused was unable

---

279 2020 ABQB 318.

280 *Jordan*, above note 1 at paras 87, 89, and 139; *R v Majeed*, 2019 ONCA 422 at paras 7–9.

281 2022 QCCS 2872.

282 *Ibid* at paras 57–64.

283 *Ansari*, above note 262.

to attend. The trial judge maintained that he was prepared to deliver his reasons for judgment on that date but for the unavailability of the accused. At the next appearance, the trial judge adjourned "because he had been off for a few weeks," which defence argued was irrelevant given the reasons for judgment had purportedly been ready to deliver at the last appearance. At the appearance after that, the judge prioritized other trial matters over providing the reasons for judgment. The judge was ill for the next appearance, and the date for the reasons for judgment was adjourned a third time. There was also evidence tendered to suggest that the judge did not consider delivery of reasons for judgment in this case a priority because the accused was on a "light bail." Defence counsel used this history as fodder to level allegations against the trial judge's integrity.[284] The Regional Senior Justice, who heard the section 11(b) motion, ultimately held that the evidence did not overcome the heavy onus created by the presumption of judicial integrity, pointing to the realities of the workload in the jurisdiction.[285] He nevertheless strongly recommended that the delivery of judgment be prioritized over trial matters and clarified that trial matters ought to be interrupted to deliver reasons for judgment.[286]

In contrast, in *R v McNeil*,[287] the Nova Scotia Court of Appeal upheld a stay for deliberation delay without any mention in its analysis of the presumption of judicial integrity.[288] In that case, the focus was on how to treat the trial judge's (medical) leave that began shortly after deliberation commenced and eventually turned into an indefinite leave that resulted in no judgment being rendered by that trial judge.

The charges in *McNeil* were sexual offences against two child complainants. When the evidence ended and closing submissions were completed, the matter was adjourned for the trial judge to render a decision. Before the appearance when the judgment was to be rendered, the judge went on leave. Over the next five months, the Crown made

---

284   *Ibid* at paras 27–39 and 65–69.

285   *Ibid* at paras 70–77.

286   *Ibid.*

287   *R v McNeil*, 2024 NSCA 57 [*McNeil (NSCA)*]; application for leave dismissed 2024 CanLII 96595 (SCC).

288   The application judge's reasons referred to the presumption of judicial integrity in stating the test, but the presumption of judicial integrity did not feature in the analysis nor was it mentioned in the decision on appeal; see *R v McNeil*, 2023 NSPC 32 at paras 28 and 31 [*McNeil (NSPC)*] and *McNeil (NSCA)*, above note 287.

regular inquiries about whether the trial judge would be able to render a decision. Responses from the Chief Judge of the Provincial Court were prompt but communicated uncertainty about the trial judge's return date. The Chief Judge described the nature of leave as being for "illness" and "medical," explaining at one point that updates were coming from "the insurer" and that the judge was "not permitted to work" nor was the Chief Judge able to ask the judge to work.[289] It was always hoped that the judge would return and render a decision. At the end of the five months, it was communicated that the trial judge's leave had become "indeterminate."[290] Pursuant to s 669.2 of the *Criminal Code*,[291] a new trial was provisionally scheduled, leaving open the possibility that the trial judge would return to deliver the verdict in the interim.[292] The trial dates were over a year away as the jurisdiction was facing a resource shortage. A few months before the new trial dates, it was confirmed that the trial judge would not render a decision.[293] As the defence would not consent to a new judge deciding the case on the basis of transcripts of the evidence, the trial had to commence anew.[294] The deliberation delay — which started when the case was in the hands of the original trial judge for a decision and ended when it was confirmed that the original trial judge would not return — was calculated as 15.7 months.[295] The application judge determined that the delay under the *Jordan* framework was not unreasonable but that the deliberation delay under the

---

289 *Ibid* at paras 11–24.

290 *Ibid* at para 25.

291 RSC 1985, c C-46, s 669.2(1).

292 *McNeil (NSCA)*, above note 287 at paras 26–28.

293 *Ibid* at para 28.

294 *Ibid*; see also *Criminal Code*, RSC 1985, c C-46, s 669.2(3).

295 In *McNeil* neither counsel invited the Court to declare a mistrial when the trial was scheduled anew. Had a mistrial been declared, the deliberation delay clock would have stopped at 7.2 months. In this case, both parties wanted to avoid recalling the evidence, both held out hope for the trial judge's return, and dates for trying the case anew were only set provisionally. In this circumstance, it would have been wise for the Crown to ask the defence to waive deliberation delay or invite the Court to declare a mistrial at an earlier date to salvage the prosecution. While the application judge found both the delay of 7.2 months (to when the provisional trial dates were set) and the delay of 15.7 months (to when it was confirmed that the original trial judge would not render a decision) to be unreasonable, had a mistrial been declared at that 7.2 month mark, thus ending deliberation delay, the result on appeal may have been different; see *McNeil (NSPC)*, above note 288 at paras 43–59 and *McNeil (NSCA)*, above note 287 at paras 42 and 52–54.

KGK framework was unreasonable in that deliberation took markedly longer than it reasonably should have been in all the circumstances and there was no defence waiver.[296] The Crown appealed the decision.

The Nova Scotia Court of Appeal unanimously agreed with the application judge. Justice Derrick, writing for the Court, held that the application judge's factual finding that the trial judge's leave was for an unknown duration and for "reasons largely unknown" was owed deference on appeal.[297] Without a factual finding that the leave was medical in nature, there was no basis for the Crown's argument that the judge's illness was a special circumstance that attenuated the "markedly longer than reasonable" standard as contemplated by the Supreme Court in *KGK*.[298] The appellate Court held that the fact of the leave of unknown duration for unknown reasons was considered but "was not a circumstance that, applying the principles in *KGK*, reduced the potency of the respondent's s. 11(b) rights."[299]

This decision again underscores the importance of providing clear information about the reason for deliberation delay.[300] It also demonstrates how the presumption of judicial integrity may not fit easily into the analysis, particularly where a judge is ill — or may be ill as the factual findings may be — and unable to communicate with the parties. Arguably, in *McNeil*, the presumption of judicial integrity was engaged by the Chief Judge's communications to counsel about the nature of the leave being illness and medical, as opposed to any other, unstated (and therefore speculative) reason, such that the nature of the leave was not "unknown." This decision serves as a reminder that deliberation delay ends when there is a decision on the merits or, in cases of illness (or death), when it is absolutely certain that the original trial judge will not render a verdict. Finally, the result in *McNeil* encourages Crowns facing similar situations to salvage the prosecution by inviting the court

---

296 *McNeil (NSCA)*, above note 287 at paras 34–42.

297 *Ibid* at para 68.

298 *Ibid.*

299 *Ibid* at para 71.

300 Where the reason for delay is "medical" in nature, in the author's view, privacy concerns dictate that information ought to be limited to the fact that the reason is medical without providing further details. This is an appropriate place for the presumption of judicial integrity to prevail. For instance, in *McNeil*, it may have been clearer had it been stated at each update that the nature of the leave was, and continued to be, medical, but more detail than that ought not be required.

to declare a mistrial at a much earlier stage, no matter how unpalatable that option may be, particularly with vulnerable witnesses. While it may be difficult to assess in evolving circumstances where there is hope a judge may return and the timeline is uncertain, it is better to act early. This is unless there an explicit defence waiver for the period(s) the defence is prepared to wait for a judge, whose return is uncertain, to return and deliberate. The defence, likewise, ought to state clearly when the accused's section 11(b) right is at risk of being infringed such that there can be no suggestion of implicit waiver.

8) Question Remaining: Interlocutory Deliberation Time

The Supreme Court's decision in *R v KGK* did not definitively answer all questions about how to treat deliberation time under the *Jordan* framework. It did not address the issue of mid-trial deliberation, such as is required on committal, pre- and post-trial motions, and for various mid-trial rulings. Often these deliberations can be determinative of a case and can require extensive consideration and processing of the evidence in order to properly assess the matter. The majority of cases have adopted the approach that delays occasioned by judges reserving mid-trial decisions are discrete events or a product of complexity that constitute exceptional circumstances, or simply that they fall outside of the *Jordan* framework because the decision by a presiding judge to reserve judgment is both unforeseen and unavoidable and entirely outside of the control of counsel.[301] The Courts of Appeal for both Quebec[302] and Alberta[303] have endorsed this approach to pre- and mid-trial deliberation time. In both Newfoundland[304] and Ontario, however,

---

301   See *Rice*, above note 85 at para 86; *R c Thanabalasingham*, 2019 QCCA 1765 at paras 81–85; *R c Dorion*, 2020 QCCQ 15125 at paras 27–32; *R c McKenzie-Fletcher*, 2020 QCCQ 8889 at paras 121–35; *Agence du revenu du Québec c Krid*, 2021 QCCQ 604 at paras 110–23; *Gravel c R*, 2021 QCCQ 5090 at para 520; *Woods c R*, 2022 QCCQ 1493 at paras 29–33; *R c Natachequan*, 2022 QCCQ 3476 at paras 35–39; *R v Stogrin*, 2021 BCPC 313 at paras 96–101; *R v Chang*, 2019 ABCA 315 at paras 76–79 [*Chang*]; *R v Lavoie*, 2017 ABQB 66 at paras 38–39; *R v Weber*, 2022 SKQB 116 at para 47; *Brown*, above note 207 at paras 72–75; *R v Lai*, 2021 BCCA 105 at para 48; *contra: Brar (SCA)*, above note 207 at paras 123–32, Woollcombe J.

302   See *Rice*, above note 85.

303   See *Chang*, above note 301.

304   *R v King*, 2018 NLCA 66 at paras 132–44.

each province's Court of Appeal has determined that such time is to be included in the ceiling count. In *R v Mengistu*,[305] Monahan JA, writing for the Court of Appeal for Ontario, held that judicial deliberation time required for the resolution of pre- or mid-trial rulings is, as a general rule, to be included in the net delay count. First, the Court determined that in *Jordan*, the Supreme Court implicitly included such time as part of the presumptive ceiling, noting that in arriving at the ceilings the inherent time needed to complete cases and the increasing complexity of criminal litigation were taken into account.[306] Second, to deduct the time for judicial deliberation would introduce an element of unpredictability to the framework. To allow for "time outs" along the timeline of the proceedings would be to undermine the predictability the framework was intended to foster.[307] Finally, in the Court's view, there is no interference with judicial independence in including pre- and mid-trial deliberation time in the net delay count, since the Supreme Court in *Jordan* has already emphasized the requirement that all actors in the criminal justice system, including judges, act with efficiency.[308]

D. FORMULA FOR CALCULATING DELAY

The Court of Appeal for Ontario has held that for the purposes of section 11(b) calculations, to convert days to months, the following formula should be applied:

number of days ÷ 30.417 = number of months.[309]

---

305 *R v Mengistu*, 2024 ONCA 575.

306 *Ibid* at paras 28–31.

307 *Ibid* at paras 31–32.

308 *Ibid* at paras 33–34.

309 The number 30.417 is approximately 365 days divided by twelve; *Shaikh*, above note 111; *R v Chung*, 2021 ONCA 188.

CHAPTER 4

Appeals and Extraordinary Remedies

In order to understand why section 11(b) protection does not apply to appeals and to discern when section 11(b) protection applies to extraordinary remedies, it is important to appreciate the overall limits of section 11(b) protection. Section 11(b) of the *Charter* protects an accused throughout the period when they have the status of "a person charged with an offence."[1] The term "person charged with an offence" has been interpreted by the Supreme Court to be a person or corporate entity[2] who is the subject of criminal proceedings.[3] A person is subject to a criminal proceeding from the time the charge is laid until the final resolution of the matter in trial court, including sentencing.[4]

As discussed in Chapter 3, the framework and tests that have developed since *Jordan* relate to various aspects of section 11(b) protection. The *Jordan* framework itself is limited to the period from the charge to the actual or anticipated end of trial, meaning "when the parties' involvement in the merits of the trial is complete, and the case is turned over to the trier of fact."[5] In the wake of *Jordan*, other frameworks

---

1 Section 11(b) of the *Canadian Charter of Rights and Freedoms*, Part I of the *Constitution Act, 1982*, being Schedule B to the *Canada Act 1982* (UK), 1982, c 11 [*Charter*], states: "Anyone charged with an offence has the right to be tried within a reasonable time;" *R v JF*, 2022 SCC 17 at paras 23–24 [*JF*]; *R v Potvin*, 1993 CanLII 113 (SCC) at paras 57–59 [*Potvin*].

2 *R v CIP Inc*, 1992 CanLII 95 (SCC).

3 *R v MacDougall*, 1998 CanLII 763 (SCC) at paras 11–13 [*MacDougall*].

4 *R v Kalanj*, 1989 CanLII 63 (SCC) at paras 16–19 [*Kalanj*]; *Potvin*, above note 1 at paras 61–62; *MacDougall*, above note 3 at paras 10 and 17–18; *R v KGK*, 2020 SCC 7 at paras 26–27 [*KGK*]; *JF*, above note 1 at para 23.

5 *KGK*, above note 4 at paras 31 and 33; *R v Jordan*, 2016 SCC 27 at para 47 [*Jordan*]; *R c Rice*, 2018 QCCA 198 at para 41.

have developed to assess deliberation delay (Chapter 3) and post-trial delay (Chapter 5). After post-*Jordan* reconsideration, as discussed in this chapter, section 11(b) protection still does not extend past the trial to appeals. Accordingly, whether the trial is complete will determine whether section 11(b) protection extends to periods when extraordinary remedy is sought.

A. APPEALS

In *R v Potvin*,[6] decided during the *Morin* era, the Supreme Court determined that a person who is a party to an appeal is not a "person charged with an offence" for the purposes of section 11(b) of the *Charter*. The Court affirmed the *Potvin* decision in this regard in the post-*Jordan* era in *R v JF*.[7] While on appeal a person is not charged with an offence and cannot resort to section 11(b) *Charter* protection.[8] If, however, the trial decision is set aside and a new trial is ordered, the accused regains the status of "a person charged with an offence."[9] The time that is subject to the presumptive ceiling of the *Jordan* framework ("the constitutional clock for calculating delay," as the Court described it) is reset to zero, commencing on the date the new trial is ordered.[10] Presumably this also includes matters that are remitted back to the trial judge to complete.[11]

B. EXTRAORDINARY REMEDIES

The issue of whether section 11(b) applies to periods when an extraordinary remedy is sought has not been expressly addressed by the Supreme Court since its decision in *Jordan* was released.[12] The various

---

6   *Potvin*, above note 1.

7   *JF*, above note 1 at paras 56–59; *Kalanj*, above note 4; *R v JEV*, 2018 ABQB 1033 at paras 19–21, affirmed in the result 2019 ABCA 359; *R v Melvin*, 2017 NSSC 149 at paras 17–19; *R v Windibank*, 2017 ONSC 855 at paras 61 and 68–69.

8   *JF*, above note 1 at para 23.

9   *Potvin*, above note 1 at para 66; *JF*, above note 1 at para 23.

10   *Ibid* at paras 3, 55–57, and 60–61.

11   *R v Masiowski*, 2020 SKPC 17 at paras 13–26.

12   The Court alluded to the risk of delay caused by interlocutory applications in *R v JJ*, 2022 SCC 28 at para 190. The Court observed that the trial judge is responsible for determining whether it is in the interests of justice to allow such an application. The Court advised trial judges to be mindful of the trial delay risks that will arise due to the bifurcation of trial. In the Court's view, "mid-trial applications should not be the norm."

decisions in the lower courts have tended to take a principled approach
to whether section 11(b) protection exists. What matters is whether the
final outcome of the trial remains pending at the time that the extraordinary remedy is sought such that the accused is a "person charged
with an offence." Where delay has been occasioned as the result of an
appeal or a *certiorari* application that occurs when the accused's trial is
completed, the time related to the adjudication of the appeal or application is not included in the *Jordan* framework's presumptive ceiling. This
is because the accused is no longer a "person charged with an offence"
for the purposes of section 11(b) protection. Where a party has brought
an interlocutory application and/or has appealed from a decision on
an interlocutory application granting or refusing *certiorari*, then section
11(b) of the *Charter* is engaged, and the *Jordan* ceilings will apply.

1)　Extraordinary Remedy After a Trial Is Complete

In *R v Manasseri*, Watt JA offered some early observations *in obiter* in
this regard.[13] In this case, the co-accused, Kenny, had been discharged
following the preliminary hearing. The Crown brought an application
for *certiorari* and a subsequent appeal to have him committed to stand
trial. This encompassed a period of just over one year and eight months.
Although the issue of whether section 11(b) of the *Charter* applies to
extraordinary remedies was not ultimately decided in that case as it
was not determinative of the appeal, Watt JA noted that it would be
incongruous to treat the time taken in pursuit of extraordinary remedies differently than that taken in appeals from convictions, acquittals,
or stays of proceedings as *Potvin* mandates.[14] Appreciating that appeals
and extraordinary remedies involve two different procedural mechan-
isms, he nonetheless observed that section 11(b) may only be invoked
by a "person charged with an offence."[15] Under *Potvin*, a person who
is a party to an appeal is not such a person and, in his view, the same
could be said of a person discharged at the conclusion of a preliminary
inquiry.[16] That person is not a "person charged with an offence" from

---

13　*R v Manasseri*, 2016 ONCA 703 at paras 335 and 337–40 [*Manasseri*].

14　*Ibid* at para 340.

15　See s 784(1) of the *Criminal Code*, RSC 1985, c C-46 [*Criminal Code*]; *Manasseri*, above
　　note 13 at para 339.

16　*Potvin*, above note 1 at para 59; *Manasseri*, above note 13 at para 340.

the date of discharge until the discharge is set aside and committal ordered or a direct indictment preferred.[17] If the matter is concluded and a review is being sought, section 11(b) of the *Charter* is not engaged.

2)   Interlocutory Applications for Extraordinary Remedy

Interlocutory applications, which include motions to quash committal or challenging disclosure orders, are distinguishable from Crown applications to challenge a discharge because the accused continues to be a "person charged with an offence." As a preliminary issue, to matter in the final calculus, the application has to have a discernible impact on the trial scheduling.[18] Where a party has brought an interlocutory *certiorari* application and/or appealed from a decision granting or refusing *certiorari*, it is open to the Crown to argue that such delay constitutes a discrete exceptional circumstance. The Court of Appeal for Ontario considered this issue in *R v Tsega* and provided an overview of how to assess delay arising from an interlocutory application for an extraordinary remedy.[19] The Court held that the time spent seeking extraordinary remedies would not automatically be included or excluded in the presumptive ceiling where the accused continues to face the charge. The court observed that such a premise would effectively nullify the Crown's ability to bring an application for extraordinary remedies without running the risk of causing unreasonable delay.[20] Whether the application fits into an exceptional circumstance depends on whether it lies outside the Crown's control in the sense that exceptional events are reasonably unforeseen or reasonably unavoidable, and Crown counsel cannot reasonably remedy the delays emanating from those circumstances once they arise. Unless the Crown's application is found to be frivolous because it is without merit, undertaken in bad faith, or executed in a dilatory manner, the time required for the application is deducted as

---

17   See s 577 of the *Criminal Code*; *Manasseri*, above note 13 at para 340; *Les Industries Garanties limitée c R*, 2017 QCCS 1504 at paras 21–24.

18   *R v Case*, 2019 ONSC 7240 at para 30; *R v 1478876 Alberta Ltd*, 2018 ABPC 6 at para 32.

19   *R v Tsega*, 2019 ONCA 111 at paras 75–83, leave to appeal refused (without reasons) 2019 CanLII 107002 (SCC) [*Tsega*]; *R v Mansour*, 2020 ONCA 586 at paras 20–26; *R v Perdomo Lopez*, 2020 ABCA 404 at paras 59–62.

20   *Tsega*, above note 19 at para 77.

an exceptional circumstance.[21] Delay arising from defence applications, so long as they are brought in good faith, is likewise to be treated as an exceptional circumstance.[22] Delay that results from defence applications that are frivolous or brought in bad faith is to be deducted as defence-caused delay.[23]

---

21   *R v Daponte*, 2021 ONCA 14 at paras 19–24; *R c Singh*, 2018 QCCM 10 at paras 96–97 and 108–10.

22   *R v Kozma*, 2017 ABQB 723 at paras 36–39; contra: *R v Brezden*, 2017 ONSC 6376 at paras 41–60; *R v Patrois*, 2018 ONSC 934 at paras 39–57; *R v Croteau*, 2020 ONCJ 55 at paras 91–96; *R v Jansen and Hall*, 2017 ONSC 2954 at paras 75–77.

23   *R v Codina*, 2017 ONSC 4886 at paras 102–13; *R v Richards*, 2016 ONSC 6372 at paras 12–15 and 28–29.

CHAPTER 5

Post-trial Delay

A. SENTENCING DELAY

1) The Pre-*Jordan* Approach to Post-Verdict Delay — *R v MacDougall* and *R v Gallant*

In the pre-*Jordan/Morin* era, the Supreme Court first considered whether and how section 11(b) of the *Charter*[1] applies to delay in sentencing in *R v MacDougall*[2] and its companion case *R v Gallant*.[3] In *MacDougall*, the accused pleaded guilty to a charge of indecent assault. As a result of the need for the preparation of a Pre-Sentence Report, Mr. MacDougall's failure to attend on one date, and, mostly, the illness of the sentencing judge, twenty-two months of delay accrued between the plea and the date the matter was ultimately stayed for delay.[4] The sentencing judge stayed the entire prosecution having regard to the total delay, from the laying of the charge to the anticipated end of the sentencing. The Crown's appeal to the Prince Edward Island Court of Appeal was dismissed.[5]

Justice McLachlin (as she then was), writing for the unanimous Supreme Court (sitting seven), held that section 11(b) of the *Charter* does

---

1   *Canadian Charter of Rights and Freedoms*, Part I of the *Constitution Act, 1982*, being Schedule B to the *Canada Act 1982* (UK), 1982, c 11 [*Charter*].

2   *R v MacDougall*, 1998 CanLII 763 (SCC) [*MacDougall*].

3   *R v Gallant*, 1998 CanLII 764 (SCC).

4   *R v MacDougall*, above note 2 at paras 3–4 and 6.

5   *Ibid* at paras 4 and 7.

apply to sentencing.[6] This conclusion depended upon how the phrase "charged with an offence" was to be interpreted, given that section 11(b) of the *Charter* is applicable to those who have been charged with an offence. Does someone whose charges have been dealt with, either by conviction after a trial or a plea of guilt, still fall into this category of individuals? To be further determined was whether a "trial" within a reasonable time included not just the trial proper, but also through to the imposition of sentence. In the Court's determination, "charged with an offence" was to be interpreted broadly and purposively, and in a way that synchronizes all of the subsections under section 11 of the *Charter*.[7] Such interpretation was also buttressed by the fact that only upon sentencing is an accused person released "from the power of the prosecutorial arm of the law."[8] Further, that the outcome of a matter is not fully known and is not complete until the sentence has been imposed led to the conclusion that a trial for the purposes of section 11(b) of the *Charter* includes sentencing.[9]

Finally, though in more limited respects, the sentencing process was found to engage the interests section 11(b) of the *Charter* was designed to protect.[10] The Court noted that as it related to prejudice to an accused's liberty interests, given that there was no guarantee the deprivation of liberty, by either imprisonment or subjection to strict bail conditions, would be taken into account on sentencing, that interest could be affected.[11] So too security interests where delay in awaiting sentencing could exacerbate the prejudice arising from a conviction and extend the period of anxiety arising from the wait for a disposition.[12] Further, an accused's fair trial rights could also be prejudiced by too long a delay awaiting sentencing, having an impact on an accused's ability to call evidence at the hearing while it is fresh and available.[13] In addition to avoiding a scenario where a convicted person may be on release through a lengthy delay to sentencing, society's interests are met by seeing a

---

6   *Ibid* at paras 11–17.

7   *Ibid* at para 11.

8   *Ibid* at para 13.

9   *Ibid* at paras 19–27.

10   *Ibid* at para 32.

11   *Ibid* at para 33.

12   *Ibid* at para 34.

13   *Ibid* at para 35.

final conclusion to any given matter.[14] Accordingly, section 11(b) of the *Charter* was found to apply to the whole period between the laying of a criminal charge, through to the final disposition of sentence. The *Morin* framework,[15] encompassing consideration of the length of the delay, the reasons for the delay, waiver of any delay periods, and prejudice to the accused, was consequently also determined to apply to the whole of the prosecution, including sentencing.

2)   Treatment of Post-trial Delay — *R v Jordan*

The Supreme Court in *Jordan* did not precisely address whether the framework it provides would be applicable to sentencing delay. Instead, in a footnote, the Court acknowledged its decision in *MacDougall*, confirming that section 11(b) is applicable to sentencing delay. The note continues:

> Some sentencing proceedings require significant time, for example, dangerous offender applications or situations in which expert reports are required, or extensive evidence is tendered. The issue of delay in sentencing, however, is not before us, and we make no comment about how this ceiling should apply to s. 11(*b*) applications brought after a conviction is entered, or whether additional time should be added to the ceiling in such cases.[16]

That it remains settled law that section 11(b) of the *Charter* applies through to the imposition of sentence was again affirmed by the Court in *R v KGK*.[17]

Though the Supreme Court has yet to revisit the issue, it has made clear that the eighteen- and thirty-month ceilings apply strictly to trial delay, defined as including the period between the swearing of an Information laying a charge and the conclusion of evidence and submissions on the trial proper.[18] How each of the provinces that has resolved the question of how to assess the reasonableness of sentencing delay is reviewed in the sections that follow.

---

14   *Ibid* at para 36.
15   Outlined in the introduction to this book.
16   *R v Jordan*, 2016 SCC 27 at fn 2 [*Jordan*].
17   *R v KGK*, 2020 SCC 7 at paras 3 and 26–28 [*KGK*].
18   See Chapter 2; *KGK*, above note 17 at paras 3, 24, and 31–50.

3)   Sentencing Delay—Ontario

In Ontario, the reasonableness of the time it took for sentencing in a given case is assessed applying the *Jordan* framework, but measured against a separate ceiling of five months, beyond which the delay is presumed to be unreasonable. In *R v Charley*,[19] the accused was convicted of offences related to a gunpoint robbery. He brought an application pursuant to section 11(b) of the *Charter* to stay the proceedings before he was sentenced for the offences.[20] At trial the judge applied the *Jordan* ceiling to the period between the laying of the charge and the anticipated date of Mr. Charley's sentencing. The entire matter was stayed as the judge determined that the net delay sat at thirty-two months and the Crown was unable to justify the delay.[21] The portion of delay between the conviction and the date the stay was imposed was seventeen months, with no suggestion that the trial delay was unreasonable on its own.

The Crown appealed the decision. While it was accepted that section 11(b) of the *Charter* applied to the whole of the trial, including to the end of sentence, the Crown argued that the *Jordan* framework did not apply beyond the end of the trial. Instead, post-trial delay should be assessed separately from the time required for trial, and the framework for assessment of delay falling below the applicable ceiling for trial delay[22] ought to apply to assess post-trial delay.[23] Counsel for the defence at trial advanced the argument that the ceilings were integral to the assessment of reasonableness and proposed a ninety-day ceiling for post-verdict delay, beyond which it fell to the Crown to justify the delay. Both parties agreed that the *Morin* framework should no longer apply to the assessment of the reasonableness of delay to sentencing.[24]

Justice Doherty, writing for the court, adopted a five-month ceiling for the assessment of what the court variously termed "post-verdict" and "sentencing" delay. In identifying the ceiling, the court was clear that it was not an aspirational target, but the point at which delay is too long and must be justified by the Crown. As well, there is an expectation that the parties will cooperate, and where the sentencing is expected to

---

19   2019 ONCA 726 [*Charley*].

20   *Ibid* at paras 5–19.

21   *Ibid* at paras 20–27.

22   Discussed in Chapter 8.

23   *Charley*, above note 19 at paras 28–31.

24   *Ibid* at paras 28 and 32–34.

be complex, the parties are to act with diligence in gathering and putting material before the court and to have developed a plan to ensure that the proceedings will conclude within a reasonable period of time. For example, that counsel for the defence at trial declined to prepare and file motion material until the Crown's section 752.1[25] assessment order application was settled was not an appropriate approach to the litigation.[26]

The *Jordan* framework, including deductions from the total delay to account for defence-caused delay and exceptional circumstances, applies in the same way, as does the transitional exception.[27] In *Charley*, the time required for the Crown to bring an application for an assessment in pursuit of a Long-Term or Dangerous Offender designation (LTO/DO) was treated as an exceptional circumstance as it was "reasonably unavoidable"[28] once the Crown determined that the criteria for pursuit of the designation were met. In circumstances where the Crown has taken steps in advance to gather the requisite material in pursuit of the application, then they have mitigated the delay arising from the exceptional circumstances and the deduction can be made.[29] As the Crown's application was exceptional, and was not frivolous, the time it required was deducted, reducing the delay to below the five-month ceiling. The Court held that, accordingly, there was no *Charter* breach.[30]

Similarly, the Court of Appeal considered how delay arising from an *R v Gardiner*[31] hearing in the sentencing proceedings ought to be characterized in the *Jordan/Charley* framework in *R v Lewis*.[32] As with a Long-Term Offender or Dangerous Offender application for an assessment and LTO/DO hearing, the Court of Appeal held that the need for a *Gardiner* hearing is not "part of the routine sentencing framework contemplated by this court in *Charley*."[33] The court, however, did not conclusively settle on whether the need for such a hearing was properly

---

25   *Criminal Code*, RSC 1985, c C-46, s 752.1.

26   *Charley*, above note 19 at para 93.

27   *Ibid* at para 105.

28   *Jordan*, above note 16 at paras 69 and 105.

29   *Charley*, above note 19 at paras 98–104.

30   *Ibid* at paras 102–5; see also: *R v Adu-Bekoe*, 2021 ONCA 136 at paras 19–26; *R v Valle-Quintero*, 2021 ONCA 390.

31   1982 CanLII 30 (SCC) [*Gardiner*].

32   2021 ONCA 59 [*Lewis*].

33   *Ibid* at para 12.

characterized as a discrete exceptional event or an indicia of complexity. The court simply found that the five months and three days required to sentence Mr. Lewis was not unreasonable in the circumstances.[34]

Application of the transitional exceptional circumstance to sentencing delay was considered by the Ontario Court of Appeal in *R v Hartling*.[35] While considered in detail in Chapter 9, in brief, the exception applies to prosecutions that were initiated prior to the release of the decision in *Jordan* on 8 July 2016 but were not completed by then. Where the parties are determined to have reasonably relied on the state of the law (that is, the *Morin* decision and the decisions that followed it applying that framework), the Crown can rely on the exception to justify delay even where on application of the *Jordan* framework, the net delay has exceeded the ceiling.[36] The exception was included as part of the *Jordan* framework to avoid a mass of stays arising from the new framework, and to allow the criminal justice system time to adjust and respond to it. In *Hartling*, the Crown could not rely on the exception. The delay to sentencing was due to a shortage of *Gladue*[37] report writers in the region of Algoma, resulting in a lengthy delay in sentencing Mr. Hartling for a conviction for aggravated assault. The Ontario Court of Appeal held that, as with trial delay, the Crown could not rely on the exception where the delay would not have been reasonable pursuant to *Morin*. Because the fourteen months of delay arising from the wait for a *Gladue* report would not have been reasonable under *Morin*, the transitional exception was inapplicable.[38]

The facts in *Hartling* can be contrasted to those in *R v JK*,[39] where the transitional exception was applied to justify post-trial delay. *JK* was also a case where delay was attributable to an outstanding *Gladue* report. However, it differed in that the report was not delayed as a result of institutional limitations but was due to an administrative error that kept the request for the report from reaching Aboriginal Legal Services. The Court of Appeal held that the transitional exception justified the delay arising from the error, as the parties were operating before the

---

34   *Ibid* at paras 12–13.

35   *R v Hartling*, 2020 ONCA 243 [*Hartling*].

36   *Jordan*, above note 16 at paras 92–104.

37   *R v Gladue*, 1999 CanLII 679 (SCC).

38   *Hartling*, above note 35 at paras 104–9.

39   2021 ONCA 256 [*JK*].

release of the decision in *Charley* and reasonably relied on the state of the law that existed at the relevant time.[40] Had they been aware of the five-month ceiling, the response to the lateness of the report would have been different and the discovery of the error likely made sooner.[41]

4)   The Remedy for a Breach of Section 11(b) at Sentencing—Ontario

Having determined that a five-month ceiling was applicable as it related to sentencing or post-trial delay, the Court of Appeal in *Charley*[42] considered what remedy or remedies pursuant to section 24(1) of the *Charter*[43] could be obtained where a breach is found. Where the trial delay is not at issue, but a breach of section 11(b) of the *Charter* has been found as it relates to the post-verdict period of delay, what is the result? Section 24(1) of the *Charter* allows the court to impose such remedy as "the court considers just and appropriate in the circumstances."[44] However, as will be fully discussed in Chapter 10, notwithstanding the broad remedial power afforded judges in section 24(1), the only remedy for a breach of section 11(b) of the *Charter* at trial is a stay of the proceedings.[45]

Though the Court of Appeal did not find a breach of section 11(b) in *Charley*, there was *obiter dicta* in this regard. Justice Doherty noted that while the law with respect to the remedy for trial delay was long settled, there was no jurisprudence as to the remedy for sentencing delay.[46] Looking to American caselaw, the Court held that a stay of a valid conviction for sentencing delay alone amounted to an "unjustified windfall."[47] While it was arguable that the remedy pursuant to section 24(1) of the *Charter* should only relate to the sentence, including potentially a stay of the sentencing or a stay of the enforcement of some portion of the sentence, the court ultimately left the question for another court to determine where a breach had been found.[48]

------

40   See also: *Valle-Quintero*, above note 30 at para 24.
41   *JK*, above note 39 at paras 69–77.
42   *Charley*, above note 19.
43   *Charter*, above note 1, s 24(1).
44   *Ibid.*
45   *R v Rahey*, 1987 CanLII 52 (SCC) [*Rahey*].
46   *Charley*, above note 19.
47   *Betterman v Montana*, 578 US 437 (2016), 136 S Ct 1609, 194 L Ed 2d 723.
48   *Charley*, above note 19 at paras 113–14.

Very shortly after the Ontario Court of Appeal's decision in *R v Charley*, Doody J considered the question as to the remedy for post-trial delay in *R v Croteau*,[49] a case that arose in the Ontario Court of Justice. Mr. Croteau had pleaded guilty to two counts of trafficking of marijuana, one related to an undisclosed amount and one under three kilograms. On the eve of the date sentencing submissions were set to commence, the Crown sought to call evidence in a *Gardiner* hearing in order to prove that one count was in an amount higher than three kilograms of marijuana, notwithstanding that the guilty pleas were accepted on the basis of an Agreed Statement of Fact. In the midst of argument in this regard, the decision in *Charley* was released. Mr. Croteau brought an application pursuant to section 11(b) of the *Charter*.[50] On application of the *Jordan* framework, the delay amounted to a year between the guilty pleas and sentencing submissions. The Crown could not rely on the transitional exceptional circumstance, having been aware that section 11(b) of the *Charter* did apply to sentencing delay and given *Jordan's* repudiation of complacency as it relates to delay.[51]

Justice Doody found that he was bound by the Supreme Court's decision in *R v Rahey*,[52] which held that the only appropriate remedy for a breach of section 11(b) is a stay.[53] A thorough discussion of the Supreme Court's decision in *Rahey* respecting the remedy for a breach of section 11(b) of the *Charter* is found in Chapter 10. For the purposes of consideration of the remedy for sentencing delay, it is sufficient to note that the majority in that decision, though for disparate reasons, held that a stay is the minimum remedy for a breach of section 11(b) of the *Charter*. While part of the majority held that this was so because jurisdiction was lost at the point of the breach, the others pointed to fairness and held that to allow proceedings to continue once a breach was found was to persist in the breach. Justice Doody held that notwithstanding that a windfall might be the result, the sentencing had to be stayed pursuant to *Rahey*. It did not require, however, that the guilty pleas be vacated.[54] In staying the passing of sentence in *Croteau*, Doody J also

---

49   2020 ONCJ 55 [*Croteau*].

50   *Ibid* at paras 2–10.

51   *Ibid* at paras 58–125.

52   *Rahey*, above note 45.

53   *Croteau*, above note 49 at para 129.

54   *Ibid* at paras 127–45.

noted that the Supreme Court's decision in *R v Nasogaluak*,[55] in his view, did nothing to denude the *Rahey* holding as to the remedy for section 11(b) of the *Charter*.[56]

The Ontario Court of Appeal, with Benotto JA writing for the Court, held otherwise about six months later in *R v Hartling*.[57] To better understand the Court of Appeal's decision in *Hartling* requires a brief description of the Supreme Court of Canada's decision in *R v Nasogaluak*.[58] In that case, the Supreme Court considered whether the sentencing judge, having found a breach of section 7 of the *Charter*, properly relied on section 24(1) to reduce an appropriate and mandatory minimum sentence as a remedy for the breach. Mr. Nasogaluak, in the course of being arrested for impaired driving offences, was punched several times by police and was left with broken ribs and a collapsed lung as a result. Arresting officers did not report the injuries and once released, Mr. Nasogaluak required emergency surgery.[59] The trial judge, finding that police had used excessive force and violated section 7 of the *Charter* in doing so, reduced Mr. Nasogaluak's sentence to a conditional sentence to remedy the breach.[60] Justice LeBel, writing for the unanimous Court, held that while a *Charter* breach can be remedied through a reduction in sentence, it is unnecessary to rely on section 24(1) of the *Charter* to take account of prejudice caused to an accused as the sentencing regime is flexible enough to allow for consideration of it.[61] The circumstances of a *Charter* breach can be taken account of in sentencing someone, "when they are relevant to the offender and to the offence."[62] Such "state misconduct,"[63] however, need not rise to the level of a *Charter* breach in order to be taken into account in fashioning a disposition. The Court made reference to several cases where courts have taken account of state misconduct as part of the sentencing process and without regard to section 24(1) of the *Charter*. While some of these cases related to such state misconduct as police use of excessive force or illegal searches, the

---

55   2010 SCC 6 [*Nasogaluak*].

56   *Croteau*, above note 49 at para 129.

57   *Hartling*, above note 35.

58   *Nasogaluak*, above note 55.

59   *Ibid* at paras 10–13.

60   *Ibid* at paras 17–18.

61   *Ibid* at paras 47–49.

62   *Ibid* at para 50.

63   *Ibid* at paras 53 and 55.

Court also referenced a number of pre-*Charter* cases where delay by the police or prosecution warranted a reduction in sentence.[64]

The Ontario Court of Appeal in *R v Hartling*[65] relied upon the *Nasogaluak*[66] decision to determine that a reduction in sentence is a permitted remedy for a post-verdict breach of section 11(b) of the *Charter*. While there was no trial delay from which a breach of section 11(b) of the *Charter* arose in this case, it took fourteen months post-conviction for sentencing. The delay was entirely due to a lack of institutional resources as a *Gladue* report could not be prepared due to a lack of writers.[67] Though the court acknowledged that a stay is the only available remedy where a breach arises from trial delay, it was determined that this is not so for sentencing delay.[68] In such instance, the conviction is not touched by the breach and to vacate it would have a negative impact on public confidence in the administration of justice.[69] Where delay to sentencing reaches the level of a *Charter* breach, the individual facing sentencing is instead entitled to *enhanced* mitigation if the sentence is to "meet the objectives and principles of sentencing codified in s. 718 of the *Criminal Code* while also providing a meaningful remedy for the *Charter* breach."[70]

Though no precise formula can be applied to determine the quantum by which the sentence ought to be reduced to account for the *Charter* breach, it ought to be arrived at by taking account of the particular circumstances in a given case, including "the offence, the offender, the length of the delay, the circumstances of the delay and any other relevant factors."[71] While Mr. Hartling's offence (an aggravated assault against his mother) was serious, the delay of more than a year to be sentenced was attributed to the failure to provide the necessary resources to serve a vulnerable segment of society. This amounted to a serious breach that warranted a five-month reduction from a sentence of thirty months.[72]

------

64   *Ibid* at paras 50–54; *R v Cooper (No 2)*, 1977 CanLII 2103 (Ont CA); *R v Simon*, 1975 CanLII 1236 (Ont CA).

65   *Hartling*, above note 35.

66   *Nasogaluak*, above note 55.

67   *Hartling*, above note 35 at paras 96–97.

68   *Ibid* at para 111.

69   *Ibid* at paras 112–14.

70   *Ibid* at para 119.

71   *Ibid* at para 122.

72   *Ibid* at paras 122–23; with the sentence already reduced to twenty-one months reflecting pre-sentence custody.

5)   Sentencing Delay—Quebec

In *Demers c R*,[73] the overall delay between the swearing of the Information and the date for the imposition of sentence amounted to forty-two months. Mr. Demers appealed against the sentence he received and against the trial judge's decision to dismiss his motion for a stay for delay pursuant to section 11(b) of the *Charter*. In argument on appeal, he advanced that while he was not entitled to a stay, he was nevertheless entitled to a reduction in sentence for the delay it took to reach his sentencing.[74] The Quebec Court of Appeal acknowledged the Supreme Court's pronouncement in *MacDougall*[75] that section 11(b) applies through to the imposition of sentence, and noted that in *Jordan*, the Court affirmed that this was so.[76] However, not yet determined by the Court was whether the section 11(b) *Jordan* clock ran through to the imposition of the sentence. Prescient of what the Supreme Court later conclusively determined in *KGK*,[77] the Court held that the ceilings were only intended to apply to the end of evidence and pleadings.[78] The Court ultimately determined that unless the steps required to complete the sentencing "drag on unduly,"[79] no breach of section 11(b) of the *Charter* could be established. No breach was found, and so the Court did not consider what remedy could apply for a breach of section 11(b) of the *Charter* in relation to the sentencing period.[80]

Rejecting the adoption of a separate ceiling for sentencing delay as was done in Ontario in *R v Charley*,[81] the Quebec Court of Appeal has maintained this "more flexible and modulated approach"[82] instead. In *Deblois c R*,[83] for example, the court attributed the eleven-month period between the conviction and sentence as attributable to the need to resolve a matter related to the imposition of a mandatory minimum sentence, which created some complexity in the litigation. The eleven

---

73   2018 QCCA 617 [*Demers*].

74   *Ibid* at para 36.

75   *R v MacDougall*, above note 2.

76   *Demers*, above note 73 at paras 39–40; *Jordan*, above note 16 at fn 2.

77   *KGK*, above note 17.

78   *Demers*, above note 73 at paras 41–42; *R c Rice*, 2018 QCCA 198 at paras 41–42.

79   *Demers*, above note 73 at para 42.

80   *Ibid* at para 50.

81   *Charley*, above note 19.

82   *Deblois c R*, 2021 QCCA 1093 at para 134 [*Deblois*].

83   *Ibid*.

months of delay was not unduly long in the circumstances.[84] The assessment of whether some period of sentencing delay is unduly long has been variously interpreted. In some courts, it has been taken to mean that the *Morin* framework survives for this purpose, applying as it would have pre-*Jordan*, to the sentencing period alone.[85] Accordingly, whether the delay is unduly long is gauged having regard to the length of the delay, the reasons for the delay, whether there has been any waiver of any of the delay, and prejudice caused to the accused.[86]

The most recent consideration of the measure of reasonableness of delay in the sentencing context at the appellant level in Quebec was in *Lévesque Paquette c R*.[87] Justice Bich, writing for the Court, affirmed the comprehensive contextual approach as outlined in *Deblois*[88] and *Demers*.[89] This approach, the court determined, is an application of the *Morin* framework as it would have applied in *MacDougall*,[90] "without necessarily requiring the level of scrutiny required by *MacDougall*,"[91] and "which keeps in mind the requirement for diligence recognized by the *Jordan* decision and the jurisprudence that followed."[92] The court, however, did not settle definitively on whether this analysis ought also to include consideration of prejudice, or the absence of any prejudice caused by the sentencing delay. The court did note, though, that since a reduction in sentence was a permissible remedy for sentencing delay, that consideration of prejudice would naturally arise in that context.[93]

6) Remedy for Sentencing Delay—Quebec

In *Lévesque Paquette c R*,[94] the Quebec Court of Appeal adopted the Ontario Court of Appeal's determination in *R v Hartling*[95] that the

---

84   *Ibid* at paras 134–36.

85   *Deschamps c R*, 2022 QCCM 44 at paras 146–49.

86   *Ibid*.

87   *Lévesque Paquette c R*, 2022 QCCA 1047 [*Lévesque Paquette*]; see also *Chemama c R*, 2024 QCCA 405 at paras 351–58.

88   *Deblois*, above note 82.

89   *Demers*, above note 73.

90   *R v MacDougall*, above note 2.

91   *Lévesque Paquette*, above note 87 at para 63.

92   *Ibid* at para 63.

93   *Ibid* at paras 72–77.

94   *Ibid*.

95   *Hartling*, above note 35.

"usual remedy" for a breach of section 11(b) of the *Charter* during the sentencing phase of proceedings is a reduction in sentence.[96]

7) Sentencing Delay—British Columbia

The Court of Appeal of British Columbia had occasion to consider the application of the framework in *Jordan* as it relates to sentencing delay in *R v SCW*.[97] The appellant pleaded guilty to sexual interference and child pornography offences. Though there were four years between the plea and sentencing, the judge at trial dismissed the appellant's application for a stay for delay pursuant to section 11(b) of the *Charter*. The Court of Appeal held that the trial judge was correct to dismiss the application but had improperly applied the *Jordan* framework to the period between the charge to the date of the imposition of sentence. In the court's view, the framework was not intended to apply to post-verdict delay. As with the Court of Appeal in Quebec, Felon JA, writing for the Court, held that the correct approach to sentencing delay was to apply the *Morin* framework, relying on *MacDougall*.[98] That jurisprudence continues to govern as it relates to sentencing delay in British Columbia, "tempered by *Jordan*'s emphasis on the importance of facilitating a more efficient justice system."[99] In contrast to the approach taken in Ontario, such an approach acknowledges that sentencing hearings will differ in length and complexity without the need to characterize periods of delay on application of the *Jordan* framework.[100]

8) Remedy for Sentencing Delay—British Columbia

There is little in the way of jurisprudence as to the remedy for a breach of section 11(b) of the *Charter* for delay between conviction and sentence in British Columbia. In one provincial court decision, the trial judge, though a breach was not found, indicated that "although I declined to order a stay of proceeding of the charge of sexual assault (s. 271), I did not

---

96   *Lévesque Paquette*, above note 87 at para 72.

97   2018 BCCA 346, leave to appeal refused (without reasons) 2019 CanLII 23872 (SCC) [*SCW*].

98   *MacDougall*, above note 2.

99   *R v Dadmand*, 2017 BCSC 1644 at para 55; *SCW*, above note 97 at para 35.

100   *SCW*, above note 97 at para 34.

foreclose the possibility of the court considering less draconian *Charter* remedies on sentencing."[101]

9) Sentencing Delay—Alberta

Though the Alberta Court of Appeal has not yet had cause to consider the approach to take in relation to delay in sentencing, there has been some developing jurisprudence in this regard. In *R v Harker*,[102] for example, Kubik J declined to adopt the Ontario approach. The court would not establish a separate ceiling to apply to sentencing delay because the protection afforded by section 11(b) is somewhat tempered in that the presumption of innocence has been displaced at this stage, and there is no concern as to the ability to make answer and defence. Further, the Court held, the effects of the COVID-19 pandemic made strict timelines for the completion of court processes less viable. The court determined to assess the delay to sentence as a matter of "reasonableness" in the circumstances.[103] There has been no reported consideration of the remedy for a breach of section 11(b) of the *Charter* at the sentencing stage in Alberta to date.

10) Sentencing Delay—Nova Scotia

In one reported Supreme Court of Nova Scotia decision, the court's approach was similar to those taken in both Quebec and British Columbia. In *R v Boyer*,[104] Coughlan J held that the *Morin/MacDougall* framework applies, but that post-*Jordan* consideration of the relevant factors in *MacDougall* "has to take into account and be modified by the principle set out in *Jordan* and *Cody* that criminal trials should proceed expeditiously to protect a citizen's right to a trial within a reasonable time."[105] The remedy for a breach of section 11(b) of the *Charter* for sentencing delay was not considered.

---

101 *R v DCR*, 2017 BCPC 326 at para 43.
102 2020 ABQB 603 [*Harker*]; see also: *R v Blanchard*, 2017 ABQB 369.
103 *Harker*, above note 102 at paras 13–19.
104 2019 NSSC 336.
105 *Ibid* at paras 22–33.

The Supreme Court of Nova Scotia, on summary conviction appeal, had recent cause to consider the issue again in *R v SPP*.[106] The respondent had pleaded guilty to sexual assault and child luring and was sentenced to a conditional sentence of eight months and three years' probation. It took nineteen months to sentence the offender, largely because the judge who took the pleas of guilty went on indefinite leave and some time had passed before the parties were advised of such.[107] The Crown appealed against the sentence, in part, on the basis that the lower court judge had erred in adopting the five-month ceiling applicable to sentencing delay in Ontario pursuant to *R v Charley*.[108] The summary appeal court agreed, holding that, "with all due respect to the Ontario Court of Appeal . . . in light of the wording in s. 720 CC and the reasoning in *KGK*,[109] sentencing-process delay is more appropriately assessed using a qualitative rather than a numerical standard of what is 'within a reasonable time' – particularly where the presumption of judicial integrity remains relevant."[110] The Court reasoned that the wording in the *Criminal Code*, which reads that "a court shall, as soon as practicable after an offender has been found guilty, conduct proceedings to determine the appropriate sentence to be imposed,"[111] as well as the wording in *KGK* that indicates the measure of whether verdict judicial deliberation time is unreasonable looks to whether it took "markedly longer than [it] reasonably should have in all the circumstances,"[112] coupled with the presumption of judicial integrity, favours an approach that is far more flexible, as in the Quebec Court of Appeal's decision in *R v DeBlois*.[113] The Court held, however, that the trial court had appropriately determined to reduce the respondent's sentence (though the quantum of the deduction ought to have been identified).[114]

In none of the remaining provinces and territories has this issue been considered in a reported decision to date.

---

106   *R v SPP*, 2024 NSSC 42 [*SPP*].

107   *Ibid* at paras 52–59.

108   *Charley*, above note 19.

109   *KGK*, above note 17.

110   *SPP*, above note 106 at para 93.

111   *Criminal Code*, RSC 1985, c C-46, s 720(1).

112   *KGK*, above note 17 at para 4.

113   *Deblois*, above note 82; *ibid* at paras 75–101.

114   *SPP*, above note 106 at paras 101–31.

B. POST-TRIAL APPLICATIONS

In some instances, the need to bring an application will only arise once the trial, that is the end of evidence and pleadings, has reached an end. How to assess the reasonableness of the time required for an entrapment application, for example, arose before the Ontario Court of Appeal in *R v Haniffa*.[115] The case took place in the context of a large investigation targeting those who hired juveniles for sexual services. On appeal, it was argued that because the application can only be brought post-conviction and because where entrapment is found, the trial judge can refuse to enter a conviction, such applications should be included as part of the trial for the purposes of the section 11(b) *Jordan* framework.[116] The Ontario Court of Appeal held that, pursuant to the Supreme Court's decision in *R v KGK*,[117] post-trial applications could not be counted beyond the end of evidence and argument.[118]

The court also rejected the contention that any post-trial applications, though unrelated to sentencing, should be counted toward the five-month ceiling applicable to sentencing delay pursuant to the Court's decision in *Charley*.[119] Instead, the time required for post-trial motions that do not relate to the sentencing itself must be considered separate and apart from the sentencing period. The time required for such motions "should not be unreasonable considering the number and complexity of the motions in the specific circumstances of the particular case."[120] As the post-trial motions in this case were necessary and litigated in an efficient fashion, there was no breach of section 11(b) of the *Charter* related to post-verdict, non-sentencing delay.[121]

To date the issue has not arisen in any reported decisions from the other provinces. However, given the flexible approach to post-verdict delay adopted by the majority of the provinces at the appellate level,[122]

---

115 2021 ONCA 326 [*Haniffa (ONCA)*]; though leave to appeal the Court of Appeal's decision with respect to the elements of entrapment was granted by the Supreme Court of Canada, leave to appeal the s 11(b) ground was refused: *Haniffa v Her Majesty the Queen*, 2021 CanLII 133770 (SCC).

116 *Haniffa (ONCA)*, above note 115 at para 32.

117 *KGK*, above note 17.

118 *Haniffa (ONCA)*, above note 115 at para 33; *KGK*, above note 17 at para 33.

119 *Charley*, above note 19; *Haniffa (ONCA)*, above note 115 at para 35.

120 *Haniffa (ONCA)*, above note 115 at para 36.

121 *Ibid* at para 38.

122 See the discussion related to sentencing delay at the outset of this chapter.

it can be anticipated that the whole portion of time taken for a prosecution that takes place post-trial, and after the period for deliberation,[123] will be assessed as a whole. It is the five-month sentencing ceiling in *Charley*[124] that necessitated a distinction as between sentencing delay and post-trial motion delay that will likely not be required in the rest of the provinces and territories.

---

123   *KGK*, above note 17; discussed in detail in Chapter 3.
124   *Charley*, above note 19.

CHAPTER 6

Waiver and Defence-Caused Delay

A. WAIVER

Delay to be subtracted from the calculation of the total delay in a prosecution to take account of defence conduct or inaction can be characterized either as (1) waiver; or (2) defence-caused delay. The accused may agree that some period of delay ought not to be counted toward the ceiling count. Such delay is frequently waived in circumstances where the defence requires an adjournment for some purpose (excluding legitimate preparation time), or where counsel of choice cannot accept earlier dates. Waiver of some period of delay can be either explicit or implicit. Explicit waiver is easy to identify. Either on record or in writing, the accused will indicate that a particular period of delay is waived. That period of delay will accordingly not be included in the calculation of net delay. It will be deducted from the total delay. It must always be recollected that waiver refers to waiver of a particular segment of time, not to overall waiver of the section 11(b) *Charter* right.[1]

Importantly, the Supreme Court has indicated that there are limits to the extent that an accused may be permitted to waive delay. As all justice system participants are tasked with ensuring that trials are concluded within a reasonable period of time, trial judges are obliged to take action where delay is simply too long, notwithstanding that it is waived. Trial judges must assess the legitimacy of steps taken by the

---

1   *Canadian Charter of Rights and Freedoms*, Part I of the *Constitution Act, 1982*, being Schedule B to the *Canada Act 1982* (UK), 1982, c 11 [*Charter*]; see *R v Conway*, 1989 CanLII 66 (SCC) at para 47; *R v Jordan*, 2016 SCC 27 at para 61 [*Jordan*].

parties as a means to *prevent* delay and as part of the overall shift in courtroom culture commanded by *R v Jordan.*[2] For example, notwithstanding that delay caused by an adjournment is waived, a court may deny such request where it would result in an unacceptably long period of delay.[3] In another matter, a conflict may arise as between right to counsel of choice and the judge's obligation to prevent unreasonable delay pursuant to section 11(b) of the *Charter*. It remains to be seen whether in all cases an accused will be permitted to delay a trial until counsel of choice is available to offer representation, or whether there is some time limit in that regard. In some jurisdictions, the issue has already been anticipated. In Manitoba, for example, the *Practice Directions* of the Court of King's Bench in that province indicate that in order to accommodate an accused's counsel of choice, the accused is permitted to waive as much as six months of delay so long as the Crown consents.[4] By necessary implication, any waiver of more than six months would not be permitted having regard to the judge's duty to prevent unreasonable delay, notwithstanding the accused's choice of counsel. Similarly, circumstances may arise where one co-accused insists upon counsel of choice and offers a waiver of the resultant delay, but the delay is not acceptable to the other accused. The judge will have to consider whether either the first accused must be forced on with or without counsel of choice or whether severance is the solution.[5] What is clear is that post-*Jordan*, "judges cannot passively sit back and let the Crown, or the accused—even if they are self-represented—'rag the puck' and unnecessarily prolong criminal proceedings."[6]

1)   Implicit Waiver

The authority predating the Supreme Court's decision in *Jordan* allowed that waiver may be inferred where the defence agreed to the setting of a particular date, so long as acceptance of that date did not amount to

---

2   *Jordan*, above note 1; see also *R v Thanabalasingham*, 2020 SCC 18 at para 9 [*Thanabalasingham*]; *R v Cody*, 2017 SCC 31 at paras 36–42 [*Cody*].

3   *Cody*, above note 2 at para 37; *Thanabalasingham*, above note 2 at para 9.

4   *R v Morris*, 2018 MBQB 85 at para 32; *Practice Directions—Manitoba Court of King's Bench*.

5   See, for example: *R v Gatt*, 2017 ONSC 3563 at para 73; *R v Kumar*, 2020 ONSC 694.

6   *R v Nowack*, 2018 ONCA 784 (unreported) at paras 11–13, leave to appeal dismissed (without reasons) [2018] SCCA No 444.

"acquiescence to the inevitable."[7] However, and perhaps paradoxically, the jurisprudence also indicated that defence waiver must be clear, unequivocal, and established by the Crown. In *R v Morin*,[8] the Court made clear that waiver must be given "with full knowledge of the rights the procedure was enacted to protect and of the effect that waiver will have on those rights." In his concurrent judgment in *Jordan*, Cromwell J observed that a rebuttable inference of waiver arising from an accused's acceptance of dates is largely incompatible with the requirement that waiver also be "clear and unequivocal."[9]

Whether the Supreme Court's decision in *Jordan* altered the law, eliminating a presumption of implicit waiver where an accused accepts dates, was considered by the Alberta Court of Appeal in *R v Chang*.[10] The court noted that other courts have concluded that the majority decision in *Jordan* did not change that waiver could be inferred in such circumstances.[11] Indeed, the Court in *Jordan* confirmed that "[w]aiver can be explicit or implicit."[12] The Alberta Court of Appeal concluded that implied waiver was still in play under the *Jordan* framework and could still justify a deduction where defence counsel is available for earlier dates but simply prefers some later date, or demonstrates "marked indifference to delay," characterized as "inaction" in the Supreme Court's decision in *R v Cody*.[13] However, simple agreement to dates, without more, could not constitute implicit waiver any more than it could pre-*Jordan*.

This is largely a matter of nomenclature, in the authors' view, with "implicit waiver" arising from the acceptance of court dates being one and the same as "defence-caused delay" within the *Jordan* framework. For example, in *R v JP*,[14] where the delay in setting a judicial pre-trial was to

---

7   *R v Smith*, 1989 CanLII 12 (SCC); *R v Morin*, 1992 CanLII 89 (SCC) at paras 37–39 [*Morin*]; *R v Askov*, [1990] 2 SCR 1199 at paras 64–66; *R v McNeil*, 2024 NSCA 57 at paras 73–93 [*McNeil (NSCA)*], leave to appeal denied (without reasons) 2024 CanLII 96595 (SCC).

8   *Morin*, above note 7.

9   *Jordan*, above note 1 at paras 186–91.

10   2019 ABCA 315.

11   *Ibid* at para 35; *Béliveau c R*, 2016 QCCA 1549; *R v Mouchayleh*, 2017 NSCA 51; *R v Schenkels*, 2017 MBCA 62, leave to appeal denied (without reasons) 2017 CanLII 78703 (SCC) [*Schenkels*].

12   *Jordan*, above note 1 at para 61.

13   *Cody*, above note 2 at paras 28 and 33.

14   *R v JP*, 2021 ONCA 866.

accommodate defence counsel's schedule, though the Crown and court had earlier dates, the Ontario Court of Appeal characterized this period of delay as "implicit, yet clear and unequivocal waiver"[15] by the defence. As will be seen below, the defence-caused delay category accounts for the "something more" the Alberta Court of Appeal identified as required before delay to trial can be properly attributed to the accused. In *JP*, the delay could have readily been attributed to defence-caused delay, as the delay was due to the unavailability of defence counsel. Similarly, the delay in securing counsel that was treated as implicit waiver by the Nova Scotia Court of Appeal in *R v Brown*[16] could have also been properly characterized as defence-caused delay.[17] In this sense, the current *Jordan* framework can be said to have subsumed implicit waiver. The Supreme Court acknowledged that this was so in *R v JF*.[18] In that case, the accused had failed to bring the application for a stay for delay in relation to delay that accrued during his first trial at that trial, instead raising it on appeal and after his second trial had already taken place. The Court rejected the argument that to have failed to bring the application amounted to waiver, though agreed that it could be a relevant factor on an assessment of whether waiver had indeed taken place. The Court also observed, however, that the framework already accounts for delay resulting from defence inaction in the form of a deduction for defence-caused delay.[19]

Either the accused will have explicitly waived delay, or some defence action or inaction will have solely or directly caused the delay, resulting in a deduction within the *Jordan* calculus. The relevant inquiry will always be: *what was the cause of this delay?*

B. DEFENCE-CAUSED DELAY

1) Rationale

While it remains the case that it is the Crown who is responsible for ensuring a matter gets to trial in a timely way, the decision in *Jordan* ushered in a shift insofar as a corresponding responsibility now

---

15   *Ibid* at paras 6–9.

16   *R v Brown*, 2018 NSCA 62.

17   *Ibid* at para 51.

18   2022 SCC 17 [*JF*].

19   *Ibid* at paras 43–52.

also attaches to all criminal justice system participants, including the accused and the judge. Every actor in the justice system is responsible for ensuring that criminal proceedings are carried out within a reasonable time. Accordingly, accused persons are not entitled to remain passive in the face of delay in the hopes of avoiding prosecution for offences while the evidence in the cases against them grows stale over time, or there is ultimately a stay for delay. Where accused persons benefit from their own delay-causing conduct, such result "operates to the detriment of the public and the system of justice as a whole."[20] Accordingly, the conduct of the defence must be examined, and any delay attributable to that conduct, or *inaction* on the part of the accused, subtracted from the total delay. It must be remembered that section 11(b) of the *Charter* is fundamentally an assessment of state conduct, and therefore conduct of the accused person or defence counsel that delays the trial cannot count toward the presumptive ceilings. Only defence delay that can be characterized as *legitimate* will be included in the count.

2) Defence-Caused Delay Defined

The delays to be subtracted at the outset consist of two components: (1) periods that are waived; and (2) periods of defence-caused delay. Defence delay comprises "those situations where the accused's acts either directly caused the delay ... or the acts of the accused are shown to be a deliberate and calculated tactic employed to delay the trial."[21] "Defence-caused delay" under the *Jordan* framework does not include "actions legitimately taken" to respond to the charges, such as time for preparation and non-frivolous applications or requests. Examples of defence-caused delay include frivolous applications and requests, and periods during which the court and Crown are ready to proceed but the defence is not.[22] However, these examples do not amount to an exhaustive list and it "will of course be open to the trial judges to find that other defence actions or conduct have caused delay."[23] Such determinations

---

20 *Jordan*, above note 1 at paras 21, 49, and 60; *Cody*, above note 2 at paras 1 and 32–33; *R v KJM*, 2019 SCC 55 at paras 81–84 [*KJM*]; *Thanabalasingham*, above note 2 at para 9.

21 *Jordan*, above note 1 at paras 60–66; *R v Williamson*, 2016 SCC 28 at paras 21–22 [*Williamson*].

22 *Jordan*, above note 1 at para 64.

23 *Ibid.*

are "highly discretionary" and "appellate courts must show a high level of deference thereto."[24]

Determining whether a given step taken by the defence is legitimate requires considerations of both substance and procedure. "The decision to take a step, *as well as the manner in which it is conducted,* may attract scrutiny."[25] Relevant to the assessment of whether some defence action is legitimate are the following factors:

- The overall number (of applications);
- Strength and importance;
- Proximity to the *Jordan* ceilings;
- Compliance with any notice or filing requirements; and
- Timeliness of applications.[26]

3) Defence Inaction

The *Jordan* and *Cody* decisions significantly changed the import of delay caused by defence *inaction* within the section 11(b) *Charter* analysis. Under *Morin* and its progeny, inaction by the accused was a factor that could only be considered either as a consideration of whether delay had been implicitly waived or at the end stage of the analysis in assessing the extent to which the accused had suffered prejudice arising from the delay. While it was acknowledged that the section 11(b) right could be employed as a shield by an accused as a means to avoid a trial on the merits, the obligation to complete a trial in a timely way nevertheless rested solely with the Crown. While action or inaction that was inconsistent with a desire for a timely trial was relevant to the assessment of prejudice, pursuant to *Morin*, defence inaction could not be considered to the extent that it could "subvert the principle that there is no legal obligation on the accused to assert the right."[27]

---

24   *Cody*, above note 2 at para 31.

25   *Ibid* at para 32 (emphasis in original).

26   *Morin*, above note 7; see also: *R v Boulanger*, 2022 SCC 2 [*Boulanger*]; *R v Lai*, 2021 SCC 52; *R v Pauls*, 2020 ONCA 220 at paras 68–72; *R v Picard*, 2017 ONCA 692 at para 40, leave to appeal denied (without reasons) 2018 CanLII 73612 (SCC); *R v Faulkner*, 2018 ONCA 174 at para 144 [*Faulkner*]; *R v Gopie*, 2017 ONCA 728 at paras 147–57 [*Gopie*]; *R v St Amand*, 2017 ONCA 913 at paras 64–78 [*St Amand*]; *R v Chung*, 2021 ONCA 188 at paras 186–89 and 191–92; *McNeil (NSCA)*, above note 7 at paras 73–93.

27   *Morin*, above note 7 at para 62.

In contrast, in *R v Cody*,[28] the Supreme Court made clear that

accused persons must bear in mind that a corollary of the section 11(*b*) right "to be tried within a reasonable time" is the responsibility to avoid causing unreasonable delay. Defence counsel are therefore expected to "actively advanc[e] their clients' right to a trial within a reasonable time, collaborat[e] with Crown counsel when appropriate and . . . us[e] court time efficiently."[29]

Accordingly, "a defence action may be deemed not legitimate ... if it is designed to delay or if it exhibits marked inefficiency or marked indifference toward delay." In this way some defence *inaction* or *omission* may also render defence action illegitimate and the delay it has caused to be excluded from the total delay count. Such a finding need not amount to professional or ethical misconduct. Instead, the assessment of legitimacy "takes its meaning from the cultural change demanded in *Jordan*," which requires that *all* justice system participants advance an accused's right to a trial within a reasonable time.[30]

The distinction between the treatment of defence inaction pre- and post-*Jordan* is perhaps most potentially significant in cases related to extradition[31] or delay in arresting the accused after a charge has been laid. The issue in such cases is whether the accused has some obligation to turn themself in once aware of charges laid against them. In *R v MacIntosh*,[32] for example, the accused had moved to India by the time allegations of sexual impropriety were made and an arrest warrant issued in February 1996. According to police, the accused was advised of the warrant over the phone and indicated that he had no intention of returning to Canada. Extradition was pursued but delayed with little explanation. The extradition request to India was not submitted until 2007. The trial judge emphasized the accused's inaction in assessing the section 11(b) *Charter* application, noting that he had been informed of the charges at the outset and had done nothing. The Nova Scotia

---

28   *Cody*, above note 2.

29   *Ibid* at para 33; *Jordan*, above note 1 at para 138.

30   *Cody*, above note 2 at paras 33–36.

31   Though it should also be noted that in *Jordan*, above note 1 at para 72, the Court identified trials with an international dimension, such as those where extradition is required, as also potentially amounting to a discrete exceptional circumstance.

32   2011 NSCA 111 [*MacIntosh (NSCA)*], appeal dismissed 2013 SCC 23 [*MacIntosh (SCC)*].

Court of Appeal found that the trial judge had erred in this regard, as it put an obligation on the accused to turn himself in to authorities.[33] The Supreme Court agreed.[34] The issue has arisen post-*Jordan* in two cases before the Ontario Court of Appeal. In *R v Burke*,[35] the court distinguished the matter from *MacIntosh* in that the accused had admitted that his purpose in fleeing was to evade capture, characterizing the resultant delay as "illegitimate defence delay." In *R v JK*,[36] a similar issue arose but was not reached by the Ontario Court of Appeal. It remains to be seen whether an accused's failure to turn himself in to authorities upon becoming aware of a charge will be attributed to defence-caused delay in future cases.

4) Defence Unavailability

Under the *Morin* framework, there was some allowance for the refusal of trial or continuation dates. Reasonable availability of defence counsel factored into a determination as to how the delay for dates counsel could not accept would be characterized. Post-*Jordan*, the oft-quoted passage from the Supreme Court's decision in *R v Godin*[37] that "s. 11(b) does not require defence counsel to hold themselves in a state of perpetual availability," thus allowing leeway for refusal of available dates by defence counsel, appears no longer to apply, though there is not agreement in the jurisprudence on this point.

The Supreme Court in *Jordan* stated plainly that "the defence will have directly caused the delay if the court and the Crown are ready to proceed, but the defence is not. The period of delay resulting from that unavailability will be attributed to the defence."[38] As a general rule, then, because the ceilings established in *Jordan* are intended as presumptive statements as to reasonable delays for which the state is responsible, actions that are not properly attributable to the state, such as where a date is available to the Crown and court but refused by defence counsel for reasons other than time required to legitimately respond to the

---

33   *MacIntosh (NSCA)*, above note 32 at paras 50–62.

34   *MacIntosh (SCC)*, above note 32.

35   2018 ONCA 594.

36   2021 ONCA 256.

37   2009 SCC 26 at para 23 [*Godin*].

38   *Jordan*, above note 1 at para 64.

charges, this is defence-caused delay. Accordingly, even where dates are proffered to the accused within a brief period, and declined due to the unavailability of the defence, that segment of time will be deducted.[39]

That *R v Godin*[40] is no longer applicable post-*Jordan* is supported by not only a plain reading of what *Jordan* has indicated but having regard to early appellate jurisprudence. The Ontario Court of Appeal's first application of the new framework arose in *R v Coulter*.[41] The court noted at the outset that "where the court and the Crown are ready to proceed but the defence is not, the defence will have directly caused the delay."[42] Applying this, where on 7 August 2012 a date two weeks out was offered for a continuing judicial pre-trial (22 August 2012), but could not be accepted by the defence, the delay to the next date that could be set (27 August 2012) was attributed to defence-caused delay and deducted (a week).[43] There was no determination that because the date was offered within a short timeframe that some consideration ought to be given that counsel's schedule cannot be presumed to be clear. Indeed, Paciocco J (as he then was) in *R v JM*,[44] held that while he had some sympathy for the holding of other lower courts that some scheduling flexibility for defence counsel ought to be permitted in applying the *Jordan* framework,[45] he was constrained to follow *Coulter* in this regard.[46] Similarly, in *R v Mallozzi*,[47] where following a mistrial, the court and Crown were available for new dates two months out, but defence counsel could not accept due to other commitments, the seven months to the new set of dates that could be set were deducted as defence-caused delay.[48]

---

39   *Boulanger*, above note 26; *Thanabalasingham*, above note 2 at para 9; *Jordan*, above note 1 at paras 63–65 and 122; *Williamson*, above note 21 at paras 21–22; *R v Coulter*, 2016 ONCA 704 at paras 72–77 [*Coulter*]; *R v Mallozzi*, 2017 ONCA 644 at paras 32–38 and 41, leave to appeal denied (without reasons) 2018 CanLII 30058 (SCC) [*Mallozzi*]; *R v Cowell*, 2019 ONCA 972 at para 32; *R v Albinowski*, 2018 ONCA 1084 at paras 32, 37–40, and 49 [*Albinowski*].

40   *Godin*, above note 37.

41   *Coulter*, above note 39.

42   *Ibid* at para 44.

43   *Ibid* at para 73.

44   *R v JM*, 2017 ONCJ 4 [*JM*].

45   *R v Edan*, 2016 ONCJ 493; *R v Ashraf*, 2016 ONCJ 584.

46   *JM*, above note 44 at paras 64–67.

47   *Mallozzi*, above note 39.

48   *Ibid* at para 36.

In *R v Albinowski*,[49] the Ontario Court of Appeal rejected the application of *R v Godin*.[50] Writing for the court, Roberts JA held that where the reason for defence counsel's unavailability for dates is due to other previously scheduled professional commitments, this

> was not related to "defence actions legitimately taken to respond to the charges," such as "preparation time" and "defence applications and requests that are not frivolous": *Jordan*, at para. 65. Thus, as *Jordan* further directs, at para. 64, their unavailability, when the Crown and court were available, fell squarely within the category of delay that counts against the defence.[51]

The Court of Appeal for Quebec has likewise flatly determined that the decision in *Jordan* has done away with the notion in *Godin*[52] that there is some flexibility for the defence to reject dates for reasons other than preparation time. In *R c Rice*,[53] the Court held that *Godin* was applicable to the old framework, and that post-*Jordan*, other than for reasonable preparation time, when the court and prosecution are ready to proceed and the defence is not, the delay that arises from unavailability is defence-caused and will not be counted.[54]

The Ontario Court of Appeal did not follow this line of authority in another case, however, where counsel were not available for continuation dates. In *R v Safdar*,[55] the application judge at trial, relying on Godin[56], did not attribute the delay arising from the unavailability of the defence for continuation dates as defence-caused: because counsel had made themselves available in other instances for continuation dates, they could not be expected to keep their schedules clear for more. Justice Feldman, writing for the Ontario Court of Appeal, held that the delay was not "solely or directly caused by the defence" because the misestimate of the time required for trial contributed to the delay. She held that counsel had legitimate basis to decline the dates and "could not compromise one

---

49   *Albinowski*, above note 39.

50   *Godin*, above note 37.

51   *Albinowski*, above note 39 at paras 28–35.

52   *Godin*, above note 37.

53   *R c Rice*, 2018 QCCA 198.

54   *Ibid* at para 72; see also *R v Vu*, 2019 QCCA 1709 at paras 47–48.

55   *R v Safdar*, 2018 ONSC 7067 at paras 118–31 [*Safdar (ONSC)*].

56   *Godin*, above note 37.

client's interests over another:"[57] the refusal of the continuation dates was because of a medical appointment in the case of one counsel and a previously scheduled hearing for the other.[58] Though in neither instance were the dates refused for legitimate preparation time, the delay was not deducted as defence-caused, relying on *Godin*[59] for the proposition that defence counsel ought to be afforded some leeway to decline dates.

While defence unavailability for continuation dates may not amount to defence-caused delay, defence unavailability may nevertheless inform the delay analysis in other ways. For example, in *R v JS*,[60] the defence did not cause the need for continuation dates but also did not respond proactively to setting them. Two dates were required and, without providing clear reasons for doing so, the defence refused all nine that the Crown and court offered. Each was proximate to the trial. While the Court of Appeal for Ontario declined to consider whether the defence unavailability constituted defence-caused delay, the Court held that, in the face of the Crown and court's proactive steps to mitigate delay, it nevertheless informed the reasonableness of the resulting adjournment and, ultimately, the discrete event deduction from the total delay.[61] Associate Chief Justice Fairburn for the Court explained:

> When the court and Crown are in a position to remedy the unforeseen circumstances in short order, but the defence cannot accommodate it through a reprioritization or otherwise, this necessarily informs the reasonableness of the length of the adjournment arising from the unforeseen circumstances.[62]

She added:

> To be clear, this should not be construed as a criticism of busy defence counsel in this case. It is a reality that busy defence counsel have many competing obligations at work and, although the record is somewhat lacking here, I accept that defence counsel would have turned his mind

---

57   2021 ONCA 207 [*Safdar (ONCA)*] at paras 49–51; see also: *R v Sandhu*, 2022 ONSC 3910 at paras 28–29; *R v Singh*, 2022 ONCJ 199 at paras 84–86; *R v Bui*, 2021 ONCJ 379 at paras 32–36.

58   *Safdar (ONSC)*, above note 55 at para 13.

59   *Godin*, above note 37.

60   2024 ONCA 794 at paras 77–83 [*JS*].

61   For a full discussion of exceptional circumstances, see Chapter 7.

62   *JS*, above note 60 at para 81.

to reprioritization and simply been unable to accommodate it. With that said, the fact remains that the Crown made reasonable efforts to respond to the unforeseen circumstances and conclude the trial under the ceiling: *Jordan*, at para. 74. The delay that ensued clearly qualifies as an exceptional circumstance and must be subtracted from the total period of delay.[63]

The Court emphasized that, due to the practical problems associated with adjourning trials, when the need for a continuation date arises, it is incumbent on all justice participants — including defence counsel — to make best efforts to accommodate the earliest possible date so that the trial can finish close to on schedule.[64] This includes assessing and reassessing priorities and being willing to adjust schedules to avoid lengthy adjournments.

5)   Quantum of the Deduction for Defence Delay

As a general rule, where the defence is not available for a date or dates when both the Crown and the court are available, the delay to the dates which the defence can accept is deducted as having been defence-caused. However, a contextual approach can in some instances be applied where, though it can be said that the delay was directly caused by the defence, it was not solely attributable to the defence. Where it can be said that there were additional causes of the delay besides defence conduct or inaction, the resultant period of delay can be parsed out as between those causes. For example, in *R v Boulanger*,[65] though defence unavailability caused some delay, the Crown's change in strategy, which led to the need for continuation dates, the court's lack of initiative in looking for dates when the need for new ones became apparent, and institutional delay also contributed to the delay. Accordingly, all of the delay to the next scheduled date was not properly characterized as having been defence-caused. As the defence was not the sole cause of the delay in that instance, it was appropriate to deduct only some of that delay.

In some instances, the Supreme Court's decision in *Boulanger*[66] has been interpreted to mean that only the portion of the delay between the

---

63   *Ibid* at para 83.
64   *Ibid* at paras 77–80.
65   *Boulanger*, above note 26 at para 9.
66   *Ibid.*

dates the defence could not accept to the next date they would have been available is the segment of the delay to be deducted as defence-caused. The remainder to the dates the court and Crown could actually set is treated as "institutional delay" in the language of *Morin* and counted toward the calculation of net delay. In *R v Hanan*,[67] because a last-minute adjournment request arose due to the unexpected refusal of the victim to testify and late Crown disclosure, and because the court could not reschedule the trial any sooner, only a portion of the delay was deducted as defence-caused. In this case, the court and Crown were available to set a six-week trial for 3 June 2019, but the defence was not. The court was next able to accommodate the trial in October and the matter was set for October 28. The Ontario Court of Appeal held that the trial judge had properly allocated only six weeks to the defence given that the court had no other space to set the trial until October. Relying on *Boulanger*,[68] because the whole period of delay was not "solely caused" by the defence, it could not be wholly attributed to defence-caused delay.[69]

In *Jordan*,[70] the Supreme Court made plain that where the court and Crown are available and the defence is not, "The period of delay resulting from that unavailability will be attributed to the defence."[71] Further, whether the defence had "solely" caused delay was not defined as being the only factor contributing to the delay. Rather, the Court indicated that delay caused solely by the defence "comprises 'those situations where the accused's acts ... directly caused the delay," then continued, "the defence will have directly caused the delay if the court and the Crown are ready to proceed, but the defence is not."[72] Accordingly, some appellate courts held that unavailability alone was properly treated as the sole cause of the delay and the delay to the next date set to be deducted as defence-caused in instances where new or continuation dates are needed. In *R v Balogh*,[73] the British Columbia Court of Appeal did not agree with the contention that because an adjournment arose

---

67   2022 ONCA 229 at paras 47–59 [*Hanan (ONCA)*], affirmed 2023 SCC 12 [*Hanan (SCC)*].

68   *Boulanger*, above note 26.

69   *Hanan (ONCA)*, above note 67 at paras 47–59; see also: *R v Mengistu*, 2022 ONSC 3624 (s 11(b) Application), appeal dismissed 2024 ONCA 575 [*Mengistu (ONCA)*]; *R v Arth*, 2022 ONCJ 216; *R v Ahmad*, 2022 ONSC 2321.

70   *Jordan*, above note 1.

71   *Ibid* at para 64.

72   *Ibid*.

73   2020 BCCA 96.

due to the trial judge, the delay to the next date set was therefore not properly treated as solely caused by the unavailability of the defence to accept proffered continuation dates. Justice Fenlon, writing for the unanimous Court, explained the application of *Jordan* to defence unavailability as follows:

> It is convenient to address here Mr. Balogh's argument that the determining factor, even under the Jordan analysis, is *the cause of the adjournment*, with the party causing the adjournment to be responsible for all delay until a new date is set. In my view, the premise is unsound because it fails to distinguish between the cause of the *adjournment* and the cause of the *delay*, which will not always coincide. Although it was the unavailability of the judge which caused the adjournment of the third trial date, the state was prepared to set a date within a few months and should only be held responsible for the delay between the third trial date and October 2015, when the court and Crown were ready to proceed to trial, but defence counsel was not. Thereafter it was only the unavailability of defence counsel that precluded the trial from proceeding.[74]

This bright-line rule that delay arising from the defence's inability to accept new dates because of unavailability is to be deducted in full in all instances was flatly rejected by the Supreme Court in *R v Hanan*.[75] Instead the Court endorsed a contextual approach to the assessment of whether delay has been "solely or directly caused" by the defence when the defence has declined new proffered dates.[76]

Though in *Boulanger*[77] the Supreme Court had confirmed the general rule as it was articulated in *Jordan*,[78] writing, "This Court did of course explain in *Jordan* that where the court and the Crown are ready to proceed but the defence is not, the resulting delay is attributable to the defence,"[79] in *Hanan*[80] the Court made clear that this will not always

---

74   *Ibid* at para 38 (emphasis in original); see also: *Poulin c R*, 2020 QCCA 1483 at para 14; *R v Mamouni*, 2017 ABCA 347 at paras 64–66, leave to appeal denied (without reasons) 2018 CanLII 89741 (SCC); *Schenkels*, above note 11 at paras 23, 27, 36, and 53; *Lecompte v R*, 2018 NBCA 33 at paras 19 and 21.

75   *Hanan* (SCC), above note 67.

76   *Ibid* at para 9.

77   *Boulanger*, above note 26.

78   *Jordan*, above note 1.

79   *Boulanger*, above note 26 at para 8.

80   *Hanan* (SCC), above note 67.

be so. The amount of delay that will be apportioned to unavailability will instead depend upon the factors contributing to the need for new trial dates (whether due to an adjournment or for continuation dates).[81] In *Boulanger*, the Court found it was "fair and reasonable" to apportion the delay between the parties.[82] This was so given that the need for continuation dates arose because of a change in Crown strategy, the need for those dates became apparent early on, but the court refused to seek out dates at the parties' requests, and when the judge did set them, did so without inquiring as to the parties' availability and chose a date that was farther out than it needed to be. Even in those circumstances, more than half of the delay to the next date set was deducted as defence-caused delay.[83] In *Hanan*,[84] which followed about a year later, the Court held that it was reasonable for the trial judge to have deducted *only* the six-week trial period the defence declined for unavailability and to have included within the ceiling the remainder of the time that followed (to when the trial could be rescheduled). This was because, when the original jury trial had to be adjourned, counsel for the defence offered to re-elect to a trial before a judge alone to avoid delay, but the Crown would not consent to it.[85] In the circumstances, it was fair for the trial judge to have attributed only the six weeks to defence-caused delay. The Court held:

> Like the majority and the dissent below, we reject the Crown's proposed "brightline" rule according to which all of the delay until the next available date following defence counsel's rejection of a date offered by the court must be characterized as defence delay. We agree with van Rensburg J.A. and Tulloch J.A., as he then was, at para. 56, that this approach is inconsistent with this Court's understanding of defence delay. Defence delay comprises "delays caused solely or directly by the defence's conduct" or "delays waived by the defence" (*Jordan*, at para. 66). Furthermore, "periods of time during which the court and the Crown are unavailable will not constitute defence delay, even if defence counsel is also unavailable" (para. 64). All relevant circumstances should be considered to determine how delay

---

81　*Ibid.*

82　*Boulanger*, above note 26 at para 10.

83　*Ibid* at paras 9–11.

84　*Hanan* (SCC), above note 67.

85　*Ibid* at para 2.

should be apportioned among the participants (*R. v. Boulanger*, 2022 SCC 2, at para. 8). We share the view of the majority and dissenting judges in the Court of Appeal that, in the circumstances of this case, it is unfair and unreasonable to characterize the entire period between June and October 2019 as defence delay (paras. 59 and 136).[86]

In *R v Bowen-Wright*,[87] Schreck J considered what factors would be relevant to an application of the *Hanan* contextual approach in assessing whether delay arising from defence unavailability ought to be parsed out as between factors contributing to the need for new dates and how much of it is to be attributed to each factor:

1. The reason for the need to reschedule and whether it was caused by the defence - Should the court or Crown have been the cause of the adjournment, none of the delay can be attributed to the defence unless they are unavailable to reschedule the matter for an unreasonable period of time. In the instant case, it was institutional limitations that caused the need for new dates. The matter was not reached when there was no judge to hear it.[88]

2. The extent to which the defence was available – Disagreeing with the proposition that *Godin*[89] is no longer good law, and in consideration of the fact that in the present case, the defence was not the cause of the need for the adjournment, Schreck J found that because the defence would have been available for four dates the court was not in a position to offer, it could not be said they were unavailable for an unreasonable period of time.[90]

3. The reasons for defence unavailability – The court was prepared to infer that the defence had declined dates due to commitments for other clients, and noted that "counsel cannot be expected to compromise one client's interests over another,"[91] relying on the Court of Appeal's decision in *R v Safdar*[92] in this regard; and

---

86   *Ibid* at para 9; see also *R v BD*, 2023 ONCJ 224 at paras 33–58.

87   2024 ONSC 293 [*Bowen-Wright*].

88   *Ibid* at paras 41–43.

89   *Godin*, above note 37.

90   *Ibid* at paras 44–46.

91   *Safdar* (ONCA), above note 57 at para 50.

92   *Ibid*.

4. The extent of the notice given of the new available date – Instances where new dates are offered that are not far enough out that the defence can be expected to be in a position to accept them was also identified as a relevant factor.[93]

In *Bowen-Wright*, because the need for new dates had nothing to do with the defence and the dates offered to the defence and declined for unavailability were offered late and were within two-and-a-half months of the adjourned trial date, none of the delay was attributable to defence-caused delay.[94] This stands in sharp contrast to the concerns expressed by the Court of Appeal in *JS* about the practical problems associated with lengthy mid-trial adjournments and the attendant need for all parties to accommodate the earliest possible continuation dates:

> The practical problems associated with adjourning trials that have already started hardly require explanation. Trial judges and counsel do not simply wait passively until the next trial date arrives. Instead, they keep working on other matters — often many other matters. As time passes, it becomes increasingly difficult to simply pick up again and continue a trial where it left off. Memories fade, they need to be refreshed, transcripts need to be ordered, notes need to be consulted, and everyone has to go through the laborious task of trying to reorient themselves to where they were and what they were thinking many months earlier. Although this can obviously be done, it is less than ideal and, in fact, highly inefficient.[95]

Some jurists have observed that the introduction of the contextual approach in the Supreme Court's decision in *Hanan* has had the effect of denuding the predictability of the *Jordan* framework. For example, in *R v Liu*, Code J opined that this approach to the assessment of defence unavailability arguably "detracts from the clarity, simplicity and predictability that *Jordan* and *Cody* intended."[96]

It seems also to be the case that, in some instances, the modern contextual approach has been read to allow the apportioning of delay arising from defence unavailability even in instances where there have been no other factors that have contributed to the need for dates

---

93 *Bowen-Wright*, above note 87 at para 48.
94 *Ibid* at paras 48–53.
95 *JS*, above note 60 at para 77.
96 *R v Liu*, 2024 ONSC 2022.

or to the length of the delay. In *R v Jacques-Taylor*,[97] for example, the contextual approach was applied not to the question of defence unavailability for new dates arising from either an adjournment or the need to add continuation dates, *but to the initial setting of trial dates*. In the context of a joint prosecution trial dates were offered. The Crown and counsel for the accused were available to accept the first dates offered for August and counsel had several other dates through August. However, counsel for the co-accused was not available. Further dates in September were offered which co-accused's counsel could accept, but counsel for the accused was not available for September. Dates in early October were set.[98] Citing *Hanan*, the Court held that a "holistic" approach should be taken, and attributed only the month of September to accused's counsel.[99] While ultimately the Ontario Court of Appeal deferred to the trial judge's assessment that the parties did not move as a collective such that the delay should be assessed communally,[100] the Court also cited *Hanan*[101] in support of the trial judge's approach in this regard.[102] In another matter, *R v Toole*,[103] the decision in *Hanan*[104] was taken as applying generally to the overall delay in a case, with Chozik J writing that "[w]here a trial is not completed within the scheduled time, all relevant circumstances must be considered in determining how to apportion delay"[105] and citing *Hanan*[106] for the proposition that an assessment of how to attribute the delay caused by a mistrial, requires, pursuant to *Hanan*, that "all relevant circumstances . . . be considered to determine how delay should be apportioned among the participants."[107] The difficulty with such broad application of the decision is that *Hanan*[108] relates

---

97   2024 ONCA 458 [*Jacques-Taylor* (ONCA)]

98   *Ibid* at paras 17–20.

99   *Ibid* at para 24.

100   Detailed consideration is given to joint prosecutions in Chapter 7.

101   *Hanan* (SCC), above note 67.

102   *Jacques-Taylor* (ONCA), above note 97 at para 7; see also *R v A(C)*, 2024 ONSC 1603 at paras 15–17.

103   2023 ONSC 7243 [*Toole*].

104   *Hanan* (SCC), above note 67.

105   *Toole*, above note 103 at para 36.

106   *Hanan* (SCC), above note 67.

107   *Ibid* at para 9.

108   *Ibid*.

to a particular scenario, namely, how to treat delay that arises from defence counsel's inability to accept dates when new or continuation dates must be set. To apply the decision more broadly to invoke its holistic and contextual approach to consideration of all segments of delay in a case, and in particular, in instances (such as the setting of initial trial dates) where neither the court nor Crown can be taken to have contributed to either the need for dates or the length of the delay, is to return to an unpredictable and endlessly flexible framework such as was repudiated in *Jordan*.[109]

In the authors' view the approach taken by Duncan J in *R v Quereshi*,[110] post-*Hanan*,[111] best encapsulates the current state of the law as it relates to defence unavailability and is still in accord with *Jordan*.[112] There is no bright-line approach that says that in any and all circumstances, where the defence is unavailable for dates, the delay to the next dates offered and accepted, no matter how far out and no matter the cause of the need for such dates, is entirely defence-caused. Nor is it correct to say that the dates the defence was not available for, and only those dates, are properly treated as defence-caused delay. What should guide the analysis in all circumstances is the extent to which it can be said that the defence "solely or directly cause[d]"[113] the period of delay on examination of the particular circumstances.[114]

6)   Categories of Defence-Caused Delay

What will constitute defence-caused delay is an open category, with trial judges best positioned to determine what segments of delay should be characterized as such in any given case.[115] That said, the following list comprises periods of delay commonly treated as defence-caused and deducted from the total delay in the *Jordan* calculus:

---

109 *Jordan*, above note 1 at para 32.

110   2023 ONCJ 202.

111   *Hanan (SCC)*, above note 67.

112   *Jordan*, above note 1.

113   *Ibid* at para 66.

114   See also: *R v JD*, 2024 SKCA 59 at paras 30–33; *R v D'Souza*, 2024 ABCA 77 at paras 11–20.

115   *Jordan*, above note 1 at para 63.

1) Where the court and Crown are available, but the defence is not, subject to a consideration of factors contributing to the need for new or continuing dates (i.e., defence unavailability);[116]

2) Where an application of little merit is brought and/or little effort is made to advance it in a timely way;[117]

3) Foot dragging in initiating and pursuing the available processes for securing funding for counsel;[118]

4) Delay caused by removal of counsel at the behest of the accused;[119]

5) Delay in securing counsel;[120]

6) Failure to order required transcripts in a timely manner where such failure has caused delay;[121]

7) Where a proceeding is conducted with marked inefficiency and indifference to delay;[122]

8) Where an accused has insisted on an unreasonably long estimate for a hearing;

9) Where the conduct of the hearing demonstrates inefficiency and indifference to delay on the part of the defence;

10) In the *Youth Criminal Justice Act* context, where extrajudicial measures are attempted, should the matter later return to court;[123] and

11) Where the defence refuses or adjourns a pre-trial or judicial pre-trial on the basis that some segment of disclosure is outstanding where the evidence was not required to conduct it. Disclosure issues are often sorted out in the context of a judicial pre-trial such that refusal to move to this step for this reason will, in most instances, amount to defence-caused delay.[124]

---

116 *Ibid* at paras 14 and 120–24; *St Amand*, above note 26 at paras 80 and 97–98; *R v Gandhi*, 2016 ONSC 5612 at para 23; *R v Jurkus*, 2018 ONCA 489 at paras 18–32 and 35, leave to appeal denied (without reasons) 2018 CanLII 116611 (SCC); *Albinowski*, above note 39 at paras 32, 37–40 and 49; *R v Locknick*, 2019 ONCA 625 at para 11; *R v Antic*, 2019 ONCA 160 at paras 7–8, leave to appeal denied (without reasons) 2019 CanLII 89653 (SCC).

117 *Faulkner*, above note 26 at paras 153–57; *R v DC*, 2017 ONCA 483 at paras 2–5.

118 *R v PA*, 2020 ONCA 673; *R v RD*, 2020 ONCA 23 at paras 27–37.

119 *R v Baron*, 2017 ONCA 772 at paras 6, 17, and 47–49; *R v Stockton*, 2019 ONCA 300 at para 8.

120 *R v Gordon*, 2017 ONCA 436 at paras 6–7.

121 *Gopie*, above note 26 at paras 147–57.

122 *Faulkner*, above note 26 at paras 158–63.

123 *KJM*, above note 20 at paras 85–89; *Youth Criminal Justice Act*, SC 2002, c 1.

124 *Hanan (ONCA)*, above note 67 at paras 43–46; *R v Carbone*, 2020 ONCA 394 at paras 51–53.

7) Lateness in Bringing the Section 11(b) Application

As discussed in Chapter 3, in most instances, it is required that the accused bring a section 11(b) *Charter* application in advance of the start of trial. This is so because once the trial date is set, the anticipated end of trial will be known. In circumstances where the delay issue does not crystallize until some later point—generally where continuation dates are required, thus pushing the anticipated end of trial date further back—the applicant must still be diligent in pursuing the application at that stage.[125]

Where an application for a stay for delay has been advanced after the start of trial, but before trial's end,[126] delay will likely have been caused by the late application. In such instances, as in most, how the delay will be characterized will depend on the particular facts. That said, where the accused has not advanced the application with diligence, but is nevertheless permitted to bring it, whatever delay is caused by the need to litigate it will likely be characterized as defence-caused delay.[127] This supposes that while late, the application was nevertheless brought before the end of the trial. Where an application related to trial delay is advanced after the trial proper has reached its end, it remains an open question as to whether the application can be advanced at all at this stage.[128]

Some courts have relied on the Supreme Court's articulation of the requirement to advance the claim in a timely way in *JF*[129] and the contextual approach to assessment of defence-caused delay that the Supreme Court developed in *Hanan*[130] to hold that a deduction is warranted where an application is brought far too late for the Crown and court to take steps to find earlier dates for the accused's matter. Where this has occurred and where there is some basis upon which to find that resort could have been made to court processes such that the matter could have been heard sooner, as much as 50 percent of the delay between the date on which the trial dates were set and the

---

125 *JF*, above note 18 at paras 3 and 30–36.
126 Defined as when the evidence on the trial proper and closing arguments have concluded.
127 *JF*, above note 18 at paras 51–52.
128 *Ibid* at para 3; see also: *R v Yizhak*, 2022 ONCJ 360 (Mistrial Application); *contra*: *R v Ibrahim*, 2022 ONCJ 450.
129 *JF*, above note 18.
130 *Hanan (SCC)*, above note 67.

first day of trial has been deducted as defence-caused.[131] Though the Court of Appeal for Ontario was asked to consider the correctness of this approach to late-breaking section 11(b) applications in two cases, in neither was there a sufficient record before the Court to allow for a determination that the matter could have been scheduled sooner had the accused indicated delay was at issue at the time, or shortly after, the trial dates were set.[132]

---

131   The basis for such a finding has included taking judicial notice of the availability, or potential availability, of earlier dates. See: *R v Wright*, 2024 ONSC 1893 (per Akhtar J.) at paras 22–34; *R v Andrew*, 2024 ONSC 607 (per Code J.) at para 18; *R v Wang*, 2024 ONCJ 177 at paras 19–29; *R v Alsouki*, 2024 ONCJ 9 at paras 13–35; *R v Lokubalasuriya*, 2024 ONCJ 46 at paras 12–23; *R v Robins*, 2024 ONCJ 12 at paras 17–35; *R v Kullab*, 2023 ONCJ 458 at paras 19–32; *R v Kowal*, 2023 ONCJ 545 at paras 42–47; *R v Nigro*, 2023 ONCJ 41 at paras 34–38; *R v MF*, 2024 ONCJ 59 at paras 15–39.

132   *R v Vallotton*, 2024 ONCA 492 at paras 29–31; *Mengistu (ONCA)*, above note 69 at paras 38–44.

CHAPTER 7

Where Delay Exceeds the Ceiling—Exceptional Circumstances

A. DISCRETE EVENTS

1) Discrete Events Defined

In instances where, after having deducted defence-caused delay, the time period remains above the eighteen-month/thirty-month ceiling, it falls to the Crown to show that the delay is reasonable because of the presence of *exceptional circumstances.* Such circumstances *"lie outside the Crown's control"* in that (1) they are reasonably unforeseen *or* reasonably unavoidable, *and* (2) the Crown cannot reasonably remedy the delays emanating from those circumstances once they arise.[1] The circumstances need not be "rare or entirely uncommon."[2] Once a period of delay is attributed to a discrete exceptional event, it must be deducted from the total delay and not reintroduced into the assessment of delay.[3]

There is not a closed list of circumstances that will be properly characterized as discrete exceptional events. In *R v Jordan*, the Supreme Court identified exceptional events such as family or medical emergencies as qualifying as exceptional circumstances.[4] An example of this can be found in *R v Baron*,[5] where the ten months between a scheduled preliminary hearing, adjourned due to the illness of one of the accused in a joint trial, and the new hearing dates, was deducted. The Court in

---

1   *R v Jordan*, 2016 SCC 27 at para 69 (emphasis in original) [*Jordan*].

2   *Ibid.*

3   *Ibid* at para 75; *R v Musclow*, 2024 ONCA 565 at paras 27–31 [*Musclow*].

4   *Jordan*, above note 1 at para 72.

5   2017 ONCA 772 at para 50 [*Baron*].

Jordan further identified cases with an international dimension, such as those requiring extradition of an accused, as potentially meeting the definition, depending on the circumstances.[6] An example of this can be found in *R v Barra*,[7] where the need to extradite both accused from the United States in one instance and the United Kingdom in the other, was conceded to constitute a discrete exceptional circumstance, but where delay in pursuing extradition by authorities warranted a reduction in what portion of the delay would be attributed to the exception and deducted from the net delay count.[8]

The Supreme Court also identified instances of unexpected and unavoidable developments in a case, for example, where a witness unexpectedly recants,[9] where a mistrial is declared,[10] or where a trial goes longer than reasonably expected in spite of best efforts to complete the trial in the time estimated in good faith by the parties.[11] In *R v Jurkus*,[12] for example, the Ontario Court of Appeal found that the delay that accrued from the need for new preliminary hearing dates, arising from both the Crown's decision to call a particular witness and the defence decision mid-hearing to call a witness, was properly treated as exceptional. The three months to the continuation date was deducted on that basis. Similarly in *R v McNeill-Crawford*,[13] the Court of Appeal for Ontario upheld the trial judge's determination that the trial time exceeding the good faith trial estimates of both parties was due to unexpected events that amounted to an exceptional circumstance and, given the Crown's responsive conduct and efforts to mitigate delay, the additional trial time was properly deducted.[14] An inadvertent oversight by the Crown might also qualify as a discrete event, as there is no standard of perfection

---

6   *Jordan*, above note 1 at para 72.

7   2021 ONCA 568 at paras 35–36 [*Barra*].

8   See also: *Boulachanis c R*, 2020 QCCA 4; *Jean c R*, 2020 QCCA 1455 at para 13; *R v Steadman*, 2021 ABCA 332 at paras 80–83.

9   *Jordan*, above note 1 at para 73.

10   See: *R v Locknick*, 2019 ONCA 625 at paras 13–18 [*Locknick*].

11   *Jordan*, above note 1 at para 73; *R v Singh*, 2016 BCCA 427 [*Singh (BCCA)*]; *R v Rai*, 2019 BCCA 377; *R v Pauls*, 2020 ONCA 220 [*Pauls*], affirmed in the result in *R v Yusuf*, 2021 SCC 2 [*Yusuf*]; *R v Lai*, 2021 BCCA 105; *R v Vader*, 2019 ABCA 191 at para 26.

12   2018 ONCA 489 at paras 37–60, leave to appeal refused (without reasons) 2018 CanLII 116611 (SCC) [*Jurkus*]; see also: *R v Antic*, 2019 ONCA 160 at para 8, leave to appeal refused, 2019 CanLII 89653 (SCC) [*Antic*].

13   *R v McNeill-Crawford*, 2020 ONCA 504.

14   *Ibid* at at paras 24–34.

placed upon the Crown, and mistakes happen.[15] It will be for the trial judge, relying on their good sense and experience, to determine whether a particular event is properly determined to be exceptional.[16]

Various other circumstances can arise through the course of a prosecution that the Crown cannot anticipate or control, and as noted, there is no exhaustive list that could possibly include them all. That said, the following comprises some instances where provincial appellate courts have attributed delay to a discrete exceptional circumstance and deducted the delay resulting from the discrete event:

- Where a judge presiding over a matter was been suspended from sitting due to an unrelated complaint to the Ontario Judicial Council.[17]
- Where the illness of the trial judge necessitated his replacement for preliminary hearing dates, and the replacement judge could not accommodate several of the previously scheduled dates.[18] However, where a judge became ill, but the loss of trial dates is attributable to the inability to replace the judge due to the lack of judges in a jurisdiction, this is not an exceptional circumstance.[19]
- Where the preliminary hearing judge assessed the content of each intercept separately, thus necessitating more time.[20]
- Where a conflict for the trial judge arose on the first day of the proceedings, necessitating a mistrial.[21]
- Difficulties with an interpreter requiring multiple audits to determine the accuracy of the interpretation.[22]
- Where the defence raised some concern, though it turned out to be unwarranted, that an Information to Obtain could reveal the identity of a confidential informer fifteen minutes before the start of the preliminary hearing.[23]

---

15   *Jordan*, above note 1 at para 90.

16   *Ibid* at para 71.

17   *Antic*, above note 12 at para 11.

18   *R v Majeed*, 2019 ONCA 422 at paras 8–9 [*Majeed*].

19   *R v Perreault*, 2020 ONCA 580 at para 7 [*Perreault*]; *R v Brown*, 2018 NSCA 62 at paras 61–71 [*Brown (NSCA)*].

20   *Locknick*, above note 10 at para 12.

21   *Ibid* at paras 13–18.

22   *R v PA*, 2020 ONCA 673.

23   *R v McManus*, 2017 ONCA 188 at paras 40–46.

- The accused's unanticipated decision during pre-trial motions to cooperate with police by providing a statement and to change his plea.[24]
- Where the Crown took ill just prior to the start of a Dangerous Offender hearing.[25]
- Delay arising from the unavailability of a *voir dire* transcript as a result of an administrative error by courthouse staff.[26]
- The unexpected discovery of video evidence.[27]
- Where the Crown's witness has failed to attend for trial though that witness had been subpoenaed.[28]
- Where a Crown witness, during his testimony at trial, disputed whether he had said something to the police that was reflected in the transcript produced from his recorded interview which related to an issue that was important to the case.[29]
- Where successive counsel have requested to get off-record for the accused.[30]
- A maternity leave for the Crown that was unexpected and unanticipated as it related to an adoption.[31]
- The prolonged medical illness of the lead investigator.[32]
- Where the accused's counsel is appointed to the bench.[33]

A consideration of how some period of delay ought to be characterized cannot be undertaken in the abstract or by reference to circumstances that could have caused delay, but by having regard to the actual cause. As the Ontario Court of Appeal recently observed, in *R v Tran*, "the material issue is not whether a trial would have been completed without unreasonable delay, had the delay attributable to the exceptional circumstance not occurred. It is whether the trial was unreasonably

---

24   *R v Gordon*, 2017 ONCA 436 at paras 10–14.

25   *R v KC*, 2022 ONCA 738 at paras 63–74 [*KC*].

26   *R v KJM*, 2019 SCC 55 at paras 5 and 20.

27   *R v Jerace*, 2018 ABCA 152 at para 29.

28   *R v Mavros*, 2020 ABCA 436 at paras 22–30.

29   *R v JS*, 2024 ONCA 794 at paras 20, 65–67 [*JS*].

30   *R v Boehmer*, 2019 SKCA 74 at paras 31–40.

31   *AE c R*, 2019 QCCA 1865 at paras 46–47.

32   *Kelly v R*, 2022 NBCA 46 at paras 13–14, 48, and 52–71 [*Kelly*].

33   *R v Cody*, 2017 SCC 31 at para 49 [*Cody*].

delayed in the actual circumstances that occurred."[34] In other words, it is speculative and does not speak to what actually caused some segment of delay to point to some other factor (in *Tran*, the ongoing provision of disclosure) that may have caused some delay had the discrete exceptional circumstances not occurred. The *Jordan* framework concerns itself with what caused each segment of delay and is not concerned with what might have happened otherwise.

2) Crown's Obligation to Mitigate Delay

The Crown cannot automatically rely on the discrete exceptional circumstances deduction where some unanticipated event it cannot control occurs and causes some delay. It is not enough for the Crown, once the ceiling is breached, to point to an unexpected event to justify that delay.[35] As a condition precedent to reliance on the exception, the Crown must not only show that the event was unanticipated or out of its control, but also that it took reasonable available steps to avoid and address the problem *before* the delay exceeded the ceiling. This might include prompt resort to case management processes to seek the assistance of the court, seeking assistance from the defence to streamline evidence or issues for trial to reduce the time the trial might require, or reaching out to the local trial coordinator in an effort to acquire earlier trial dates or "any other appropriate procedural means."[36] The extent to which such efforts will be sufficient to rely on the exception will depend on the circumstances.

In *R v Williamson*,[37] the companion case to *Jordan*, the accused had twice appeared for preliminary hearing dates, and twice those dates were lost when on the day they were meant to start, some mix-up prevented that from occurring. Once in the superior court, a shortage of available courtrooms that could accommodate a jury meant further delay in scheduling the trial. The courtroom shortage was less about a resourcing issue, and more in the nature of a discrete exceptional circumstance as the trial was to occur in Kingston, Ontario, a relatively

---

34   *R v Tran*, 2023 ONCA 532 at paras 45–46 [*Tran*]; see also *Musclow*, above note 3 at paras 32–34.

35   *Jordan*, above note 1 at para 70.

36   *Ibid*.

37   2016 SCC 28 [*Williamson*].

smaller jurisdiction, where a large, lengthy, multi-accused homicide trial before a jury had created a burden on the courthouse that was out of the ordinary. Likewise, the confusion that resulted in the loss of two sets of preliminary hearing dates might have arguably been characterized as discrete events. In the face of these difficulties, however, the Crown took no steps to attempt to expedite the setting of dates for trial. For example, as suggested by the Ontario Court of Appeal, the Crown could have reached out to neighbouring jurisdictions in an effort to find space for the trial. The Supreme Court noted that

> [t]he record does not disclose whether the Crown could have been successful if it had attempted to expedite the trial. However, the point is simply that the Crown made no effort. As the Court of Appeal wrote, "the Crown … [did not take] seriously the obligation to bring this relatively straightforward case to trial in a reasonable time" (para. 67).[38]

Though it is imperative for the Crown to demonstrate that it took reasonable steps to mitigate the delay arising from a discrete exceptional circumstance, the Supreme Court in *Jordan* emphasized that the Crown is not required to show that the steps it took were ultimately successful. Rather, the Crown need only show that it took reasonable steps in an *attempt* to mitigate the delay.[39] The Crown may take steps to try to mitigate delay arising from an unexpected event, but the delay arises notwithstanding those efforts. So long as sufficient efforts have been made, the Crown can rely on the exception and the delay arising from the exceptional event will be deducted in calculating the net delay. As well, the Crown is not required to "exhaust every conceivable option for redressing the event in question to satisfy the reasonable diligence requirement."[40] For example, in *Kelly v R*,[41] where the investigating officer went on extended medical leave, it was sufficient that the Crown modified its case to the extent it could in an attempt to mitigate the delay the officer's absence caused but was not required to gut its case by proceeding without an essential witness.[42] Likewise, in *R v Mitchell*,[43]

---

38   *Ibid* at para 28.

39   *Jordan*, above note 1 at paras 69–71.

40   *Cody*, above note 33 at para 54.

41   *Kelly*, above note 32.

42   *Ibid* at paras 66–71.

43   2017 ABQB 717 at paras 20–25 [*Mitchell*].

where some last-minute evidence arose from an additional witness in the context of an ongoing investigation, but just prior to the start of the preliminary hearing, the Crown was not obliged to call that witness. Instead, it was reasonable to adjourn the preliminary hearing in order to review the new disclosure, provide it to counsel for the accused, and also to allow counsel time to consider it. As it happened, the new statement resulted in a new charge against the accused. As the Crown had immediately advised the defence of the new disclosure material, and ultimately pursued a Direct Indictment in order to mitigate the delay arising from the adjournment of the preliminary hearing date, it had done what was reasonably required to rely on the discrete exceptional circumstance. The Supreme Court made a similar determination in *R v Cody*[44] as it related to some late-breaking disclosure obligation. Where it came to light that one of the investigating officers in a drug operation had himself come under investigation, the Court found that while the Crown might well have determined to move forward without reliance on that officer's evidence or sought an Agreed Statement of Facts, it was sufficient and reasonable for the Crown to have promptly advised the accused's counsel of the new disclosure issue and sought the earliest available dates following that.

So long as the Crown has made reasonable efforts to remediate the error and minimize the resultant delay, the time should be deducted as a discrete event.[45] The Court in *Jordan* noted, though, that where such issues arise close in time to the actual or estimated end of the trial, it will likely not be possible for the Crown to mitigate the delay it has caused.[46] In such circumstances, it will be more likely that the Crown will have fewer options to attempt to avoid or mitigate the delay arising from the exceptional circumstance. Accordingly, the extent to which the Crown can be said to have made sufficient effort to mitigate delay must be informed by the stage of the proceedings when the discrete event arose. Transitional considerations (discussed below) may also be taken into account where a case was already in the system when *Jordan* was released.

---

44   *Cody*, above note 33 at para 54.
45   *Jordan*, above note 1 at para 73; *JS*, above note 29 at paras 68–76.
46   *Jordan*, above note 1 at para 74.

3)   Quantum of the Deduction for Discrete Events

Generally, the whole of the period of delay arising from the discrete exceptional event will be deducted where the Crown can demonstrate reasonable efforts to mitigate that delay. However, any and all delay will not be deducted as attributable to a discrete exceptional event where the delay is simply far too long, and a portion of it is therefore more properly attributable to institutional delay, or where the Crown could have reasonably mitigated a portion of the delay that arose from the discrete event.[47] This is so as to do otherwise would be to foster the culture of complacency that *Jordan* was devised to address.[48]

Two cases can be contrasted in terms of their facts as to whether a deduction could be made in whole, in part, or not at all, having regard to the Crown's efforts to mitigate the delay arising from a discrete exceptional circumstance.

In *R v KC*,[49] the Crown assigned to conduct a Dangerous Offender hearing took ill mere weeks before the hearing was scheduled to start. While counsel for the accused conceded that the Crown's illness was properly characterized as a discrete exceptional event, counsel advanced the argument that a year to the rescheduled hearing was simply too long and evidenced a lack of diligence on the part of the Crown in taking steps to mitigate the delay arising from the Crown's illness. Several factors convinced the trial judge that the whole period of delay should be deducted. The Crown did take steps to reschedule the trial, including seeking dates in two jurisdictions, in an attempt to mitigate the delay. Further, though a lack of resources could be blamed for something like half of the delay in rescheduling the hearing, as this was a transitional matter, the jurisdiction was allowed some period of time to get in line with *Jordan*. The prejudice to the accused (still relevant under the transitional exception), now convicted and sentenced on the predicate offence, was attenuated in the circumstances. Further, the matter could not go before another judge, but only the judge seized of the matter given that this was a sentencing hearing. In the circumstances,

---

47   *R v Carbone*, 2020 ONCA 394 at para 57; *Jordan*, above note 1 at para 75; *R v Safdar*, 2021 ONCA 207 at para 57, affirmed in the result 2022 SCC 21.

48   *R v Villanti*, 2020 ONCA 755 at paras 35–40 [*Villanti*].

49   *KC*, above note 25.

the Ontario Court of Appeal held that the judge at trial had not erred in deducting the full year between hearing dates.[50]

The outcome in *R v KC* can be contrasted to the outcome in *R v Villanti*,[51] a matter that was considered and distinguished by the Ontario Court of Appeal in *KC*.[52] Four accused were charged with fraud over $5,000 and conspiracy to commit an indictable offence in an alleged tax avoidance scheme in the amount of $13 million. The charges were laid in March 2014 and a twelve-week jury trial was set to begin in September 2017. A section 11(b) *Charter* application was dismissed in advance of the trial, and once dismissed, two of the accused sought an adjournment of the trial to retain counsel. The trial was rescheduled for February 2018, but those dates were lost as the assigned judge was reassigned to other matters to cover the illnesses of two other judges in that jurisdiction. As there were limited judicial resources, new trial dates were only available to be set nearly a year later. On the second section 11(b) application, the judge accepted that the judges' having taken ill was a discrete event but would only deduct three months of the eleven months of delay to the anticipated end of the new trial dates. The proceedings were stayed.[53]

Justice Lauwers, writing for the Court on the Crown's appeal against the stay, held that notwithstanding that this was a transitional case, the trial judge's determination that eleven months of delay was not acceptable post-*Jordan* was entitled to deference. Much of the delay was attributable to a shortage of judges in the Toronto courthouse, which permitted no flexibility in rescheduling matters when two judges had become ill. The Court of Appeal agreed with the application judge's assessment that though the Crown took steps to attempt to mitigate the delay, eleven months was simply too long for a new set of trial dates and could not wholly be attributed to the discrete events of the illnesses in light of the resourcing issue of which the judge at trial had taken proper notice.[54]

50　*Ibid* at paras 67–70.
51　*Villanti*, above note 48.
52　*KC*, above note 25 at paras 71–73.
53　*Villanti*, above note 48 at paras 5–8.
54　*Ibid* at paras 22–40; see also *Locknick*, above note 10 at paras 15–17; *R v JCP*, 2018 ONCA 986 at paras 15–16; *Perreault*, above note 19 at para 7; *Brown (NSCA)*, above note 19 at paras 61–71.

Though the *KC*[55] and *Villanti*[56] matters dealt with a delay of about a year attributable to a discrete exceptional circumstance and in both cases, illness, the quantum of the permitted deduction differed widely. This was so notwithstanding the Crown's diligent efforts to mitigate the delay arising from the discrete event in each case. Comparison of the two cases illustrates that an assessment of how long is too long to allow a full deduction for a discrete event is not a measure of the passage of time alone but will be informed by all of the relevant circumstances, including whether some portion of the delay is more properly attributable to some other factor beyond the discrete event.

When the need to mitigate delay arises as a result of a discrete event, defence conduct will also inform the reasonableness of the period of time deducted. In *R v JS*,[57] two continuation dates were required because of a discrete event relating to a Crown witness. The Crown and the Court worked proactively to obtain nine continuation date options relatively proximate to the trial and before an extended period in which the *per diem* out-of-town trial judge[58] would become unavailable. The defence, in contrast, refused all of the proposed dates without providing clear reasons for doing so. The Court of Appeal for Ontario declined to consider whether this constituted defence-caused delay but held that defence unavailability in the face of the Court and Crown's proactive steps to mitigate delay informed the reasonableness of the delay resulting from the discrete event. Associate Chief Justice Fairburn for the Court explained, "When the court and Crown are in a position to remedy the unforeseen circumstances in short order, but the defence cannot accommodate it through a reprioritization or otherwise, this necessarily informs the reasonableness of the length of the adjournment arising from the unforeseen circumstances."[59]

A discrete exceptional circumstance is the only basis upon which the Crown will be able to justify delay that exceeds the applicable ceilings. That there was no apparent prejudice to the accused arising from the delay, that the offences charged are serious, or that the applicable

---

55   *KC*, above note 25.

56   *Villanti*, above note 48.

57   Above note 29 at paras 77–83.

58   An out-of-town judge was required as the accused was a police officer with the local police service.

59   *Ibid* at para 81.

ceiling is only slightly exceeded are irrelevant considerations in applying the *Jordan* framework and cannot save a prosecution that exceeds the ceiling from a stay. If, after consideration of defence-caused delay and exceptional circumstances, the delay still exceeds the ceiling (subject to an assessment of the complexity of the matter, discussed later in this chapter), a stay of the proceedings must follow.[60]

4) Discrete Events in Context: Pandemic Delay

The COVID-19 pandemic plainly qualified as a discrete exceptional circumstance. It could not be foreseen or avoided, and nothing could be done to reasonably remedy the immediate delays arising out of the crisis. That the COVID-19 pandemic amounted to a discrete exceptional circumstance is uncontroversial and has been confirmed to be so by courts throughout the provinces and territories of Canada.[61]

Some courts have held that the inquiry as to whether the Crown took reasonable steps to mitigate delay is fundamentally not about inquiry into whether sufficient resources were allocated to the province's response to the pandemic, or to whether in a given locality the decisions as to when and whether particular matters (such as jury trials) could run were the best decisions in the circumstances. Pointing, for example, to low numbers of cases in a particular jurisdiction, to expert evidence that the courts could have safely done differently, or to disparate approaches to the closure of the courts as between provinces are not relevant considerations to the inquiry under section 11(b) of the

---

60   *Jordan*, above note 1 at para 81.

61   *R v Agpoon*, 2023 ONCA 449 [*Agpoon*] leave to appeal refused (without reasons) 2024 CanLII 15047 (SCC); *R v Drummond*, [2020] OJ No 3908 (SCJ) [*Drummond*]; *R v Gutierrez*, 2020 ONSC 6810 [*Gutierrez*]; *R v Khattra*, 2020 ONSC 7894 [*Khattra*]; *R v Simmons*, 2020 ONSC 7209 [*Simmons*]; *R v Truong*, 2020 ONCJ 613 [*Truong*]; *R v Stack*, 2020 ONCJ 544 [*Stack*]; *R v Walker*, 2020 ONSC 8153 [*Walker*]; *R v GR*, 2020 ONCJ 578 [*GR*]; *R v Pinkowski*, 2021 ONCJ 35 [*Pinkowski*]; *R v Koustov*, [2021] OJ No 191 (CJ) [*Koustov*]; *R v Topp*, 2022 ONCJ 83 at para 11; *R v Buoc*, 2022 ONSC 1067 at paras 35–39 [*Buoc*]; *R v Consolidated Homes Ltd*, [2022] OJ No 1161 (CJ) [*Consolidated Homes Ltd*]; *R v Brooks*, [2022] OJ No 243 (SCJ) at paras 27–28 [*Brooks*]; *R v Buabeng*, [2022] OJ No 1732 (SCJ) at paras 92–110 [*Buabeng*]; *R v Burgess*, 2022 NSSC 335 at para 6 [*Burgess*]; *R v Clifford*, 2022 ABQB 509 [*Clifford*]; *R v Harker*, 2020 ABQB 603 at paras 18–22; *R v Archibald*, 2021 CanLII 87325 (NL Prov Ct); *R v Awasis*, 2020 SKPC 41; *R v Shamrat*, 2022 MBPC 33; *R v Ali Ismail*, 2020 BCPC 144; *R v Berard*, 2020 ABQB 345; *R v Morrison*, 2020 SKPC 28; *R v Campbell*, 2020 ABQB 624; *R c ML*, 2020 QCCM 108; *R v Cathart*, 2020 SKQB 270; *R v KGY*, 2020 ABPC 171.

Charter. The only issue for the court's determination on the application is whether there was a discrete exceptional circumstance, and whether the Crown did what it could reasonably do to mitigate the delay that resulted. Where the argument on the section 11(b) *Charter* application relates to resources or the correctness of the government's response to the pandemic, it has generally been unsuccessful and in some instances, summarily dismissed.[62]

The Ontario Court of Appeal most recently made clear that an accused cannot rely on an argument that responses taken to the pandemic, be they at the provincial or local level, could have been different such that her case could have been heard sooner.[63] The Court noted that through the course of the pandemic, there were province-wide closures, both regional and province-wide jury blackout periods, and courthouse restrictions and closures at a local level that were undertaken in response to local circumstances. Further, on a local level, the availability of court facilities were limited as courtrooms had to be outfitted for safety.[64] As to efforts to triage cases for priority in the face of the backlog of cases the pandemic caused, the Court observed that "Regional Senior Justices were given significant discretion over how best to address the backlogs in their courts, but in most regions ... prioritized in-custody criminal matters over out-of-custody matters, and continuing over new trials."[65] The Court then held as follows:

> Going forward, where access to courts has been limited in these ways, the attributable delays are to be treated by the reviewing court as discrete exceptional circumstances in assessing delay for *Jordan* purposes. Although the focus of this decision has been on jury trials, similar principles apply to the availability of judge-alone trials in the Superior Court of Justice, and, with necessary modifications, to the Ontario Court of Justice.[66]

This approach is subject to the right of the defence to argue that the delay is unacceptable nonetheless as set out in *Jordan.* That said, it is not

---

62   *R v Shen*, [2022] OJ No 2673 (SCJ) [*Shen*]; *R v Redufe*, [2021] OJ No 4134 (SCJ) at paras 13–36; *R v Rahi*, 2023 ONSC 905 at para 32 [*Rahi*].

63   *Agpoon*, above note 61.

64   *Ibid* at paras 27–31.

65   *Ibid* at para 32.

66   *Ibid* at para 33.

open to the defence to second-guess the policy decisions made that limited access to courts in the ways set out above on a case-by-case basis.[67]

a)   Mitigation of Pandemic Delay

As with any discrete event, the Crown must demonstrate that reasonable steps were taken to mitigate the delay caused by the crisis where and when possible to have done so. As local conditions and systemic circumstances regularly have an impact on the time it takes to get cases to trial, trial judges are expected to employ their knowledge of their own jurisdiction and its typical delay in deciding the reasonable time requirements of the case.[68] Accordingly, the court can apply its knowledge of proactive local Crown initiatives that have reduced the normal delay to trial, even if they have not proven successful in every case. That said, in any individual case, the Crown is still obliged to show that it had resort to case management processes or attempted to find earlier dates in an effort to mitigate the delay caused by the pandemic, even where the prosecution is not ultimately successful in this regard.

In *R v Ghraizi*,[69] for example, the Alberta Court of Appeal accepted that the pandemic and resultant court closures plainly amounted to a discrete exceptional circumstance as it is defined in *Jordan*. However, the court did not agree with the summary conviction court that the Crown could do little to mitigate the delay that arose from it. Instead, the court emphasized that some effort to mitigate the delay caused by the exceptional circumstance was required to rely on the exception for a deduction, whether or not such effort succeeded.[70] Similarly in *R v Kande*,[71] the Crown could not rely on the pandemic for a deduction from the first trial date, vacated as a result of the pandemic, to the next, a period of thirteen months. This was so as the Crown had taken no steps to try to mitigate the delay the pandemic had caused.

As discussed earlier in this chapter, mitigation of delay caused by a discrete exceptional circumstance does not require that the Crown take

---

67   *Ibid* at paras 33–34.
68   *Jordan*, above note 1 at paras 87, 89, and 139; *Majeed*, above note 18 at paras 7–9; *R v Gopie*, 2017 ONCA 728 at para 173 [*Gopie*]; *R v RD*, 2020 ONCA 23 at paras 39–42.
69   2022 ABCA 96 [*Ghraizi*].
70   *Ibid* at paras 12–14; see also: *Burgess*, above note 61 at paras 21–22; *R v Hazizaj*, [2022] OJ No 3795 (CJ).
71   2020 ONCJ 446.

every proposed or possible step, only that reasonable steps have been taken. For example, in *R v Ansari*,[72] the Court held that mitigation of delay attributable to the pandemic did not require that the Crown sever the accused's matter from his co-accused where it was in the interest of justice for the Crown to have proceeded jointly (see Section B (8) below for a discussion related to joint prosecutions).

Though the Crown is obliged to try to mitigate the delay arising from the pandemic in the given case, the Crown is not obliged to prioritize one individual case over another where thousands of matters were adjourned and await a trial. So long as the Crown can point to having made prompt resort to remote case management processes (established for most matters in Ontario by 6 April 2020) to get the matter back on track and rescheduled promptly, this will generally be sufficient to establish the reasonable diligence requirement. The oft-quoted passage from the Ontario Court of Appeal's decision in *R v Allen*[73] is apposite in these unique circumstances:

> No case is an island to be treated as if it were the only case with a legitimate demand on court resources. The system cannot revolve around any one case but must try to accommodate the needs of all cases. When a case requires additional court resources the system cannot be expected to push other cases to the side and instantaneously provide those additional resources.[74]

Placing a timeline of events related to the adjournment of non-urgent trial matters and the availability of remote access for other matters before the court will be important. First, from the Crown's point of view, it can be relied upon to show what steps were taken to get cases back on the rails as soon as possible in a general sense across the province. For individual cases where the Crown has utilized remote technology to conduct some aspect of the prosecution, promptly pursued a judicial pre-trial for the purpose of rescheduling a matter, or pursued

---

72   2021 ONSC 186; see also: *R v Khiar*, 2021 ONSC 4677 [*Khiar*].

73   1996 CanLII 4011 (Ont CA).

74   *Ibid*; *R v KGK*, 2020 SCC 7 at para 61; *R v Brissett*, 2017 ONSC 401 at paras 29–30 [*Brissett*], affirmed in *R v Brissett*, 2019 ONCA 11; *R v Benjamin*, 2019 ONCA 10; *R v Peltier*, [2022] OJ No 822 (SCJ) at para 82 [*Peltier*]; *Stack*, above note 61; *R v Lieu*, 2021 ONCJ 402; *R v Budesa*, [2021] OJ No 3458 (CJ); *R v Ruchlewicz*, 2021 ONCJ 538 [*Ruchlewicz*]; *R v Fisher*, 2022 ONSC 5889 [*Fisher*]; *Rahi*, above note 62 at para 33.

any other available means to mitigate the effects of pandemic delay, the pandemic can be relied upon as a discrete exceptional event. Further, it will be important to take note of the dates that certain hearings or appearances *could have* been conducted remotely and the process for scheduling such matters, and where their availability was taken advantage of by the accused when offered or were declined. A timeline and/or judicial notice of closures can conversely be relied upon by the accused applicant to demonstrate that though pursued, access to remote hearing dates, a judicial pre-trial for the purpose of rescheduling a matter, or an offer to get their matter into a courtroom when other matters collapse, were not options proffered in a timely way, though such processes were available. While no case is an island, this does not mean that a case can be ignored and allowed to languish though the accused made efforts to get the matter back on track and processes were in place to assist with that. It will be imperative that the parties keep track of all correspondence between them to evidence what efforts were or were not attempted or offered to mitigate pandemic delays.

In most instances it will be neither necessary nor advisable to call evidence as to the impact of the pandemic on scheduling trial or preliminary hearing dates beyond a prepared timeline. A list of all Notices related to pandemic closures is readily available online. In addition to the provincial notices, check the Superior Court website to review local notices, as well.

By operation of two provisions of the *Canada Evidence Act*,[75] reproduced below, judicial notice may be taken of any of the orders and notices made by the courts with regard to pandemic closures and procedures upon reopening.[76] Providing a copy of any of these orders will be sufficient. Filing the orders and notices in summary form in a timeline chart will only assist the court.

Judicial Notice

Imperial Acts, etc.

17 Judicial notice shall be taken of all Acts of the Imperial Parliament, of all ordinances made by the Governor in Council, or the lieutenant governor in council of any province or colony that, or some portion of which, now forms or hereafter may form part of Canada, and of all the Acts of the

---

75   RSC 1985, c C-5.

76   *Agpoon*, above note 61 at fn1.

legislature of any such province or colony, whether enacted before or after the passing of the *Constitution Act, 1867*.

Documentary Evidence

Proclamations, etc., of lieutenant governor

22(1) Evidence of any proclamation, order, regulation or appointment made or issued by a lieutenant governor or lieutenant governor in council of any province, or by or under the authority of any member of the executive council, being the head of any department of the government of the province, may be given in all or any of the following ways:

(a)   by the production of a copy of the official gazette for the province purporting to contain a copy of the proclamation, order, regulation or appointment, or a notice thereof;

(b)   by the production of a copy of the proclamation, order, regulation or appointment purporting to be published by the government or Queen's Printer for the province; and

(c)   by the production of a copy or extract of the proclamation, order, regulation or appointment purporting to be certified to be true by the clerk or assistant or acting clerk of the executive council, by the head of any department of the government of a province, or by his deputy or acting deputy, as the case may be.

The Ontario Court of Appeal has also acknowledged that local judges are fully entitled to take judicial notice of local circumstances in assessing the reasonableness of delay having regard to the pandemic. In *R v Agpoon*, the Court held:

> Finally, there is the local perspective. The *Jordan* court noted the need for trial judges to "employ the knowledge they have of their own jurisdiction, including how long a case of that nature typically takes to get to trial in light of the relevant local and systemic circumstances": at para. 89; see also paras. 87 and 101. This instruction applies with necessary modifications to the assessment of pandemic-related delay for *Jordan* purposes.[77]

b)   Quantum of the Deduction for Pandemic Delay

Where the Crown could not have reasonably mitigated the delay caused, the whole period of delay caused by the exceptional event is to be subtracted. In instances where some other factor besides the pandemic

---

77   *Ibid* at para 26.

also contributed to the delay (e.g., the failure to take steps to reschedule a matter for too long or Crown unavailability for proffered dates to reschedule the matter), it cannot be said that the whole period of delay was necessarily caused by the pandemic. In such instances, the court may determine that the entire delay period ought not to be deducted. In Ontario, a series of cases have determined that the pandemic amounts to an exceptional circumstance, and the whole of the delay to the next scheduled trial date is to be deducted where that period can be said to have been entirely caused by the pandemic and having regard to the system's response in mitigating the delay the crisis has caused.[78] In instances where the delay from either the first date of the declaration of the global pandemic (16 March 2020) or the anticipated end of the first scheduled trial to the anticipated end of the rescheduled trial was caused entirely by the pandemic, that whole period of delay will generally be deducted from the total delay count.

In instances where a matter was set for trial (or a preliminary hearing) *prior* to the declaration of the pandemic and court shutdowns, it cannot be said that the whole period between the court shutdowns (on 16 March 2020) and the rescheduled date is attributable to the pandemic. In those cases, the period of delay between the original date (set before the pandemic was declared, and therefore not set later than would have otherwise been the case due to the pandemic) and the anticipated end of the rescheduled hearing is the portion to be deducted.[79] While in two cases the court treated the whole period between 16 March 2020 and the rescheduled date as the proper period to be deducted, in both instances, the courts can be taken to have included the period between the court closures and the first date set for trial in the deduction as a way to account for backlog delays attributable to the pandemic.[80] Backlog delay is discussed later in this chapter.

78　*Drummond*, above note 61; *Gutierrez*, above note 61; *Stack*, above note 61; *Simmons*, above note 61; *R v Reyes*, unreported decision of Doorly J, 9 December 2020 (Ont CJ) [*Reyes*]; *Truong*, above note 61; *Walker*, above note 61; *GR*, above note 61; *Pinkowski*, above note 61; *Koustov*, above note 61; *Khattra*, above note 61; *R v LaPlante*, [2021] SJ No 11 (QB); *R v Venne*, 2021 ONCJ 80; *R v Belzil*, [2021] OJ No 516 (SCJ) [*Belzil*]; *R v Gharibi*, [2021] OJ No 523 (CJ); *R v Ali*, 2021 ONSC 1230; *R v Henry*, 2021 ONSC 3303; *R v Olmstead*, 2021 ONCJ 327; *R v Coates*, [2021] OJ No 2915 (CJ); *R v Lawson*, 2021 ONCJ 389.

79　See: *Consolidated Homes Ltd*, above note 61; *Khattra*, above note 61; *R v Osei*, 2022 ONSC 1607 [*Osei*]; *Buabeng*, above note 61.

80　See: *Brooks*, above note 61; *R v Hyacinthe*, [2022] OJ No 1327 (SCJ) [*Hyacinthe*].

c) Jury Trials in the Pandemic

On 20 April 2020, in Ontario, the court issued a notice to the profession advising that most jury trials would be suspended. Jury trials were only up and running again sporadically through the period that followed, though jury trials were set to resume on 28 February 2022. This was due to a third wave of the pandemic, which caused even further disruption to regular court operations. Given the closures, most of the jurisprudence respecting the pandemic as a discrete exceptional event in the context of jury trials has allowed for a full deduction to when a jury trial could be either scheduled or rescheduled depending on the circumstances.[81] As well, that there were brief periods during which a jury trial could be heard through this more than two-year shutdown period did not require that any particular matter had to be prioritized and squeezed into those short segments of time when jury trials could be offered.[82] Justice Harris expressed it thusly in *R v Hyacinthe*:[83]

> I agree with the opinion voiced in the caselaw that generally the entire two-year period ought to be regarded as an exceptional circumstance even though, theoretically, a jury trial could have been heard if the timing was precisely right and all the stars magically aligned. Cognizance must be taken of the reality that only a select few of the multitude of backlogged jury trials could fit into the few spaces in the court docket that were available: see *Khattra* at paras. 62, 79–83. There was a significant domino effect which affected this case and the vast majority of other jury trials. The entire waiting period caused by COVID in my view constitutes exceptional delay.[84]

---

81   *R v Smith*, [2021] OJ No 2615 (SCJ); *Buoc*, above note 61; *R v Obregon-Castro*, 2021 ONSC 1096 [*Obregon-Castro*]; *Drummond*, above note 61; *Gutierrez*, above note 61; *Simmons*, above note 61; *Belzil*, above note 78; *Khattra*, above note 61; *R v Robinson*, [2021] OJ No 1796 (SCJ) [*Robinson*]; *R v Dumpfrey*, [2021] OJ No 6607 (SCJ); *R v Huang*, 2021 ONSC 8372 [*Huang*]; *Consolidated Homes Ltd*, above note 61; *Brooks*, above note 61; *Hyacinthe*, above note 80; *R v KL*, 2022 ONCJ 60 [*KL*]; *Osei*, above note 79; *Khiar*, above note 72; *R v MT-S*, 2022 ONSC 2471; *R v Cann*, [2022] OJ No 2129 (SCJ) [*Cann*]; *R v Titus*, 2022 ONSC 3484 [*Titus*]; *R v Sandhu*, 2022 ONSC 3910 [*Sandhu*]; *Fisher*, above note 74; *R v Thompson*, 2022 ONSC 2712; *R v Demisse*, 2022 ONSC 6200 unreported decision of Code J, 2 November 2022 (SCJ) [*Demisse*]; contra: *R v JP*, [2020] OJ No 5047 (SCJ), reversed on appeal, 2021 ONCA 866.

82   *Khattra*, above note 61; *Osei*, above note 79; *Demisse*, above note 81.

83   *Hyacinthe*, above note 80.

84   *Ibid* at para 17.

For a trial by jury in the context of the global pandemic, a unique scenario arises in that *Charter* rights can come into conflict. While section 11(b) of the *Charter* codifies the right to a trial within a reasonable time, section 11(f) of the *Charter* guarantees anyone charged with an offence the benefit of a trial by jury where the maximum punishment for the offence is five years or more. The issue that arises is whether, in the unprecedented circumstances of the global pandemic, one right must give way to the other. Recent jurisprudence indicates that where an accused has persisted in choosing a trial before a jury notwithstanding court closures, the delay to that trial will be fully deducted in applying the *Jordan* framework. In that sense, the right to a trial within a reasonable time must give way to the right to a trial by jury where that is the mode of trial selected.

In *R v Sharma*,[85] the total delay amounted to forty-three months. The accused applicant was charged with a series of sexual assaults and related offences with regard to his common law partner. The Information was sworn in February 2019. The courts shut down three months in advance of the June 2020 dates scheduled for the preliminary hearing, and so that was adjourned until it could be heard in June 2021. After committal on the charges, a trial of six to eight days before judge and jury was set for 22 September 2022.[86] The year between the originally scheduled preliminary hearing and the rescheduled hearing was wholly deducted as having been caused by the discrete exceptional circumstance of the global pandemic.[87] As for the delay in the Superior Court for the setting of a jury trial, Harris J held that while the accused applicant was entitled to pursue a jury trial, to do so was to accept the delay necessarily resulting from that choice. This was particularly so since the consequences of a choice of a trial before a judge and jury was well known at the time that decision was made.[88] Similarly in *R v Belzil*,[89] Goodman J held as follows:

> The applicant elected to have his trial by a Superior Court judge sitting with a jury. That remains his constitutional right. However, the COVID-19

---

85   2022 ONSC 5192 (unreported).
86   *Ibid* at paras 1–4.
87   *Ibid* at paras 12–20.
88   *Ibid* at paras 21–22.
89   *Belzil*, above note 78.

pandemic continues to preclude the parties from setting new trial dates. It is beyond dispute that this situation was completely unforeseeable and still cannot not be remedied by either of the parties, despite the Superior Court re-opening on a limited basis on July 6, 2020. In fact, that re-opening was short lived, in that jury trials are still suspended at the time of this writing.[90]

That the right to a trial by jury pursuant to section 11(f) of the *Charter* is not without limit and might have to give way in particular unique circumstances was anticipated by the Supreme Court of Canada in *Reference Re s 94(2) of the Motor Vehicle Act, 1985*.[91] As discussed in detail in Chapter 1, the primary purpose of section 11(b) of the *Charter* is the protection of the individual rights of accused: (1) the right to security of the person, (2) the right to liberty, and (3) the right to a fair trial.[92] That everyone has the right to life, liberty, and security of the person is codified in section 7 of the *Charter of Rights and Freedoms*. Section 1 of the *Charter* indicates that the rights it codifies are guaranteed, "subject only to such reasonable limits prescribed by law as can be demonstrably justified in a free and democratic society."[93] As Code J notes in his decision in *R v Obregon-Castro*,[94] Lamer J, for a majority of five (of seven) in *Reference Re s 94(2) of the Motor Vehicle Act, 1985*,[95] held that "[s]ection 1 may, for reasons of administrative expediency, successfully come to the rescue of an otherwise violation of s. 7, but only in cases arising out of exceptional conditions, such as natural disasters, the outbreak of war, epidemics and the like."[96] Noting that the discrete exceptional circumstance category of the *Jordan* framework is not "endlessly elastic,"[97] Code J wrote that

> [d]epending on how long the pandemic continues, and the extent to which the Court and the Crown are able to mitigate its effects on s. 11(b) *Charter* rights, particularly in the context of the s. 11(f) *Charter* right to trial

---

90   *Ibid* at para 90.

91   1985 CanLII 81 (SCC) [*Re BC Motor Vehicle Act*].

92   *R v Morin*, 1992 CanLII 89 (SCC).

93   *Canadian Charter of Rights and Freedoms*, Part I of the *Constitution Act, 1982*, being Schedule B to the *Canada Act 1982* (UK), 1982, c 11, s 1.

94   *Obregon-Castro*, above note 81.

95   *Re BC Motor Vehicle Act*, above note 91.

96   *Ibid* at para 85 (emphasis added).

97   *Obregon-Castro*, above note 81 at para 41.

by jury, there may come a time when s. 1 reasonable limits need to be considered.[98]

It remains to be seen whether, going forward, the backlog of jury trials resulting from the more than two years of court closures in Ontario will require resort to section 1 of the *Charter* to return the system to pre-pandemic caseload numbers.

Notably, in response to the suspension of jury trials, many Ontario Crown's offices offered to consent to re-election to judge-alone trials for those set for jury trials pursuant to sections 561 and 561.1 of the *Criminal Code*,[99] allowing accused persons to re-elect from judge and jury to judge-alone trials. Where this offer has been made and refused by the defence in favour of a trial by jury, not only will the delay attributable to court shutdowns for jury trials likely be deducted, but the Crown will also be able to point to having made the offer to consent to re-election as an effort to mitigate the delay caused by the crisis. Given that re-elections to judge-alone trials before the Ontario Court of Justice were offered and accepted for the purpose of getting to trial sooner in such instances, and that prosecutions are more likely to be pursued by the Crown before the Ontario Court of Justice in order to circumvent the backlog problem related to jury trials in the superior courts, it can be anticipated to increase caseloads in Ontario Courts of Justice for the foreseeable future. In this sense, the delay in the superior courts related to jury trials will have carried over to the Ontario Court of Justice, amounting to something of a Catch-22 for the criminal justice system. As Wendl J recently observed in *R v Fraser*:[100]

> I wish to note that 95 percent of all criminal matters in Ontario resolve in the Ontario Court of Justice. In Hamilton, the Ontario Court of Justice deals with a significant amount of complex criminal litigation where the Crown is proceeding by indictment such as project cases, youth murder trials, Garofoli applications, child pornography and sexual assaults.
> On a sexual assault charge, where the maximum penalty is 10 years when the Crown proceeds by indictment, a preliminary hearing is not available. These types of matters often involve multiple days of trial preceded by pre-trial motions which can also take multiple days. The same applies for

---

98   *Ibid*; see also: *Sandhu*, above note 81.
99   RSC 1985, c C-46, ss 561 and 561.1.
100   2022 ONCJ 580.

firearms offences which have a maximum of 10 years, they usually involve multiple days of trial and complex Charter applications. On these matters if the accused elects trial in the Superior Court, the delay ceiling is 30 months, while in the Ontario Court of Justice, the exact same case must proceed to trial in 18 months. There is nothing to account for the 12-month difference except for the defence election to either the Superior Court or the Ontario Court of Justice.

Furthermore, even if a preliminary hearing was available and requested in matters such as this it would likely have proceeded by way of 540(7) application which would have added little time to no time in the matter.

The reality is that *Jordan*, the streamlining of preliminary hearings under 540(7) and the elimination of preliminary hearings with respect to matters which have less than a 14-year maximum, is having the effect of increasing elections to the Ontario Court of Justice. It is simply a matter of common sense that the election of a complex matters to the Ontario Court now has a higher chance of being stayed for delay than an election to the Superior Court.[101]

d) Pandemic Backlog Delay

The impact of the pandemic will not always be readily quantifiable. Some Ontario Courts of Justice and Superior Courts of Justice in Ontario have held that consideration ought to be given to the obvious fact that, in spite of all efforts, a backlog in scheduling and rescheduling cases will be inevitable and returning to normal at courthouses in terms of trial scheduling will take longer than the actual course of the pandemic itself. In instances where there is some portion of delay that exceeds the ceiling, these courts have determined that such delay may be reasonably deducted as attributable to backlog depending on the circumstances.

The pandemic can be taken to have had an impact on the criminal justice system in various ways. Application judges, in most instances, will be in a position to take judicial notice of the following contributors to delay arising from the COVID-19 crisis and consequent closures of the courts:

---

101   *Ibid* at paras 28–31.

- The need to take steps at the outset of the pandemic to get the system up and running again, including: the need to set judicial pretrials for adjourned matters, time required to retrofit courtrooms for safety, and time required to shift to remote courtrooms.
- That even on "reopening" only a certain number of courtrooms may have been opened and that the process of reopening was necessarily gradual rather than immediate given that both adjourned and new matters had to be dealt with.
- Changes to usual court processes that took time to implement or added time (such as the requirement to set a remote meeting with a trial coordinator to obtain dates rather than simply attending at office as before).
- That through court closure periods, matters continued to enter the system, thus creating a backlog of cases that persists at present (having regard to court closures and what occurred locally over that period).
- Any other local difficulties or changes in procedure that the judge would be aware of, and which would have contributed to overall delay.[102]

Though not readily quantifiable, it cannot be gainsaid that the pandemic has and will continue to have an impact on the system's ability to move cases forward, and for some period of time, even well beyond its end. This was acknowledged by Nakatsura J in *R v Simmons*,[103] where he wrote:

> [T]he impact of the COVID-19 pandemic on the criminal justice system is not limited to those periods of time when the court had to adjourn scheduled cases or when jury trials were suspended. It has had numerous and far-reaching impacts upon how we do things, and, on the people, who do them. Not the least has been the necessity to take measures to protect the health and safety of justice participants and the public. The way trials are conducted needed to be transformed. Physical courtrooms had to be changed. Some trials are now conducted virtually. This in turn, has had a significant impact on scheduling. Scheduling new trials and rescheduling existing trials have become more complex and difficult. A backlog of cases

---

102 *Agpoon*, above note 61 at paras 26–34.
103 *Simmons*, above note 61.

has ensued. A lack of resources was not the cause. Rather, COVID-19 was. It has had a system-wide impact of unprecedented proportions, never seen before in our lifetime.[104]

A number of decisions have cited the above-noted passage and acknowledged that once the net delay count has been arrived at, some reasonable period of delay should also be deducted to account for the additional pressures and backlog arising out of the pandemic.[105] In one recent Ontario Superior Court decision, *R v Hamblett*,[106] Akhtar J took judicial notice of the impact of the pandemic on the workings of the criminal justice system, calling it the "ripple effect." He agreed that some account should be taken of the overall effect of the backlog of cases due to cases flowing into the criminal justice system through the period that the courts were closed because of the COVID-19 pandemic. Similarly, in *R v Titus*,[107] Dunphy J noted that "[t]here has never been an emergency in the history of the administration of justice in this country that has resulted in this degree of court closures lasting for anything close to this amount of time. Ever."[108] Likening the impact of

---

104　*Ibid* at para 70.

105　See: *R v Meir*, [2022] OJ No 1177 (CJ); *Peltier*, above note 74; *Brooks*, above note 61; *R v Toor*, 2022 ONCJ 8; *R v Delves*, 2022 ONCJ 141; *R v Hamidi*, [2022] OJ No 5878 (CJ); *Consolidated Homes Ltd*, above note 61; *Hyacinthe*, above note 80; *R v Farooq*, unreported decision of Kelly J, 23 March 2022 (Ont CJ); *R v Khan*, 2021 ONCJ 195 [*Khan 2021*]; *Reyes*, above note 78; *Ruchlewicz*, above note 74; *R v Ajgirevich*, 2022 ONCJ 237; *Titus*, above note 81; *Cann*, above note 81; *R v Hamblett*, [2022] OJ No 4548 (SCJ) [*Hamblett*]; *R v Nagy Willis*, 2022 NSPC 29 at paras 15–22 and 93–109; *Clifford*, above note 61 at paras 14–21; *Robinson*, above note 81; *R v Buri*, 2021 ONSC 2222; *R v Metatawabin*, 2021 ONSC 7168; *Huang*, above note 81; *Obregon-Castro*, above note 81; *Shen*, above note 62; *R v Korovchenko*, 2022 ONCJ 388; *Sandhu*, above note 81; *R v GS*, 2022 ONCJ 427; *R v Martiuk*, 2022 ONSC 3285; *Fisher*, above note 74; *Demisse*, above note 81; *R v AA*, [2022] OJ No 4811 (CJ); *R v Hassan*, [2022] OJ No 5157 (SCJ); *R v Langford*, 2022 ONSC 4542; contra: *R v Yang*, 2021 ONCJ 537; *R v Mengistu*, 2022 ONSC 3624 (s 11(b) Application); *R v Giaman*, [2022] OJ No 3306 (CJ); *R v Mohamed*, 2022 ONCJ 512; *R v SM*, 2022 ONCJ 513; *R v Schardt*, 2021 ONSC 3143 [*Schardt*]; *R v Greenidge*, 2021 ONCJ 57; *R v CP*, [2022] OJ No 4821 (SCJ); *R v DB*, [2022] OJ No 4776 (CJ); *R v Hannah*, [2023] OJ No 2828 (SCJ); *R v Lauterpacht*, 2023 ONCJ 51; *R v Balasubramaniam*, [2023] OJ No 218 (CJ) (Downes J) [*Balasubramaniam*]; *R v Buick*, [2023] OJ No 130 (SCJ); *R v Nawabi*, 2022 ONSC 7258; *R v Malhi*, 2023 ONSC 7; *R v Khan*, 2022 ONSC 7310; *R v Brown*, [2023] OJ No 39 (SCJ); *R v Kirkopoulos*, 2022 ONSC 6440; *R v SC*, 2022 ONCJ 486; *Rahi*, above note 62 at paras 29–32.

106　*Hamblett*, above note 105 at paras 46–49.

107　*Titus*, above note 81.

108　*Ibid* at para 18.

the pandemic on the system as the proverbial "pig in a python,"[109] he held that it will take some time for the courts to digest the impact of court closures and return to normalcy and this fact should be accounted for in assessing the reasonableness of trial delay.[110]

It remains to be seen how long some reliance can be placed on the ripple effect of the pandemic crisis to account for delay. Once the impact of the pandemic has been digested and given that the transitional exception grace period for compliance with the *Jordan* framework has long expired, delay to trial that cannot be characterized as defence-caused, attributable to a discrete event, or arising from case complexity (discussed later in this chapter), must be counted toward the net delay figure. In the Ontario Superior Court, for example, there has been a shift from the characterization of delay as attributable to pandemic backlog to a determination that such delay is properly attributable to a lack of resources (i.e., a shortage of judges) because pandemic backlog has long been known to government.[111] Likewise, in *R v Kirkopoulos*,[112] the Ontario Court of Appeal held that the judge at trial did not err in attributing some delay to the pandemic backlog and the rest to institutional delay, noting that the judge was best-positioned to take notice of the circumstances in their own jurisdiction in this regard.[113]

e)   When Pandemic Delay Will Not Be Deducted

In relying on the overall effect of the pandemic or backlog delay, it has been held to be inappropriate to identify the COVID-19 crisis as the cause of some segment of delay where it would have been appropriately treated as included in the ceiling prior to the pandemic. In the absence of some evidence that it took longer than it normally would have to get to trial, a deduction to account for backlog is inappropriate.

---

109   *Ibid* at para 17.

110   *Ibid* at paras 17–20.

111   See: *R v Liu*, 2024 ONSC 2022 at paras 26–40 (per Code J); *R v Constantine*, 2024 ONSC 2626 at paras 55–68 (per Rhinelander J); *R v Downey*, 2024 ONSC 2157 at paras 40–46 (per Penman J); *R v Alli*, 2023 ONSC 5829 at paras 17–31 (per Forestell J); *R v Bowen-Wright*, 2024 ONSC 293 at paras 49–50 (per Schreck J); *R v Constantino*, 2024 ONSC 491 (unreported) (per Campbell J).

112   2024 ONCA 596 [*Kirkopoulos*].

113   *Ibid* at paras 27–53.

For example, as in *R v McCudden*,[114] if before the pandemic a judicial pre-trial would have to have been scheduled in some matter, and the application judge has taken judicial notice that the time required to set that during the pandemic was largely the same as it would have been prior, or perhaps took only slightly longer, it will not be appropriate to ask that that whole segment of delay be deducted from the net count as attributable to pandemic delay.

Likewise, in instances where the application judge has taken notice that the time to set a preliminary hearing or trial date was the same as what it would have been before the pandemic, the delay to this stage of the prosecution cannot be attributed in whole or in part to pandemic delay. In *R v Li*,[115] for instance, Misener J took notice that, in that jurisdiction, the time to trial was the same as what it would have been pre-pandemic given the Crown's efforts to expedite the matter. Accordingly, the pandemic made no contribution to the delay in that particular case that warranted any deduction. Similarly, in *R v YD*,[116] while the court acknowledged the existence of backlog delay, it was held that in this particular case, where there was little in the way of attempts to mitigate the delay, seventy days between a Crown pre-trial and judicial pre-trial was not properly attributable to pandemic backlog.[117]

Though a prosecution took place during some or all of the course of the pandemic, this does not necessarily mean that some account must be taken of backlog delay in all instances. Recalling that the *Jordan* framework is ultimately concerned with making determinations as to the cause of various segments of delay, it will be important to consider whether the pandemic actually even impacted the time to trial in a particular case. For example, in a case where, notwithstanding the pandemic's overall effects, the court was able to fit the matter into a vacated spot and the matter had not yet come into the system during the period that the courts were changing procedures in response to the pandemic and/or were closed, there may be little basis to ask for consideration for backlog delay. The COVID-19 crisis must have *caused* some period of delay before that delay can be properly deducted.

---

114   2022 ONCJ 138.
115   *R v Li*, [2021] OJ No 7392 (CJ).
116   2022 ONCJ 376.
117   *Ibid.*

For example, in *R v Spencer*,[118] the Saskatchewan Court of Appeal considered whether the application judge at trial erred in the determination that though a portion of the prosecution had taken place in the context of the pandemic, it had no impact on the delay in the case. Prior to the declaration of the pandemic in March 2020, a trial had been set to start on 8 June 2020 for charges of sexual exploitation and sexual assault. The date was lost for trial as the defence had brought a section 11(b) *Charter* application, for which the 8 June date was in part to be used. In advance of that, both the defence and Crown brought motions to strike the content of affidavits the other had filed on the motion, thus requiring the whole day to litigate that. The section 11(b) application was adjourned as a result to September, having regard to the trial judge's availability, and to December for trial. The court upheld the trial judge's determination that the pandemic had only minimally impacted the delay in the prosecution given that the delay was more properly attributed to the above-noted factors and there was no evidence on record as to the availability of counsel prior to the setting of the original 8 June trial dates.[119] In another case, *R v Lee*,[120] where an Information was laid, and the accused's whereabouts were well-known to police (he was in custody), but a period of eight months passed before police arrested him, without explanation, this was the actual cause of delay. Backlog delay was not a factor as, once arrested, the parties made efforts to get the matter heard as quickly as possible.

In other instances, where some period of delay can more properly be attributed as having been caused by some other aspect of the prosecution, the fact that the matter took place in the context of the global pandemic will not be relevant to the assessment of the reasonableness of the delay to the end of trial. For example, in instances where delay in the provision of disclosure has delayed the prosecution, and would have done so notwithstanding pandemic delay, several courts have ruled that the delay cannot be attributed to the pandemic. For example, in *R v Ryan*,[121] where the Crown was not diligent with respect to the provision

---

118   2022 SKCA 135 [*Spencer*]; *R v Gyamfy*, 2022 ONCJ 472.
119   *Spencer*, above note 118 at paras 16–19, 30, and 64–65; *R v Deol*, [2021] OJ No 5106 (CJ).
120   [2022] OJ No 169 (CJ).
121   [2020] OJ No 4382 (CJ); see also: *R v Ottewell*, 2020 ONCJ 623; *R v ASL*, 2021 ONCJ 269;
      R v Van Dyke, [2021] OJ No 4635 (CJ); *R v Delaney*, 2021 ONCJ 467; *R v MS*, 2021 ONCJ
      543; *R v DL*, 2021 ONCJ 385; *R v Gagnon*, [2021] OJ No 6888 (CJ); *R v Brown*, 2021 ONCJ

of essential disclosure, the matter could have been returned to military court to be heard sooner, and because the trial date had been set prior to the onset of the pandemic, the Crown could not rely on the pandemic to reduce the net delay count. It has generally not been accepted that delay in the provision of essential disclosure is irrelevant to the assessment since pandemic delay ran parallel through the same period. Similarly, in *R v Zahid*,[122] the Crown could not rely on the pandemic to argue that but for the crisis, an earlier date would have been sought where the defence had, well before the declaration of the pandemic, raised the delay issue, but the Crown had not responded promptly.

Importantly, the assessment of whether and the extent to which prosecution delay can be attributed to the pandemic, or to some other cause, is largely a factual determination that is well within the trial judge's purview to make. Accordingly, where the motion judge is of the view that delay in setting a matter for trial is more properly the result of some other factor or combination of factors, such determination is entitled to deference. For example, in *R v LL*,[123] the judge at trial was of the view that backlog arising from the pandemic had not contributed to the delay to trial. Instead, late disclosure (occurrence reports), which in that case had properly delayed the setting of the judicial pre-trial, was responsible. The motions judge took notice that the delay before a trial could be set was largely the same as it would have been prior to the pandemic. On appeal, the Ontario Court of Appeal held that in the absence of some evidence that would show otherwise, that determination could not be interfered with.[124]

Similarly, the judge at trial might reach a conclusion as to the *cause* of backlog delay, relying on their experience and knowledge of their own jurisdiction. For example, in *R v Jakovac*,[125] Caponecchia J, though acknowledging that there had been court closures arising from the pandemic that may well have contributed to delays to trial in that jurisdiction, also observed that the courthouse in which the trial was to have

---

663; *R v Racanelli*, 2022 ONCJ 390; *R v MK*, 2022 ONCJ 392; *R v Bohnsack*, 2022 ONCJ 603; *R v Shahid*, 2021 ONCJ 723.

122   [2020] OJ No 4573 (CJ); *R v Vorontsov*, 2021 ONCJ 169; *Schardt*, above note 105; *R v Naseer*, 2021 ONCJ 239; *contra: Khan 2021*, above note 105.

123   2023 ONCA 52 [*LL*].

124   *Ibid* at paras 15–16 and 22–23; *R v Pereira*, 2023 ONCJ 20; *R v Jakovac*, 2023 ONCJ 27 [*Jakovac*]; *R v Aoun*, 2023 ONCJ 36; *R v MacMillan*, 2022 ONCJ 594.

125   *Jakovac*, above note 124.

taken place had for years been chronically under-resourced, particularly with regard to the number of judges on the bench. In the circumstances, the Crown could not rely on pandemic backlog delay to seek a further deduction from the net delay count.[126] In a contrasting example, in *R v Balasubramanium*,[127] Downes J had regard to his role as the local administrative judge in his jurisdiction to take notice of the global pandemic's impact on trial scheduling, and made a deduction to account for it.

While it has largely been accepted in the Ontario Superior Courts that backlog delay attributable to the pandemic exists and can be readily taken notice of, a divide had arisen in the lower courts in this regard. In some instances, account had not been taken of pandemic backlog delay because the Crown had failed to call evidence to establish its existence, while in others, the court had taken notice of the pandemic's impact without any need for evidence to establish it. In *R v Ivarone*,[128] Leitch J aptly described this divide in the jurisprudence as the "causal evidence" versus "conservative" approaches. The first required the Crown to marshal statistical evidence to demonstrate the extent of the impact in a given case, failing which no deduction could be made for backlog delay. The second approach allowed for notice to be taken of pandemic backlog delay and a deduction of generally between three to six months to be made to account for it, with the requirement for the Crown to call some evidence arising only where it sought a deduction in excess of what is generally taken. Justice Leitch adopted the conservative approach as the correct one. In *R v Hassan-Bashir*,[129] Lai J noted that such approach was consistent with the Ontario Court of Appeal's decision in *LL*,[130] wherein the court deferred to the trial judge's factual determination as to the impact of the pandemic in the case before her, which she arrived at through "her own knowledge of the culture at the court location where she sits." Similarly, in *R v Singh*,[131] Blacklock J held that the *LL* decision supports the view that evidence need not be called, with the factual determination as to the pandemic's impact in a given case relying on the trial judge's knowledge of their own jurisdiction.

---

126   *Ibid* at paras 28–30.

127   *Balasubramaniam*, above note 105 at paras 23–24.

128   *R v Ivarone*, 2023 ONCJ 69 at paras 4–16.

129   [2023] OJ No 1066 (CJ) at para 34.

130   *LL*, above note 123 at paras 21–23.

131   *R v Singh*, unreported decision of Blacklock J, 10 March 2023 at paras 28–44 (Ont CJ).

Ultimately, in *R v Agpoon*,[132] the Court of Appeal for Ontario settled definitively that judicial notice, without the need for evidence, could be relied upon to make a deduction for pandemic backlog delay.

f)   Disclosure Delay in the Pandemic

There may be instances where the provision of disclosure was delayed due to the pandemic, for example, staff shortages because of illness or the need to change the manner in which such material would be turned over to the Crown and/or vetted early on in the pandemic. However, this is not an instance where the court can be expected to take judicial notice that the pandemic caused such delay. The Crown will likely be required to call evidence through the officer, who can explain what occurred during the relevant period and how much sooner the material would have been provided but for difficulties caused by the pandemic.[133] It will likewise be necessary to call evidence from the agency where the provision of some required report from that outside agency is delayed for COVID-19-related reasons.[134] The judge will not be in a position to take judicial notice of the impact of the pandemic on the ability of third parties or outside agencies to provide such materials.

B.   COMPLEX CASES

1)   Particularly Complex Cases Defined

While the presumptive ceilings of the *Jordan* framework reflect the increase in complexity of criminal matters since *Morin*, the Court also acknowledged that some cases will necessarily be more complex than others.[135] Particularly complex cases require an inordinate amount of preparation and/or trial time due to (1) the nature of the evidence or (2) the nature of the issues.[136] Accordingly, under the *Jordan* framework, complexity can justify delay as an exceptional circumstance.[137] No stand-alone deduction will arise from a finding of particular complexity in

---

132   *Agpoon*, above note 61.

133   *KL*, above note 81.

134   *R v Panchal*, [2022] OJ No 3859 (CJ); *R v Jadav*, [2022] OJ No 3858 (CJ); *R v Hinterberg*, 2022 ONSC 4860.

135   *Jordan*, above note 1 at paras 42 and 53; *Cody*, above note 33 at para 63.

136   *Jordan*, above note 1 at para 77.

137   *Ibid* at paras 77–78.

a given case. Instead, a qualitative rather than quantitative assessment of the whole of the case is made in order to determine whether the net delay was reasonable in the circumstances. Once a finding is made that a case is particularly complex, such that the overall time the case has taken is justified and the delay is reasonable, no further analysis is required, and no stay will issue.[138]

2) Complexity Is a Qualitative Assessment

Unlike defence-caused delay or discrete events, complexity is not a quantitative calculation from one date to another date that results in a quantified deduction. Instead, after the calculated periods of defence-caused delay and discrete events are deducted, a qualitative assessment of the net delay will be undertaken to determine whether the complexity of a case, as a whole, justifies any additional time to the end of trial above the presumptive ceiling.[139] Complexity of the case "as a whole" refers to the entirety of the prosecution, not the state of the prosecution at day one of trial.[140] Complexity leading up to the trial — such as the extent of disclosure, the time needed for narrowing of issues in the context of continuing judicial pre-trials, and settlement upon agreed facts — must be considered along with the complexity of the trial itself. It is legal error to fail to consider the complexity at the outset of a prosecution as such factors add to the time required to get the matter to trial.[141] It is similarly an error to attribute delay to complexity where a prosecution becomes more complex over time due to what can more properly be characterized as discrete events adding to the time required for trial.[142]

---

138 *Ibid* at para 80.

139 *Ibid* at paras 77–78; *Cody*, above note 33 at paras 64–65; *R v Picard*, 2017 ONCA 692 at para 40, leave to appeal refused (without reasons) 2018 CanLII 73612 (SCC) [*Picard*]; *R v Millar*, 2019 BCCA 298 at para 88 [*Millar*]; *R v Zahor*, 2022 ONCA 449 at para 106 [*Zahor*]; *Huang*, above note 81 at para 196; *Kelly*, above note 32 at paras 52–59.

140 *Picard*, above note 139 at paras 57 and 62; *Baron*, above note 5 at para 71; *R v Lopez-Restrepo*, 2018 ONCA 887 at paras 36–38 [*Lopez-Restrepo*]; *Barra*, above note 7 at para 41; *Zahor*, above note 139 at paras 106 and 109; *contra*: *R v Powell*, 2020 ONCA 743 at para 8 (in *obiter*) [*Powell*].

141 *Picard*, above note 139 at para 62; *Baron*, above note 5 at para 71; *Lopez-Restrepo*, above note 140 at paras 36–38; *Barra*, above note 7 at para 41; *contra*: *Powell*, above note 140 at para 8 (in *obiter*).

142 *Zahor*, above note 139 at paras 107–13.

3) Hallmarks of Complexity

Hallmarks of complex cases as they relate to the evidence[143] in the case include:

- voluminous disclosure;
- a large number of witnesses;
- significant requirements for expert evidence; and
- charges covering a long period of time.

Hallmarks of complexity related to the issues[144] in a case include:

- a large number of charges;
- a large number of pre-trial applications;
- novel or complicated legal issues;
- a large number of significant issues in dispute;
- matters proceeding jointly against multiple co-accused, where it is in the interests of justice to do so;
- an international dimension to a case; and/or
- procedural delays processing legal aid applications.[145]

With respect to the final item of procedural delays processing legal aid applications underscores the point that although the Crown cannot do much, it must be seen to do whatever it can to avoid or mitigate delay.

4) Complexity Is a Factual Determination

The determination that complexity in the evidence and issues that arise in a case justifies the time to trial is a "determination fall(ing) well

---

143 *Jordan*, above note 1 at paras 77–79; *R v CG*, 2020 ONCA 357 at paras 16, 18, 23–24, and 44–56 [*CG*]; *Locknick*, above note 10 at paras 19–22; *Lopez-Restrepo*, above note 140 at paras 33–34; *Gopie*, above note 68 at paras 169–75; *Singh (BCCA)*, above note 11 at paras 85–94; *R v Reinbrecht*, 2019 BCCA 28 at paras 69–71 [*Reinbrecht*]; *R v Bulhosen*, 2019 ONCA 600 at para 79, leave to appeal refused (without reasons) 2020 CanLII 17613 (SCC) [*Bulhosen*]; *Zahor*, above note 139 at para 105; *Baron*, above note 5 at paras 67–69.

144 *Jordan*, above note 1 at paras 77–80; *Xanthoudakis v R*, 2020 QCCA 446 at para 34; *Reinbrecht*, above note 143 at paras 69–71; *Locknick*, above note 10 at paras 19–22; *R v Spencer*, 2017 SKCA 54 at para 108; *Bulhosen*, above note 143 at para 79; *Zahor*, above note 139 at para 105.

145 *R v Pastuch*, 2022 SKCA 109 at paras 150–54; *R v Case*, 2019 ONSC 7240 at para 15.

within the trial judge's expertise."[146] However, deference to that factual determination is premised on the requirement that the exception be interpreted correctly as a matter of law.[147]

5) Mitigation of Complexity Delay

Before a Crown can rely on complexity to justify delay above the ceiling, the judge will also consider whether the Crown developed and followed a concrete plan to help minimize the delay caused by the identified complexity.[148] The Crown may need to demonstrate this plan to establish that the circumstances resulting in delay were outside of its control either because they were unavoidable or unforeseeable.[149] The Court of Appeal for Ontario has adopted the following test to scrutinize Crown proactivity: whether the Crown's plan for dealing with a particularly complex case, considered as a whole, reasonably attempted to minimize delay occasioned by such complexity.[150]

A line of jurisprudence has developed in some provinces wherein evidence must establish a "causal connection" between the complexities of the case and the delay. In those cases, the courts have called for the complexity-causing delay to be particularized and proven in a detailed way to determine whether it explains and justifies delay.[151] Arguably, the requirement to particularize a causal connection between the complexity and the delay invites judges to fall into error by assessing portions of the trial process in isolation, contrary to the Supreme Court's direction

---

146 *Jordan*, above note 1 at para 79; *Cody*, above note 33 at paras 31 and 63–64; *R v Wookey*, 2021 ONCA 68 at para 88 [*Wookey*]; *Majeed*, above note 18 at paras 10–11; *R v Way*, 2022 ABCA 1 at para 9; *Ghraizi*, above note 69 at para 10.

147 *Ontario (Labour) v Nugent*, 2019 ONCA 999 at paras 24–28 [*Ontario (Labour) v Nugent*]; *R v TWS*, 2020 ABCA 157 at para 23; *Majeed*, above note 18 at paras 10–11; *R v Regan*, 2018 ABCA 55 at paras 32–33 [*Regan*], leave to appeal refused 2018 CanLII 99645 (SCC); *R c Rice*, 2018 QCCA 198 at paras 29–33 and 53 [*Rice*]; *R v Lemioer*, 2019 SKCA 95 at para 70 [*Lemioer*].

148 *Jordan*, above note 1 at para 79; *R c Boulanger*, 2021 QCCA 815.

149 *Wookey*, above note 146 at paras 83–98; *R v Lee*, 2023 NSCA 3 at para 20 [*Lee (NSCA)*].

150 *Ontario (Labour) v Nugent*, above note 147 at paras 24–50; *Powell*, above note 140 at para 7; *Wookey*, above note 146 at paras 83–98.

151 *R v Roberts*, 2020 BCCA 307 at paras 88–89; *Millar*, above note 139 at paras 84–89; *R v Christhurajah*, 2019 BCCA 210 at para 109; see also: *Lemioer*, above note 147 at para 71; contra: *R v Klassen*, 2018 ABCA 258 at paras 98–104.

to consider the case as a whole[152] and to the Court of Appeal for Ontario's determination in *R v Picard*[153] that the complexity assessment has regard to the state of the prosecution from the outset of the charges, not the first day of trial. Indeed, reliance on the complexity exception requires that the Crown has taken steps to manage and reduce the complexity of the case from the outset. To have done so is a condition precedent to a finding that some portion of delay that exceeds the ceiling after the net delay has been calculated as reasonable because of case complexity. That the issues and evidence were made less complex over the course of a prosecution and by the time of the start of the trial ought not to detract from the overall picture indicating that a case was initially very complex and would have remained so but for the efforts made in advance, which is precisely what *Jordan* calls on counsel to do.

6) Crown Responsibility

In order to rely on complexity as an exception justifying delay, the Crown must act reasonably and according to a concrete plan in prosecuting a complex case. Such a plan may be relied on to demonstrate that, considering the case as a whole, the Crown acted reasonably and proactively to avoid or mitigate delay and did not wait for the ceiling to be breached to take steps.[154] Issues frequently litigated in this area are the Crown's exercise of prosecutorial discretion, the adequacy of the Crown's planning, and the extent to which the Crown is required to work collaboratively with other parties.

a)   Prosecutorial Discretion

As the Court made clear in *Jordan*, the Crown must be alive to the fact that any delay resulting from their prosecutorial discretion must conform to the accused's section 11(b) right and be in the interests of justice.[155] Accordingly, the Crown's decisions — such as proceeding with

---

152   *Jordan*, above note 1 at para 81; *Picard*, above note 139 at para 62; *Baron*, above note 5 at paras 67–72; *Lopez-Restrepo*, above note 140 at paras 36–38.

153   *Picard*, above note 139 at para 62.

154   *Jordan*, above note 1 at para 70; *R v Auclair*, 2014 SCC 6 at para 2; *Kelly*, above note 32 at paras 60–71; *R v Manasseri*, 2016 ONCA 703 at para 308 [*Manasseri*]; *Majeed*, above note 18 at paras 10–11.

155   *Jordan*, above note 1 at para 79.

multiple counts or, as discussed in more detail below, to try multiple accused together—factor into the complexity analysis.[156] The courts have been careful to recognize that they play no supervisory role in decisions of the Crown. The courts have also indicated that, for the purposes of a *Jordan* analysis, such discretionary decisions must not be arbitrary or in bad faith in order to be found not delay-causing. Reasonable and principled exercises of discretion that have resulted in additional time have been found to be consistent with complexity as opposed to inconsistent with the duty of the Crown to prevent and/or mitigate delay.[157]

b) Imperfect Planning

Further, the Crown is not held to a standard of perfection,[158] nor is it required to have succeeded in every respect in reducing the delay attributable to the complexity of its case in order to rely on the effort.[159] The Crown may be forgiven for making mistakes provided it takes proactive steps to correct them. It will suffice if the Crown takes the initiative and makes consistent efforts to anticipate and prevent delay from occurring and/or to mitigate the extent of delay caused.[160] The purpose of the *Jordan* framework—to prevent complacency and encourage proactivity—provides the guiding principle to this contextual analysis. For example, where time estimates are inadequate, what matters is whether the Crown made best efforts in the first place to prevent delay, whether the Crown proactively identified the potential delay, and whether, in doing so, the Crown took proactive steps to address it and/or to mitigate it.[161] In *R v CG*,[162] though the Crown had underestimated the length of time the trial would require and the Court contributed to the delay

---

156 *Ibid*, citing *R v Rodgerson*, 2015 SCC 38.

157 *Jordan*, above note 1 at para 79; *Gopie*, above note 68 at paras 169–75; *Bulhosen*, above note 143 at paras 81–84; *R v Saikaley*, 2017 ONCA 374 at para 37 [*Saikaley*]. For pre-*Jordan* comment about the Court's lack of supervisory role over the exercise of prosecutorial discretion, see: *R v Nguyen*, 2013 ONCA 169 at para 61.

158 *Jordan*, above note 1 at paras 79 and 90; *Majeed*, above note 18 at paras 10–11; *Regan*, above note 147; *Ontario (Labour) v Nugent*, above note 147 at paras 24–50.

159 *Manasseri*, above note 154 at para 308; *Bulhosen*, above note 143 at para 83.

160 *Manasseri*, above note 154 at para 308; *R v Morash*, 2021 ONCA 335 at paras 15–17 and 23–35 [*Morash*]; *Locknick*, above note 10 at paras 19–22.

161 *Morash*, above note 160 at paras 15–17 and 23–35; *CG*, above note 143 at paras 22 and 46–53; *contra: Lee (NSCA)*, above note 149 at paras 16–30.

162 *CG*, above note 143 at paras 3, 12, and 16–17.

by requiring that continuation dates be set in blocks due to the complexity of the evidence, the resultant delay was properly attributed to complexity and deducted because the Crown had made its estimate in good faith and acted proactively, both before the trial started and throughout the trial, to mitigate the delay.

c)   Planning Past the Applicable Ceiling

The availability of the complexity exception is not necessarily contingent on a plan to meet the applicable ceiling.[163] Some cases are so complex that even the most efficient approach in the circumstances will exceed the applicable ceiling. In such cases, a plan to minimize the delay caused by a particularly complex case is neither undermined nor rendered inadequate because it does not aim to conclude a case within the applicable ceiling.[164] As the Court of Appeal for Ontario explained in *Ontario (Labour) v Nugent,* as "the very purpose of the particularly complex case exception is to justify delay for cases that require time beyond the presumptive ceiling, the availability of the exception cannot be conditioned on attempts to meet that ceiling."[165]

d)   Working Collaboratively

To be proactive, *Jordan* encourages the Crown and defence to work collaboratively.[166] This does not require the Crown to abdicate its responsibility to prosecute meritorious cases in order to achieve expediency, or bend to every suggestion proposed by the defence to expedite matters.[167] Efforts on both sides must be reasonable.

7)   Defence Responsibility to Reduce Needless Complexity

All justice participants bear responsibility to ensure that complexity is managed. In *R v Faulkner,* Watt JA for the Court of Appeal for Ontario held: "case complexity is not a sole proprietorship, the exclusive business of the Crown."[168] Where the defence's approach

---

163   *Ontario (Labour) v Nugent,* above note 147 at para 39.
164   *Ibid.*
165   *Ibid.*
166   *Jordan,* above note 1 at para 138.
167   *Saikaley,* above note 157 at paras 36–48.
168   2018 ONCA 174 at para 178.

to the litigation injects a degree of complexity into the proceedings in the form of motions of doubtful merit, failure to adhere to filing deadlines, pointless or repetitive cross-examination, or lack of preparation, these factors are also relevant to the reasonableness of the delay.[169]

8)   Complexity in Context: Joint Prosecutions of Multiple Accused

a)   Crown Discretion to Proceed Jointly

The Crown's decision to proceed jointly against co-accused is justified as an exceptional circumstance adding to the complexity of a proceeding, where proceeding jointly is in the interests of justice.[170] Generally, it is in the interests of justice that individuals charged jointly with an offence be tried together; this conserves judicial resources, avoids inconsistent verdicts, and does away with the need for witnesses having to testify more than once.[171] The Crown must be "alive to the fact that any delay resulting from their prosecutorial discretion must conform to the accused's s. 11(b) right."[172]

Where the Crown shows that it has done what it reasonably can to mitigate the delays associated with such a case, a prosecution involving multiple accused persons is a factor which increases the complexity of a case and justifies a lengthier time to trial. While delay occasioned by the actions of one co-accused is not necessarily delay attributable to all, so long as it is in the interests of justice to proceed jointly, such delays are taken into account under the exceptional circumstances analysis.

---

169 *Rice*, above note 147 at paras 64–65; *Gopie*, above note 68 at para 175; *R v Vassell*, 2016 SCC 26 at paras 6–7 [*Vassell*]; *R v Phan*, 2020 ABCA 370 paras 26–27; *R v Pipping*, 2020 BCCA 104 at paras 129–39; *see also: Zahor*, above note 139 at para 125.

170 *Vassell*, above note 169 at paras 6–7; *Jordan*, above note 1 at paras 77–79; *Cody*, above note 33 at para 32; *Gopie*, above note 68 at paras 123–42 and 167–75; *Manasseri*, above note 154 at paras 311–14, 323, and 329; *Singh (BCCA)*, above note 11 at paras 89–91; *R v Ny*, 2016 ONSC 8031 at paras 37–38 and 47; *Baron*, above note 5 at para 68; *Jurkus*, above note 12 at paras 63–72; *Lopez-Restrepo*, above note 140 at paras 39–40; *Antic*, above note 12 at para 8; *Brissett*, above note 74 at paras 14–15; *Pauls*, above note 11 at paras 45–54, affirmed in the result in *Yusuf*, above note 11; *R v Eheler*, 2021 BCCA 316 at para 71.

171 *R v LG*, 2007 ONCA 654 at para 63.

172 *Jordan*, above note 1 at paras 77–79.

b) Severance

The Crown has an obligation to continually assess whether the decision to proceed jointly remains in the best interests of justice or whether severance is necessary. One accused cannot be held "hostage" by his co-accused's actions or inactions.[173] That said, severance is "not a panacea when delay issues arise in a multi-party indictment."[174] The framework in *Jordan* does not require severance in all instances where some additional delay is caused where a prosecution proceeds jointly. In *R v Singh*,[175] the British Columbia Court of Appeal relied on the comments of Fraser JA in *R v Koruz*,[176] in support of this proposition:

> Moreover, if the suggestion is that every time a number of defendants are charged with conspiracy, the Crown should be required to sever charges if and when timing problems arise, the implications for prosecuting these kinds of cases could be profound. Although the right to trial within a reasonable time is an individual right, one cannot ignore the practicalities of what is involved in the Crown's prosecution of a conspiracy case. The mere fact that an accused has been charged with conspiracy does not confer upon him some inherent advantage in asserting a claim for a s. 11(b) breach if and when one of his co-defendants causes a delay in the proceedings. To suggest severance as a simple solution ignores the very real cost to the Crown and the public involved in prosecuting separate actions: *R. v. McNamara* (No. 1) (1981) 56 C.C.C. (2d) 193 (O.C.A.), affirmed (1985) 19 C.C.C. (3d) 1 (S.C.C.). In the end this kind of approach will only serve to contribute to further delays in the administration of justice.[177]

c) Communal Versus Individual Application of the Framework

An individualized approach must be taken to the attribution of defence-caused delay in cases of jointly charged accused in order to avoid attributing to an accused the delay caused by the actions or inactions of a co-accused that are inconsistent with the approach and language of *Jordan*.[178] However, where delay begins due to a co-accused but is

---

173   *Vassell*, above note 169 at para 7; *Manasseri*, above note 154 at para 323.

174   *Singh (BCCA)*, above note 11 at para 81.

175   *Ibid.*

176   *R v Koruz*, 1992 ABCA 144, affirmed in *R v Koruz*, 1993 CanLII 130 (SCC) [*Koruz*].

177   *Singh (BCCA)*, above note 11 at paras 80–82; *Koruz*, above note 176 at para 83; see also *R v Boghossian*, 2019 ONCA 169 at para 22.

178   *Gopie*, above note 68 at paras 128 and 136.

prolonged by an accused, the accused will be responsible for the delay they contributed. For example, where a co-accused seeks to adjourn a trial date, but the accused is not available for new dates for an unreasonable length of time, the delay between the first new dates offered by the court and the new dates counsel could accept is attributable to the accused.[179] Similarly, if an accused acquiesces to delay caused by a co-accused for their own purposes, that delay is attributable to the accused.[180]

The Ontario Court of Appeal has held that the individualized approach will not apply where the delay was common to all accused because the defence has proceeded collectively. Where "the defence proceeded through the system as a collective, the delay caused by scheduling challenges must be analyzed in the same manner — that is, communally."[181] Such a scenario does not represent one in which a co-accused is "dragged along" because of the inaction of another.[182] This argument about communal conduct was made at the Supreme Court in *R v Yusuf*[183] but the Court, in upholding the Court of Appeal for Ontario's decision in the result, opted to "leave for another day" the issue of whether and in what circumstances multiple accused should be treated communally as opposed to individually when assessing defence delay under section 11(b). The Supreme Court noted that this issue (and other novel issues raised in *Yusuf*) would be best decided in a case where there were intervenors, which did not involve the transitional exception, and where the accused had made meaningful efforts to move the trial process ahead in cooperation with the Crown and the trial court.[184]

The distinction between cases where delay has been attributed to all as a collective — in contrast to those where delay applies to one accused but not the other — largely turns on the extent to which a co-accused can be said to have advanced their case forward in contrast to what their co-accused has done in causing delay. In *R v Manasseri*, for example, one accused (Manasseri) was charged with murder, and his

---

179   *R v Grant*, 2022 ONCA 337 at paras 27–51.

180   *Brissett*, above note 74 at paras 14–16.

181   *R v Albinowski*, 2018 ONCA 1084 at paras 37–38 [*Albinowski*]; *Brissett*, above note 74 at paras 14–16; *Pauls*, above note 11 at paras 45–54, affirmed in the result in *Yusuf*, above note 11; *R v Chung*, 2021 ONCA 188 at paras 194–95.

182   *Vassell*, above note 169 at paras 11–12; *Manasseri*, above note 154 at para 326; *Gopie*, above note 68 at paras 128 and 136; *Albinowski*, above note 181 at paras 36–39.

183   *Yusuf*, above note 11 at paras 3–5, affirming *Pauls*, above note 11 at paras 45–54.

184   *Yusuf*, above note 11.

co-accused (Kenny) originally faced a charge of assault with respect to the victim, which the Crown upgraded to assault causing bodily harm and manslaughter three weeks prior to his assault trial and charged him jointly with Manasseri. As there had been a delay in the production of an expert report, the previously scheduled preliminary hearing date was lost. Manasseri's counsel was not available for new dates for another year and the Crown was in agreement with that schedule, over counsel for Kenny's objections. In the circumstances, Watt JA, writing for the Ontario Court of Appeal, held that while it was open to the Crown to proceed jointly, "A joint trial is not some magic wand the Crown can wave to make a co-accused's s. 11(b) rights disappear. The 'right' to a joint trial only prevails to the extent that such a proceeding is in the interests of justice both pre- and post-*Jordan*."[185] The Crown could have severed Kenny's matter from Manasseri's or preferred an indictment as a means of preserving Kenny's section 11(b) rights. Instead he was dragged along with Manasseri's matter such that his right to a reasonable trial was violated. Similarly, in *R v Vassell*,[186] the appellant before the Supreme Court of Canada sought to have his conviction for possession of cocaine for the purposes of trafficking set aside by the Court. Vassell had been co-accused with six others, eventually reduced to two others. In contrast to his co-accused, counsel for Vassell had promptly reviewed disclosure, pursued early pre-trial discussions, and had "from start to finish" advanced the matter along. In the circumstances, the Court held that the Crown had not been proactive with regard to his section 11(b) rights, allowing him to be dragged along with the others in spite of his efforts to move matters forward.

The above-noted cases can be contrasted to what occurred in *R v Albinowski*.[187] It was scheduling challenges as between counsel for the defence for the jointly-charged accused that produced the delay. As the co-accused had proceeded collectively in this regard, and it was in the interests of justice for the Crown to have proceeded jointly, the delay was attributable to all accused. That the co-accused had proceeded as a collective was evidenced even by their approach to the section 11(b) *Charter* litigation, with one counsel making submissions for all.

---

185   *Manasseri*, above note 154 at para 373.
186   *Vassell*, above note 169 at paras 5–12.
187   *Albinowski*, above note 181 at paras 36–39.

In *R v Tran*,[188] the Ontario Court of Appeal found a middle ground between the individual rights of each co-accused and the communal nature of a joint trial that ensures efficiency and consistent verdicts. The court determined, without specifying whether it is a discrete event or complexity, that the "exceptional circumstance" excused delay caused as the result of the prosecution of a joint trial, because (1) the joint trial was being undertaken in the interests of justice; (2) the delay arose because of the joint trial; (3) the delay was unforeseen or reasonably unavoidable; and (4) the Crown could not reasonably have ameliorated that delay.[189] The court emphasized that the nine-day delay beyond the presumptive ceiling in that case was not the result of something that the Crown could have ameliorated and was distinguishable from the extreme circumstances of *Manasseri*.[190] The court made clear that, even without the demonstrated communal approach described in *Albinowski*, it is generally in the interests of justice for trials to proceed jointly and the Crown will not be held responsible for delay caused solely by the unavailability of multiple defence counsel.[191]

---

188   *Tran*, above note 34.

189   *Ibid* at para 40.

190   *Ibid* at paras 41–44.

191   *Ibid*.

CHAPTER 8

Where Delay Falls Below the Ceiling

A.   ONUS AND TEST TO MEET

After account has been taken of defence-caused delay, any exceptional circumstances, the complexity of the case, and the net delay sits below the applicable eighteen-month (in provincial court) or thirty-month (in superior court) ceiling, the onus will be on the defence to demonstrate that the delay is unreasonable in the circumstances.[1] Recalling that, in formulating the ceilings, the Supreme Court already took account of tolerable levels of institutional delay, it will be rare for cases to be stayed due to unreasonable delay where the net delay falls below the applicable ceiling as "stays beneath the ceiling [will] be granted only in clear cases."[2]

To establish that a matter with delay below the applicable ceiling for net delay is nevertheless unreasonable, the defence must satisfy each of the following criteria:

1)   that the defence took meaningful steps demonstrating a sustained effort to expedite the proceedings; and
2)   that the case took "markedly longer" than it reasonably should have.

Where each of these requirements cannot be established, "the s. 11(b) application must fail."[3]

---

1   *R v Jordan*, 2016 SCC 27 at para 82 [*Jordan*].
2   *Ibid* at paras 48 and 83; *R v SA*, 2024 ONCA 737 at paras 21–24 [*SA*].
3   *Jordan*, above note 1 at paras 82–83; *R v KJM*, 2019 SCC 55 at paras 4, 70, and 114 [*KJM*]; *R v RD*, 2020 ONCA 23 at para 38 [*RD*]; *R v Coulter*, 2016 ONCA 704 at paras 58 and

B. MEANINGFUL STEPS

The first criterion requires a consideration of "action or non-action by the accused that is inconsistent with a desire for a timely trial."[4] "Token efforts,"[5] such as placing a statement on the record that an earlier date was wanted, will not suffice. The defence must demonstrate that it tried to set the earliest trial date, cooperated with the Crown and the court, put the Crown on timely notice when delay had become problematic, and conducted all applications (including the section 11(b) *Charter* application) "reasonably and expeditiously."[6]

In *R v RD*,[7] the Court of Appeal for Ontario held that the application judge at trial had not erred in determining that this criteria had not been met where counsel for the accused at trial had indicated, in a judicial pre-trial in February 2016, an intention to file a third-party records application, but did not bring that application until September of that year. In *R v Coulter*,[8] the Court of Appeal for Ontario held that the trial judge had not erred in holding that the accused had failed to establish this criteria where the delay fell below the ceiling. In that case, when the accused's application could not be heard on the originally scheduled date, the trial coordinator reached out to counsel for the accused to reschedule the date and subsequently offered earlier dates. The defence did not accept the dates offered though available and though the Crown indicated its willingness to accept short service of the application material.[9]

The defence need not demonstrate it took every possible step, however, in particular where to have done so would have been futile.[10] For

---

87–89 [*Coulter*]; *R v Daponte*, 2021 ONCA 14 at paras 25–27 [*Daponte*]; *R v Safdar*, 2021 ONCA 207 at paras 64–65 [*Safdar (ONCA)*], affirmed (on other grounds) 2022 SCC 21 [*Safdar (SCC)*]; *R v Campbell*, 2022 ONCA 223 at para 20 [*Campbell*]; *R v Musclow*, 2024 ONCA 565 at paras 22 and 27 [*Musclow*]; *SA*, above note 2 at para 25.

4   *Jordan*, above note 1 at para 84.

5   *Ibid* at para 85.

6   *Ibid.*

7   *RD*, above note 3 at para 41.

8   *Coulter*, above note 3.

9   *Ibid* at para 95.

10   *Jordan*, above note 1 at paras 48 and 82–86.

example, in *R v Campbell*,[11] the accused was not obliged to bring a severance application to meet this criteria.[12]

The distinction between the actions of an accused through the course of a prosecution that are simply regular steps, expected to be performed as a party to the litigation and required as a function of the cultural shift ushered in by *Jordan*, and the actions of an accused that amount to "meaningful steps" can be a difficult one to make. To have taken normal steps as required through the course of a matter will be a condition precedent to attempting to establish that the defence took meaningful steps in this context, though likely not sufficient to meet the criteria. What is required is a "sustained effort to expedite the proceedings."[13] Thus in *R v LCJ*,[14] the Alberta Court of Appeal, though acknowledging that counsel for the defence at trial "took some cooperative steps that exceeded professional expectations"[15] through the course of the case, including proceeding with a preliminary hearing though late disclosure was received, it would not interfere with the judge at trial's determination that this was insufficient to meet the first criteria for a stay for delay below the ceiling. In contrast, in *R v Safdar*,[16] though counsel for the defence at trial had been unable to accept continuation dates due to other commitments and had brought a late-breaking section 11(b) *Charter* application, the Court of Appeal for Ontario nevertheless held that the defence, "had certainly acted in the spirit of co-operation," sufficient to meet the criteria given that "the defence had taken more steps to expedite the matter than the Crown had."[17] In *AE c R*,[18] the Court of Appeal of Quebec held that where the defence did not raise the section 11(b) delay issue with the court or Crown when it arose, consented to a postponement of the trial, and might have been more diligent in applying for legal aid assistance, the defence could not meet the criteria.[19]

---

11   *Campbell*, above note 3.

12   *Ibid* at paras 20–23.

13   *Jordan*, above note 1 at paras 82–83.

14   2019 ABCA 484.

15   *Ibid* at paras 23–24.

16   *Safdar (ONCA)*, above note 3; see also: *Daponte*, above note 3.

17   *Safdar (ONCA)*, above note 3 at paras 66–67.

18   2019 QCCA 1865.

19   *Ibid* at paras 58–69.

C.   CASE TOOK MARKEDLY LONGER THAN IT SHOULD HAVE

The second criterion, whether the prosecution took markedly longer than it reasonably should have, "involves consideration of such factors as case complexity, local circumstances, and whether the Crown took reasonable steps to expedite the proceedings."[20] Determining whether the time taken for a case markedly exceeds what was reasonably required is not a matter of precise calculation. Instead of parsing each day or month to determine whether each step was reasonably required, the Court in *Jordan* made clear that trial judges should step back from the *minutiae* and adopt a "bird's eye" view of the case.[21] In *R v Musclow*, Justice Coroza for the Court of Appeal for Ontario made clear that this "bird's eye" view is a qualitative assessment of the remaining delay, and is not an opportunity to reintroduce issues related to periods already deducted from the total delay.[22] In considering the case's reasonable time requirements, trial judges should use "the knowledge they have of their own jurisdiction, including how long a similar case typically takes to get to trial in light of relevant local and systemic circumstances."[23] Whether a prosecution took markedly longer than it should have, is a question of fact, well within the trial judge's expertise.[24] That said, the trial judge must be careful not to stray into hypothetical or speculative circumstances.[25] The trial judge must remain case- and fact-specific in determining whether it took markedly longer than it should have when compared to what is typical for similar cases in that jurisdiction at the time and cannot stray outside of the actual local circumstances.[26]

The issue of how to consider local circumstances arose squarely in *R v SA*.[27] In that case, the application judge found that the delay under the presumptive ceiling was unreasonable as a result of seven judicial vacancies.[28] Her analysis used a hypothetical yardstick for measuring the reasonableness of the below-ceiling delay, i.e., what would

---

20   *Jordan*, above note 1 at paras 51 and 87; *KJM*, above note 3 at para 75; *SA*, above note 2 at para 25.

21   *Jordan*, above note 1 at para 91; *SA*, above note 2 at para 26.

22   *Musclow*, above note 3 at paras 24–30.

23   *Jordan*, above note 1 at para 89; *SA*, above note 2 at para 26.

24   *Jordan*, above note 1 at para 91; *SA*, above note 2 at para 26.

25   *Musclow*, above note 3 at paras 29 and 32; *SA*, above note 2 at paras 29, 33, and 42.

26   *Musclow*, above note 3 at paras 29 and 32; *SA*, above note 2 at paras 29, 33, and 42.

27   Above note 2.

28   *Ibid* at para 17.

have happened had there been no judicial vacancies?[29] In staying the prosecution, she found that this case (and other cases in the jurisdiction) would have been heard sooner if the court had not been under-resourced. While it was reasonable to posit that the matter would have been reached earlier had there been no judicial vacancies, the question was whether this resourcing issue was relevant to the assessment of delay below the ceiling and capable of rebutting the presumption of reasonableness such that the defence met its onus.[30] In overturning the stay, Associate Chief Justice Fairburn for the Court of Appeal for Ontario determined that the application judge erred in considering not what was typical in her jurisdiction but what should be typical or would be typical if the court were not under-resourced.[31] Whether a case took markedly longer than it should have is not about measuring the time the matter took against how long it might have taken to get to trial in ideal and non-existent circumstances. This is because the yardstick for measuring the reasonableness of delay below the ceiling cannot be hypothetical circumstances. It must be actual local circumstances. In *R v SA*, the Court of Appeal for Ontario relied on the majority decision of the Supreme Court in *R v KJM*, which held that "the test is not whether the case should reasonably have been completed in less time, but whether it took *markedly* longer than it reasonably should have."[32] In *R v SA*, the Court made clear that the issue is not whether the matter could have been heard any sooner if the circumstances had been better or whether the circumstances should have been better such that the case could have been heard sooner. The issue is whether the case took markedly longer than it should have when compared to what is, in fact, typical for similar cases in that jurisdiction around the same time.[33]

The first trial date set does not amount to a ready-made yardstick against which to measure how long the case ought to have taken to get

---

29   *Ibid* at paras 29–33.

30   This is distinct from delay above the ceiling where, in the author's view, under-resourcing alone may not be used to explain delay above the presumptive ceiling. Importantly, the application decision in *R v SA*, 2023 ONSC 5829 (unreported) sparked a series of decisions from the Superior Court of Justice in Toronto where judicial resourcing was the sole basis for delay: see *R v Bowen-Wright*, 2024 ONSC 293; *R v Constantino*, 2024 ONSC 491 (unreported); and *R v Liu*, 2024 ONSC 2022 [*Liu*]. SA was the only case where the delay in issue was under the presumptive ceiling.

31   *SA*, above note 2 at paras 33 and 44.

32   *KJM*, above note 3 at paras 107 and 111; *SA*, above note 2 at para 35.

33   *SA*, above note 2 at paras 34–37.

to trial.[34] Put another way, that a matter is not reached on the first trial date set is not an indicator that the time to trial was a rare and clear instance where the matter took markedly longer than it should have.[35] It is well known, particularly in busy jurisdictions, that trial dates are often set optimistically to ensure courts run efficiently and for the purpose of moving matters forward.[36] Stacked courtrooms are common in busy jurisdictions and are to be encouraged lest matters collapse, courtrooms wind up empty, and court time is wasted.[37] It is understood that this practice involves a risk that the predicted collapse rate will be inaccurate and a matter may not be reached on its first date.[38] This is particularly the case during a backlog or where resources are tight. The assessment of whether a matter set for trial under the presumptive ceiling took markedly longer than it should have must be undertaken with the understanding that, "[i]n the real world . . . resources are, in fact, finite . . ." and that "no case is an island to be treated as if it were the only case with a legitimate demand on court resources."[39] Essentially, the under-the-ceiling test provides room for local realities, including resource issues, by comparing what happened in the case to what is typical in similar cases at the time.[40]

Neither Crown nor defence counsel are held to standards of perfection in the review of their conduct. Where the Crown has done its part to ensure that the case proceeds expeditiously, it is unlikely that the reasonable time requirements of the case will be found to have been markedly exceeded.[41] However, as the Supreme Court held in *R v KJM*,[42] in the youth criminal justice context, the failure of either party to take steps to move the matter forward expeditiously is less likely to be tolerated on the second criterion. That said, the enhanced need for timeliness in youth matters is simply one case-specific factor to consider in determining whether a case has or will have taken longer than it should have and is not dispositive.[43]

---

34   *Campbell*, above note 3 at paras 24–37.

35   *SA*, above note 2 at paras 38–41.

36   *Campbell*, above note 3 at para 24; *SA*, above note 2 at para 38; *Liu*, above note 30 at paras 26–27.

37   *SA*, above note 2 at para 40.

38   *Ibid* at paras 34 and 40–41.

39   *R v Allen*, 1996 CanLII 4011 (ON CA) at para 27; *Jordan*, above note 1 at para 57; *SA*, above note 2 at para 23.

40   *SA*, above note 2 at paras 41–43.

41   *Jordan*, above note 1 at paras 85, 90 and 112; *SA*, above note 2 at para 27.

42   *KJM*, above note 3.

43   *Ibid* at paras 68–84.

Ultimately, the determination of whether the remaining delay *markedly* exceeds the time requirements of the case — viewed in context of case-specific factors such as complexity, the circumstances of what is typical in the local jurisdiction for similar cases, and the Crown's conduct — requires applying the bird's-eye view approach.[44] In *R v Daponte*,[45] for example, the Court of Appeal for Ontario considered whether a ten-day trial in a drug prosecution, in London, Ontario, and involving two accused, markedly exceeded the time requirements of the case. The net delay amounted to twenty-seven-and-a-half months. The court considered that the trial judge found that the case itself was not a complex one in that most of the Crown's witnesses were police officers, and the issues for trial relatively narrow. The court agreed with the judge at trial that had the Crown been on top of its obligation to continually reassess whether it ought to disclose confidential informer information it could have avoided late-breaking disclosure that added delay to the proceedings. Nevertheless, the parties agreed that all had moved smoothly to that point, the defence was able to take the next set of dates, and, at the time, made no complaint that the trial had markedly exceeded its time requirements. While there was little on the record as to the usual time requirements for such a trial to take place in the jurisdiction, the judge at trial did indicate that the case had proceeded normally through the Ontario Court of Justice. Standing back and assessing these factors, the court determined that the time requirements of the case had not been markedly exceeded, and no breach of section 11(b) of the *Charter* was found.[46]

In *R v Safdar*,[47] the Court of Appeal for Ontario held that the accused (respondent on the appeal) could not meet this criteria in the circumstances. The matter was not without some complexity, as the court noted that it was, "a difficult case of alleged very serious domestic abuse involving three defendants and a significant medical dispute that required "voluminous disclosure" of medical records. It was supposed to take six weeks to try, but took another three weeks in circumstances where the initial number of witnesses was significantly reduced. In light of these factors the matter could not be said to be of unreasonable length though the net delay came in under the thirty-month mark.

---

44   *Campbell*, above note 3 at paras 24–37; *Musclow*, above note 3 at paras 24–30.

45   *Daponte*, above note 3.

46   *Ibid* at paras 29–37.

47   *Safdar* (ONCA), above note 3 at para 68.

CHAPTER 9

Transitional Exception (Charges Laid Before 8 July 2016)

A. RATIONALE

The transitional exception has a limited application. It only applies to cases that were "in the system" on 8 July 2016, which was the day on which the *R v Jordan* decision was released.[1] This included matters where charges had just been laid to matters pending appeal at the time of the decision. The creation of the transitional exception was the Supreme Court's way of immediately imposing the *Jordan* framework while acknowledging that the parties would have placed reasonable reliance on the legal framework provided in *R v Morin* and its progeny and could not have been aware of the *Jordan* framework prior to the release of the decision in *Jordan*.[2] This exception was intended to prevent a recurrence of the situation that ensued after the release of Court's decision in *R v Askov*, where the Court's abrupt change in law, in Ontario alone, led to the stay or withdrawal of tens of thousands of criminal charges.[3] As the Court in *Jordan* noted, "[s]uch swift and drastic consequences risk undermining the integrity of the administration of justice."[4]

At this point, it is highly unlikely that any transitional cases remain pending. Nevertheless, it is important to understand how the transitional exception has been applied in order to comprehend the outcome

---

1   *R v Jordan*, 2016 SCC 27 at paras 5, 6, and 95 [*Jordan*].

2   *Ibid*, above note 1 at paras 92–104; *R v Morin*, 1992 CanLII 89 (SCC) [*Morin*].

3   *Jordan*, above note 1 at paras 93–94; *R v Askov*, [1990] 2 SCR 1199.

4   *Jordan*, above note 1 at para 92.

requirements of the case must reflect this high level of tolerance for institutional delay in particular localities.[15]

When time taken to the end of trial falls below the presumptive ceiling, the two criteria—(1) defence initiative and (2) whether the time taken markedly exceeds what was reasonably required—are applied contextually, sensitive to the parties' reliance on the previous state of the law.[16] For example, since defence initiative was not expressly required by the *Morin* framework, it would be unfair to expect the defence to demonstrate that they took the initiative to expedite matters for the period prior to the release of the decision.[17] In close cases, any defence initiative would assist in meeting the under-the-ceiling test.[18] In any event, *Morin* required consideration of defence action or inaction by the accused and whether it was inconsistent with a desire for a timely trial.[19] Similarly, prejudice experienced by the accused would be a relevant, albeit not a determinative, factor for the limited purpose of considering the transitional exception.[20] Additionally, if institutional delay that was reasonably acceptable in the relevant jurisdiction under the *Morin* framework before the *Jordan* decision was released caused the delay in question, that institutional delay would be a component of the reasonable time requirements of the cases that are subject to the transitional exception.[21]

---

15   *Ibid.*

16   *Ibid* at para 99.

17   *Ibid.*

18   *Ibid.*

19   *Ibid*; citing *Morin*, above note 2.

20   *KN*, above note 10 at para 37.

21   *Jordan*, above note 1 at para 100.

CHAPTER 10

Remedy for Trial Delay

Section 24(1) of the *Charter of Rights and Freedoms* allows for broad potential remedies in the event of a *Charter* breach. It reads that "Anyone whose rights or freedoms, as guaranteed by this *Charter*, have been infringed or denied may apply to a court of competent jurisdiction to obtain such remedy as the court considers appropriate and just in the circumstances."[1] In spite of this broad remedial power, however, it has been determined that the minimal remedy for a breach of section 11(b) of the *Charter* due to unreasonable delay to trial is a stay of the proceedings. Once a breach has been found, the prosecution comes to an end, without exception. A review of the history of the Supreme Court's consideration of the appropriate remedy for a breach of section 11(b) of the *Charter* follows below. It demonstrates that the underlying basis for the determination that only a stay will suffice to remedy the breach was not initially agreed upon. However, those who did agree that only a stay would suffice, shared the concern that to persist with a trial once a breach was found would amount to perpetuating the *Charter* breach.

In the pre-*Jordan*[2] era, the appropriate remedy for a breach of section 11(b) of the *Charter* was first considered by the Supreme Court in *R v Mills*.[3] Justices McIntyre, Beetz, Chouinard, and La Forest held that the infringement of a *Charter* right does not give rise to jurisdictional error. They further held that section 24(1) is a broad provision that allows a

---

1   *Canadian Charter of Rights and Freedoms*, Part I of the *Constitution Act, 1982*, being Schedule B to the *Canada Act 1982* (UK), 1982, c 11, s 24(1) [*Charter*].
2   *R v Jordan*, 2016 SCC 27 [*Jordan*].
3   1986 CanLII 17 (SCC) [*Mills*].

court of competent jurisdiction to impose whatever remedy it deems just and appropriate in the circumstances. Per La Forest J, a stay should be reserved for "the more compelling cases."[4] In dissent, Dickson CJ and Lamer J held that a stay was the lone remedy available for a breach of section 11(b), as once breached, the court's jurisdiction to continue to try the accused was lost. To continue with the proceedings beyond the point at which a breach was found would be to persist in the breach.[5] Justice Wilson agreed with Lamer J insofar as she would "dispose of the appeal as my colleague proposes," imposing a stay of proceedings.[6]

The following year the Supreme Court gave further consideration to the remedy issue in *R v Rahey*[7] in the context of an eleven-month delay for the determination of a motion for a directed verdict at trial. The majority (Dickson CJ, Beetz, Estey, Lamer, Wilson, and LeDain JJ) held that a stay is the minimum remedy for a breach of section 11(b) of the *Charter*. Chief Justice Dickson and Estey, Lamer, and Wilson JJ held that this was because the court had lost jurisdiction to proceed.[8] Justices LeDain and Beetz were of the view that jurisdiction was not lost but that "a stay is the just and appropriate remedy for an infringement of the right to be tried within a reasonable time."[9] As in *Mills*, La Forest and McIntyre JJ held that section 24(1) allowed for broad remedial responses to *Charter* delay. To characterize a breach of section 11(b) as resulting in a loss of jurisdiction was to impede the broad discretion afforded to judges by section 24(1) to address the problem.[10]

This issue of the proper remedy or remedies for a breach of section 11(b) of the *Charter* was once again raised before the Court in its seminal decision in *R v Morin*.[11] Though the Crown had again raised the argument that remedies other than a stay of proceedings could suffice to address a breach, as the Court found that no breach of section 11(b) had been established, it was not necessary for the Court to consider the remedy issue.

---

4   *Ibid*, Lamer J at paras 78, 82, and 239–41; McIntyre J at paras 276–78; ilson J at para 286; La Forest J at paras 297–301.

5   *Ibid*, Lamer J at paras 78, 82, and 239–41.

6   *Ibid*, Wilson J at para 286.

7   1987 CanLII 52 (SCC) [*Rahey*].

8   *Ibid*, Lamer J at paras 1 and 48–53.

9   *Ibid*, LeDain J at paras 54 and 58.

10   *Ibid*, La Forest J at paras 103–11 and 125.

11   1992 CanLII 89 (SCC).

The broad discretion to fashion any remedy that is appropriate and just in the circumstances where an accused's *Charter* right has been breached was next revisited by the Supreme Court in *R v Potvin*,[12] albeit by the minority alone, the majority having determined that section 11(b) of the *Charter* did not apply to appellate delay. For Lamer CJ, McLachlin and Major JJ, "charged with an offence" meant a person subject to the power of the criminal process, with section 11(b) of the *Charter* intended to protect the fairness of the process at all stages. Accordingly:

> The many circumstances which may prevail at the post-verdict, post-stay stage required a flexible approach to remedies. The *Charter* empowers the court to grant such remedies as may be just in all the circumstances. Factors such as the length of the delay, seriousness ... should be considered in selecting a remedy in such circumstances.[13]

That some lesser remedy than a stay of proceedings could be employed to remedy a breach of section 11(b) of the *Charter* was not revisited again until some twenty-five years later, and only in passing, in the Supreme Court's decision in *R v Jordan*.[14] The majority, having overhauled the entire approach to the assessment of the reasonableness of delay pursuant to section 11(b) of the *Charter*, indicated in a footnote to the decision that "We were not invited to revisit the question of remedy. Accordingly, we refrain from doing so."[15] The Court also noted that the fact that the perimeters of the *Morin* framework, a backward-looking analysis, had been strained by the courts over time was not surprising given that judges have "only one remedial tool at their disposal—a stay of proceedings."[16]

Though the Supreme Court has not directly considered whether some further remedies beyond a stay of the proceedings ought to be available for a breach of section 11(b) of the *Charter*, it can arguably be taken from recent jurisprudence from the Court that there is unlikely to be change in this regard. In *R v KGK*,[17] the Court made a determination as to whether the *Jordan* analysis and ceilings would apply to the

---

12   1993 CanLII 113 (SCC).
13   *Ibid* (McLachlin J).
14   *Jordan*, above note 2.
15   *Ibid* at fn 1.
16   *Ibid* at para 35.
17   2020 SCC 7 [KGK].

period between the end of evidence and closing argument to the rendering of a verdict.[18] In determining that judicial deliberation time did not fall within the *Jordan* analysis, the Court listed two bases for placing the onus on the accused to meet the high test to establish a breach in this period—the presumption of judicial integrity and the significance of stays in this context. The Court noted that "[s]tays in this context are significant and, although distinct from stays below the ceiling, they too are likely to be 'rare' and limited to 'clear cases.'"[19] The following year, the Court denied an application for leave to appeal (without reasons) raising the remedy issue in *R v Ellis*,[20] a matter arising out of Nova Scotia. As well, in *R v Yusuf*,[21] the court determined to leave for another day "whether a s. 11(b) application can be brought post-conviction and if so, whether a remedy other than a stay of proceedings is available."[22]

The Supreme Court similarly declined to revisit the remedy issue in *R v Ste-Marie*.[23] In September 2009 the accused were charged with laundering proceeds of crime and criminal organization offences. The judge at trial, applying the *Morin* framework (as the decision was released prior to the Supreme Court's decision in *Jordan*), held that the seventy-seven months of delay amounted to a breach of section 11(b) of the *Charter*, but would not enter a stay on the basis that the accused had suffered no prejudice beyond that arising from the charges themselves, and that some lesser remedy than a stay was warranted in the circumstances. The application for a stay was dismissed.

Before the Quebec Court of Appeal,[24] the only issue the court set about to decide was whether the judge at trial, having found a breach of section 11(b) of the *Charter*, erred in determining not to enter a stay of proceedings. Justice Healy, writing for the Court, held that the trial judge erred, both in assessing prejudice or harm as relevant to remedy, in particular given that prejudice is of limited relevance pursuant to *R v Jordan*, and in refusing to enter a stay in the face of the clear direction

---

18   A detailed consideration of the decision can be found in Chapter 3.

19   *KGK*, above note 17 at para 65.

20   2020 NSCA 78, leave to appeal refused 2021 CanLII 44587 (SCC).

21   2021 SCC 2.

22   *Ibid* at para 4; note that as discussed in Chapter 3, the Court later determined, in *R v JF*, 2022 SCC 17, that a post-conviction application for a stay for delay can only be brought post-conviction in exceptional circumstances.

23   *R v Ste-Marie*, 2022 SCC 3 [*Ste-Marie (SCC)*].

24   *Ste-Marie v R*, 2020 QCCA 1118.

in *R v Rahey* that a stay is the minimum remedy for a violation of section 11(b) of the *Charter*.[25] The Court therefore stayed the proceedings. Interestingly, on the appeal before the Supreme Court, the Quebec Crown did not pursue the argument that the trial judge had properly determined that a stay was inappropriate in the circumstances or ask the Court to revisit the remedy issue. Instead, it argued, and the Court agreed, that the Quebec Court of Appeal had erred in determining that the record of admissions before it was insufficient to assess the reasonableness of the delay and had erred in failing to find that much of the delay was properly attributable to defence-caused delay such that there was no *Charter* breach. The Supreme Court therefore set aside the stay and sent the matter back to the Quebec appellate court to consider the grounds of appeal it had not reached given their determination that a stay at trial was warranted.[26] Though the Attorney General of Ontario was granted leave to intervene on the basis of an argument that the Court should revisit *R v Rahey*, the Supreme Court did not consider the argument in its written judgment.

The Court of Appeal for Ontario has held that the decision in *R v Rahey* remains the binding authority that the only remedy for a breach of section 11(b) of the *Charter* as it relates to trial delay is a stay of the proceedings. In *R v Charity*,[27] the Crown proposed that, post-*Jordan*, the court assessing the section 11(b) *Charter* application should be permitted to consider alternative remedies to a stay, having regard to the level of harm the breach can be said to have caused to the accused. The Court held that the Crown was precluded from raising the issue for the first time on appeal.[28] However, Tulloch JA, writing for the Court, also specified that "the reformulated test [in *R v Jordan*] does not make a stay of proceedings any less appropriate of a remedy for unreasonable delay, nor does it re-open the question of what an appropriate remedy would be."[29] The court also noted that in both *R v Charley*[30] and in *R v Hartling*,[31] in the context of a consideration of the appropriate remedy

---

25   *Ibid* at paras 16–18.

26   *Ste-Marie (SCC)*, above note 23 at paras 6–14.

27   2022 ONCA 226 [*Charity*].

28   *Ibid* at paras 25–35.

29   *Ibid* at paras 38–47.

30   2019 ONCA 726.

31   2020 ONCA 243.

for sentencing delay,[32] that it is settled law that the only remedy for a section 11(b) *Charter* violation for delay to trial is a stay of proceedings.[33]

Similarly, in *R v Hanan*,[34] heard with the appeal in *R v Charity*,[35] though the court upheld the trial judge's refusal to grant a stay applying the transitional exception, the court went on to note the following:

> In light of my conclusion, I should address the respondent's submission that a remedy short of a stay should be considered when a s. 11(b) breach is found. The Supreme Court of Canada has, in many cases, said that the remedy for a s. 11(b) breach is a stay of proceedings. Indeed, in *Jordan* at para. 35, the court referred to it as the "one remedial tool." In my view, if some other remedy is to become available for a s. 11(b) breach, that availability will need to be determined by the Supreme Court of Canada. I refer to the discussion of this issue in *R v Charity* being released concurrently with the reasons in this matter.

Though the Supreme Court of Canada has not yet had occasion to hear full argument with respect to whether it ought to revisit its decision in *R v Rahey*, it seems unlikely to do so. First, as reviewed above, jurisprudence from the Court since presumes the remedy remains a stay where a breach has been established. Second, to ask the Court to develop an analysis for selecting an appropriate remedy is to ask it to reintroduce the need to assess prejudice or harm to the accused. This is antithetical to the *Jordan* framework, which presumes the presence of such prejudice when the ceiling is reached (and, going further, arguably treats prejudice as entirely irrelevant to the analysis). Third, to reintroduce assessments of harm or prejudice would be to increase the complexity and length of section 11(b) applications. Fourth, to reintroduce considerations of prejudice to the accused would be to impose a burden on the accused to establish harm though she has already established the existence of a breach. Alternatively, if a burden is imposed on the Crown in this regard, the Crown will have the difficulty of somehow

---

32   See Chapter 5 for a discussion about the application of s 11(b) of the *Charter* to sentencing delay.

33   *Charity*, above note 27 at para 47.

34   2022 ONCA 229.

35   *Charity*, above note 27. These two cases were heard with another called *R v Campbell*, 2022 ONCA 223, where the issue was also raised but was not reached in the Court's judgment.

demonstrating the absence of some harm in order to argue for a lesser remedy. While this is possible in terms of, for example, the absence of any concern as to loss of evidence, it seems doubtful that it is even possible for the Crown to present some evidence as it relates to the accused's security of the person interests. Fifth, for the *Jordan* framework to be stringently interpreted and applied in part depends upon the starkness of the remedy in the event of a breach. Just as the *Morin* framework was stretched beyond all limits by judges due to the strict remedy of a stay, so too is there a danger that *Jordan* will be loosely applied where the consequences for a breach amount to little.

Finally, post-*Jordan*, it is not clear that there are many alternatives to a stay for a breach of section 11(b) of the *Charter*. As *Jordan* imposes a forward-looking, rather than a backward-looking, approach to delay, remedies proposed as alternatives to a stay prior to the release of *Jordan*, such as orders for an expedited trial and release on bail, for example, are no longer in play. As to an expedited trial, *Jordan* already requires the Crown to seek an earlier trial where delay has become problematic and the accused has raised the issue. Under the *Jordan*, forward-looking framework, it is a *preventative measure* employed to avoid delay, not a remedy. Release on bail pre-*Jordan* was a means to reduce prejudice and therefore increase the likelihood that a stay for delay would be avoided. As already noted, prejudice is irrelevant to the *Jordan* analysis. Release on bail does nothing to alter the calculus in reaching the net delay count. All that realistically remains is a sentence reduction as an alternative to a stay. However, this runs into the same problem in that to assess the quantum of the reduction in any given case would be to require a reintroduction of the assessment of prejudice with all the problems that brings, as discussed above. It also does not contend with the rationale underlying the *Rahey* decision in that to continue on to trial and sentencing is to persist in the breach and is of no assistance to an accused who is ultimately acquitted.

CHAPTER 11

Appellate Review

A. STANDARD OF REVIEW

The applicable standard of review having regard to assessments of the reasonableness of delay pursuant to section 11(b) of the *Charter* was articulated in several provincial appellate decisions,[1] including *R v Pauls*,[2] as follows:

> [T]he standard of review is well established. Deference is owed to a trial judge's underlying findings of fact. Characterizations of periods of delay and the ultimate decision concerning whether there has been unreasonable delay are reviewable on a standard of correctness.[3]

Though the respondents in that case had sought to have the court revisit the standard of review, the Court of Appeal declined to do so on the basis of prior appellate authority on this issue.[4] The Supreme Court of Canada later affirmed the standard of review in the same case, noting

---

1   See: *R v Jurkus*, 2018 ONCA 489 at para 25, leave to appeal refused (without reasons) 2018 CanLII 116611 (SCC) [*Jurkus*]; *R v Albinowski*, 2018 ONCA 1084 at para 27 [*Albinowski*]; *R v Bulhosen*, 2019 ONCA 600 at para 73, leave to appeal refused (without reasons) 2020 CanLII 17613 (SCC) [*Bulhosen*]; *R v Warring*, 2017 ABCA 128 at para 5; *R v KN*, 2018 BCCA 246 at para 13; *R v Regan*, 2018 ABCA 55 at para 32, leave to appeal refused 2018 CanLII 99645 (SCC); *R v JEK*, 2016 ABCA 171 at para 10.

2   2020 ONCA 220 [*Pauls*].

3   *Ibid* at para 40.

4   *Jurkus*, above note 1 at para 25; *Albinowski*, above note 1 at para 27; *Bulhosen*, above note 1 at para 73.

that the Ontario Court of Appeal, "applying the appropriate standard of review,"[5] had allowed the appeal and restored the convictions.[6]

Though the standard of review was well settled in the *Morin*[7] era, in several cases post-*Jordan*, as in *Pauls*,[8] the argument was advanced that the Supreme Court majority in *Jordan* had modified the standard, or at least the nature of the role of trial judges in making attributions, such that the applicable standard of review ought to be revisited by the Court.[9] This likely arose out of the Supreme Court's decisions in both *Jordan* and *R v Cody*.[10] In *Jordan*, for example, in the discussion related to what will constitute a discrete exceptional circumstance, the Court noted that "[u]ltimately, the determination of whether circumstances are 'exceptional' will depend on the trial judge's good sense and experience."[11] Similarly, as to potential categories of conduct that could amount to defence-caused delay, the Court held that "[b]eyond defence unavailability, it will of course be open to trial judges to find that other defence actions or conduct have caused delay."[12] As to determinations of what will amount to legitimate defence conduct as it is understood for the purposes of the *Jordan* analysis, the Court likewise indicated that

> The determination of whether defence conduct is legitimate is "by no means an exact science" and is something that "first instance judges are uniquely positioned to gauge" (*Jordan*, at para. 65). It is highly discretionary, and appellate courts must show a correspondingly high level of deference thereto.[13]

The standard as affirmed by the Supreme Court requires that deference be given by the appellate court to the trial judge's findings of fact, reviewable only where the appellate court has found palpable and overriding error. A lesser degree of deference applies to legal

---

5   *R v Yusuf*, 2021 SCC 2 [*Yusuf*].

6   *Ibid* at para 2.

7   See *R v Conway*, 1989 CanLII 66 (SCC); *R v Schertzer*, 2009 ONCA 742 at para 71, leave to appeal refused [2010] SCCA No 3; *R v Widdifield*, 2014 BCCA 170 at para 76; *R v Horner*, 2012 BCCA 7 at para 90; *R v CD*, 2014 ABCA 333 at paras 26–28.

8   *Pauls*, above note 2.

9   See also *Jurkus*, above note 1 at para 25.

10   2017 SCC 31 [*Cody*].

11   *R v Jordan*, 2016 SCC 27 at para 71 [*Jordan*].

12   *Ibid* at para 64.

13   *Cody*, above note 10 at para 31.

determinations, that is, the attributions made to each block of time in the *Jordan* assessment and the ultimate assessment of the reasonableness of the delay must be correct in law. The distinction between factual findings and legal determinations concerning proper characterizations may, at times, be difficult, particularly given the Court's direction in *R v Cody* that a high degree of deference is owed to the trial judge's determination of whether defence conduct is legitimate. In the authors' view, the only way to read *R v Cody* in a manner that reconciles it with the applicable standard of review is to presume that what the Court intended in *Cody* was to convey that trial judge's determinations as to what the defence did or did not do through the course of the prosecution is a factual finding in a particular case and is subject to a high degree of deference. Once the facts have been settled upon, however, the categorization of a segment of delay pursuant to the *Jordan* framework — such as how defence conduct (arising from the facts as found) ought to be classified and deducted or not from the total delay — is a legal determination that must be correct in law.

An example will illustrate how the distinction between factual determinations and *Jordan* attributions can be difficult to draw. In *R v Safdar*,[14] the Ontario Court of Appeal was tasked to apply the standard of review as to the appropriate characterization of a section of delay arising from the inability of the defence to accept continuation dates because one had another trial scheduled and the other a medical appointment. The judge at trial determined that the delay was attributable not to defence-caused delay, but was properly treated as legitimate defence conduct and therefore did not deduct the delay in applying the *Jordan* calculus. In the decision on the appeal, the Court held as follows:

> In my view, based on the trial judge's factual findings, he was entitled to conclude that this period of delay was not solely or directly caused by the defence. First, and importantly, the April dates were offered as continuation dates in the midst of the ongoing trial. The inadequacy of the trial estimate was therefore part of the cause of the delay. Second, these dates were offered on relatively short notice. Third, as the trial judge found, defence counsel had agreed to all other dates that were offered, including other dates offered with little notice. The April dates were the only exception. Finally, defence counsel had legitimate reason to decline

---

14   2021 ONCA 207 [*Safdar* (ONCA)], affirmed (on other grounds) 2022 SCC 21.

these continuation dates. One counsel was booked on a serious Superior Court matter for a client who was in custody, while another was scheduled for medical treatment. The trial judge appropriately recognized that counsel could not, in good faith, "compromise one client's interests for another."The trial judge made no error by not treating defence counsel's legitimate unavailability on the April dates as defence delay in all the circumstances.[15]

This passage is illustrative of the tension between what is legally correct and the direction in *Cody* that appellate courts ought to defer to the trial judge's assessments as to what is legitimate defence conduct. In *R v Safdar*, the Court of Appeal regarded the following as *factual findings* underlying the trial judge's determination that no deduction should be made having regard to counsel for the defence's inability to accept continuation dates:

1) *The delay was not solely caused by the defence as the misestimate of the time needed for trial contributed to the need for the dates.* The Court did not consider, though, whether the delay was nevertheless *directly* caused by the defence in that they were simply not available to accept new dates. Was this a factual determination subject to deference or more properly treated as a legal decision as to whether delay was defence-caused?

2) *The dates were offered on short notice.* This is factually accurate, but is it relevant to whether this was defence-caused delay or legitimate delay in that it amounted to defence preparation time?

3) *One counsel declined the dates due to another court commitment and the other for a medical appointment.* The question that arises is whether the trial judge, best suited to make such determinations pursuant to *Cody*, was properly accorded a high level of deference by the appellate court for his determination that to have declined continuation dates for the above-noted reasons was legitimate (with legitimacy being a question of fact[16]) *or* not properly legally characterized as

---

15   *Ibid* at paras 50–51.

16   Note: The Court in *Jordan* indicated explicitly that in circumstances where the delay falls below the ceiling, whether the matter took markedly longer than it reasonably should have, which is one of two criteria the accused must meet to establish a breach of s 11(b) of the *Charter*, is a question of fact. A detailed discussion related to the assessment of reasonableness for below-ceiling cases is found at Chapter 8.

"actions legitimately taken to respond to the charges"[17] applying the standard of review as endorsed by the Supreme Court in *R v Yusuf*.[18]

B. RECORD ON APPEAL

On appeal, the parties are not limited to the record that was before the trial court. Where the record at trial was deficient in terms of the transcripts, those missing portions of the record must be placed before the appellate court. In *R v Allen*,[19] Doherty JA held, in response to a preliminary objection that the Crown was not permitted to include additional transcripts to what had been filed on the original application, that "When s. 11(b) is in issue, this court has come to expect that full transcripts of the proceedings under review will be placed before it. A fair assessment of an alleged breach of s. 11(b) is best made after a review of all available transcripts pertaining to the challenged proceedings."[20] However, additional further evidence must be submitted through a fresh evidence application. Pursuant to the decision in *Palmer v The Queen*,[21] if the proffered evidence does not meet the criteria for admissibility, that is, due diligence, relevance to the issue before the court, credibility, and whether if believed, the evidence could reasonably be expected to have affected the result, it cannot be admitted.

C. CONCESSIONS MADE AT TRIAL

An appellate court is not bound by the concessions made in the context of classifying periods of delay that are erroneous.[22] Delay attributions are questions of law.[23]

---

17   *Jordan*, above note 11 at para 65.

18   *Yusuf*, above note 5 at para 2.

19   1996 CanLII 4011 (ON CA) [*Allen*].

20   *Ibid*.

21   1979 CanLII 8 (SCC).

22   *Jurkus*, above note 1 at para 71; *R v Steele*, 2012 ONCA 383 at para 19; *R v Tran*, 2012 ONCA 18 at para 31; *M v H*, 1999 CanLII 686 (SCC) at paras 45 and 210–11 [*M v H*]; *Ocean Port Hotel Ltd v British Columbia (General Manager, Liquor Control and Licensing Branch)*, 2001 SCC 52 at para 44.

23   *Ibid* at para 44; *R v Silveira*, 1995 CanLII 89 (SCC); *M v H*, above note 22.

Suggested Reading

ALBERTA JUSTICE AND SOLICITOR GENERAL, CRIMINAL JUSTICE DIVISION. "Injecting a Sense of Urgency: A New Approach to Delivering Justice in Serious and Violent Cases." Report by G. Lepp (April 2013), online: https://open.alberta.ca/publications/6983714.

BALA, NICHOLAS. "Youth as Victims and Offenders in the Criminal Justice System: A Charter Analysis—Recognizing Vulnerability" (2008) 40 *Supreme Court Law Review*, 2d ed 595.

BALA, NICHOLAS & SANJEEV ANAND. *Youth Criminal Justice Law*, 3d ed (Toronto: Irwin Law, 2012).

BULMAN, PHIL. *Delays in Youth Justice*, 2014. Washington, DC: US Department of Justice Office of Justice Programs, National Institute of Justice Office of Juvenile Justice and Delinquency Prevention, online: www.purl.fdlp.gov/GPO/gpo71104.

BUTTS, JEFFREY A., GRETCHEN RUTH CUSICK & BENJAMIN ADAMS. *Delays in Youth Justice*, University of Chicago, National Institute of Justice, Office of Justice Programs, 2009, online: www.purl.fdlp.gov/GPO/LPS125772.

CANADA, DEPARTMENT OF JUSTICE. "The Final Report on Early Case Consideration of the Steering Committee on Justice Efficiencies and Access to the Justice System" (2006), online: www.justice.gc.ca/eng/rp-pr/csj-sjc/esc-cde/ecc-epd/toc-tdm.html.

CODE, MICHAEL A. *Trial Within a Reasonable Time: A Short History of Recent Controversies Surrounding Speedy Trial Rights in Canada and the United States* (Toronto: Carswell, 1992).

COUGHLAN, STEVE. "*R. v. Jordan*: A Dramatically New Approach to Trial Within a Reasonable Time" (2016) 29 *Criminal Reports*, 7th ed 311.

———. "Early Patterns in the New Section 11(b) Framework" (2016) *Criminal Reports*, 7th ed 386.

———. "Patterns in the *Jordan* Case Law One Year after *Cody*" (2018) *Criminal Reports*, 7th ed 342.

———. "Making Trial Within a Reasonable Time a Right Once More" *The Supreme Court Law Review: Osgoode's Annual Constitutional Cases Conference* 81 (2019), online: www.digitalcommons.osgoode.yorku.ca/sclr/vol81/iss1/11.

COWPER, D GEOFFREY. *A Criminal Justice System for the 21st Century* (2012) Report Commissioned by the BC Justice Reform Initiative.

FITZGERALD, OLIVER. "*Jordan* and Classifying Decision Delay: A Need for Guidance" (2017) 40 *Criminal Reports*, 7th ed 72.

GOLD, ALAN D., MICHAEL LACY & LAURA METCALFE. *A Practical Guide to the* Charter: *Section 11(b)* (Toronto: LexisNexis Canada, 2019).

HARRIS, PETER, BRIAN WEAGANT, DAVID COLE & FERN WEINPER. "Working 'in the Trenches' with the *YCJA*" (2004) 46 *Canadian Journal of Criminology and Criminal Justice* 3 at 367–90.

JONES, BROCK, EMMA RHODES & MARY BIRDSELL. *Prosecuting and Defending Youth Criminal Justice Cases: A Practitioner's Handbook* in B.H. Greenspan & V. Rondinelli, eds, Criminal Law Series (Toronto: Emond Publishing, 2016).

LESAGE, PATRICK J. & MICHAEL A. CODE. *Report on the Review of Large and Complex Criminal Case Procedures*, 2008. Report Commissioned by the Ontario Ministry of the Attorney General.

PACIOCCO, PALMA. "The Hours Are Long: Unreasonable Delay After *Jordan*" (2017) 81 *Supreme Court Law Review*, 2d ed 233.

PILLA, ANDREW & LEVI VANDERSTEEN. "Re-Charting the Remedial Course for Section 11(b) Violations Post-*Jordan*" (2019) 56 *Osgoode Hall Law Journal* 436.

SHERRIN, CHRISTOPHER. "Reconsidering the *Charter* Remedy for Unreasonable Delay in Criminal Cases" (2016) 20 *Canadian Criminal Law Review* 263.

———. "Understanding and Applying the New Approach to *Charter* Claims of Unreasonable Delay" (2017) 22 *Canadian Criminal Law Review* 1.

STREZOS, LOUIS P. "The Uncertain Reach of *Jordan*" (2018) 46 *Criminal Reports*, 7th ed 394.

STUART, DON. *Charter Justice in Canadian Criminal Law*, 7th ed (Toronto: Thomson Reuters, 2018).

TREHEARNE, JENNIFER A.Y., R. CRAIG BOTTOMLEY & JOSHUA FROST. *Justice Delayed: A Practitioner's Guide to Section 11(b) of the* Charter (Toronto: Thomson Reuters, 2020).

Table of Cases

Index

About the Authors

Tracy Kozlowski, BA (Hon), LLB, has worked as Crown Counsel at Crown Law Office—Criminal since 2005, both arguing appeals and prosecuting trials. She has appeared for the Ontario Crown in the Supreme Court of Canada on several seminal section 11(b) cases, including *R v Williamson*, 2016 SCC 28; *R v Cody*, 2017 SCC 31; *R v Safdar*, 2022 SCC 21; *R v JF*, 2022 SCC 17; and *R v Hanan*, 2023 SCC 12. Her appearances before the Court of Appeal for Ontario on the subject include *R v Picard*, 2017 ONCA 692; *R v JK*, 2021 ONCA 256; *R v Haniffa*, 2021 ONCA 326; and *R v Adu-Bekoe*, 2021 ONCA 1136. She frequently appears as a lecturer and acts as an advisor to Crown colleagues and provincial prosecutors on all matters related to section 11(b) of the *Charter of Rights and Freedoms*.

Joanne Stuart, BA (Hon), LLB, has worked as Crown Counsel at Crown Law Office—Criminal since 2008, arguing appeals at the Court of Appeal for Ontario and the Supreme Court of Canada, including as Intervenor for the AG Ontario on seminal cases related to section 11(b) of the *Charter of Rights and Freedoms*, namely *R v KJM*, 2019 SCC 55 and *R v KGK*, 2020 SCC 7. Her appearances before the Court of Appeal for Ontario on the subject include *R v CG*, 2020 ONCA 357; *R v Grant*, 2022 ONCA 337; and *R v SA*, 2024 ONCA 737. She has also worked as a trial Crown in Toronto at the Toronto West (Etobicoke) Crown Attorney's Office, and most recently, at the Toronto East (Scarborough) Crown Attorney's Office. Prior to working as a Crown, she spent three years working as an Associate at Greenspan Humphrey Lavine (now Greenspan Humphrey Makepeace) doing trials and appeals as defence counsel.